PARABLES OF RAMA

STORIES IN ENGLISH USED BY SWAMI RAMA TIRTHA TO ILLUSTRATE THE HIGHEST TEACHING OF VEDANTA

SWAMI RAMA TIRTHA

Made with ♥ on the Notion Press Platform
www.notionpress.com

To Brahman

Contents

Contents

Foreword

What is Practical Vedanta?

Pushing, marching labour and no stagnant Indolence,
Enjoyment of work, as against tedious drudgery,
Peace of mind and no canker of suspicion,
Organisation and no disaggregation,
Appropriate reform and no conservative customs,
Solid real feeling, as against flowery talk
The poetry of facts, as against speculative fiction,
The logic of events, as against the authority of departed authors;
Living realisation and no mere dead quotations, Constitute Practical Vedanta.
"Vedanta says that your relations and connections ought to be an aid to you and not an obstacle. Everything you meet in this world should be a stepping stone instead of a stumbling block. Convert your stumbling block into a stepping one".

Preface

While going through the Complete Works of Swami Rama, "In Woods of God Realization" one is struck with the vast number of simple stories, so profusely used by Swami Rama to illustrate the highest teaching of Vedanta. The most difficult and intricate problems of philosophy and abstract truths, which may very well tax the brains of the most intellectual, are thus made not only simple and easy to understand but also brought home to us in a concrete form in such an interesting and attractive style that even a dullard or a child finds delight and pleasure in reading them and can easily apply their truths in daily life and practice.

And yet there are some who cannot at once go in for the full set of Complete Works owing to financial difficulty, or are rather not well inclined to go through a work bearing any such label as Vedanta, thinking it to be either too abstruse for their comprehension or to be prejudicial to their own particular forms of faith or ways of belief. For such specially, and generally for those who take interest mostly in light reading only, as of stories and fables, and are averse to study any subject requiring serious attention, it is a great pleasure to us that we have been able to bring out in this cheap and handy volume a complete and classified collection of all the illustrations and stones spread throughout the Complete Works of Swami Rama; for abstract Truths, otherwise most difficult to comprehend and to remember are easily understood, kept in mind, and applied in life, if available in the form of interesting stories.

To make these Parables still more useful and easier to remember, they have been numbered and divided subject-wise, each with an appropriate heading giving the subject dealt with and a subheading giving the actual story related. A brief and fitting moral is also drawn for daily practice and added in bold type at the end of each story.

Each story is given a number above the heading to denote its general serial position, a number on the left of heading denoting its number in the subject dealt with, a number on the right of the main subject giving the total number of stories under that subject, while all the subjects are also alphabetically arranged and numbered serially in Roman figures. A reference, as to the Volume of Swami Rama's Works of Fifth Edition and its pages from which the story is taken, is also given at the end of the moral of each story. The morals of all the stories in the book have also been collected together and given at the end as 'Bouquet, of Morals'. There are altogether 171 stories with morals, given in 27 chapters. The table of Contents is also arranged chapter wise, with headings and subheadings, to serve as an Index for all the subjects used in the book. Thus the classification and arrangement is made as complete as possible.

To give the general public a taste of spiritual food in the most delicious and wholesome form, easy of digestion and giving full spiritual vigour and strength at a nominal cost the present, edition under the name of 'Parables of Rama' has been brought out as one more addition to the series of similar volumes of 'Heart of Rama" and 'Poems of Rama' already published.

We are confident that this volume will appeal equally to the highest cultured as well as the man in the street, and will not only serve its purpose to give a foretaste for the study of Rama's Complete Works but will also create an ardent desire for an unprejudiced and unbiased search after Truth, and a real and earnest longing to live the Higher Life of Self-realization and Eternal Happiness.

CHAPTER ONE

Ambition

The Case of Ambition (Shahjahan in Prison)

In India the Emperor, Shahjahan, was put into prison by his son Aurangzeb. He was put into prison because his son wanted to possess the whole kingdom. The son put his father into prison so that he might satisfy his hunger after lucre. At one time the father wrote to his own son to send him some students so that he might amuse himself by teaching them something. Then the son said, "Will you hear this fellow, my father? He has been ruling over the kingdom for so many years and even now he cannot give up his old habit of ruling. He still wants to rule over students, he wants somebody to rule over. He cannot give up his old it habits."

So, it is. How can we give up our old habits? The old habits cling to us. We cannot shake it off. The real Self of yours, the emperor Shah-e-Jahan (the literal meaning of the word is, ruler of the whole world, and so the name of that Emperor Shah-e-Jahan, means the Emperor of the whole Universe) is the Emperor of the Universe. Now, you have put the Emperor into a prison, into the black-hole of your body, into the quarantine of your little self. How can that real Self, that Emperor of the Universe, forget his old habits? How can he give up his nature? Nobody is capable of shaking off his own nature. Nobody can jump out of his own nature. So the Atman, the True Self, the real Reality in you,—how can that give up its nature? You have confined that in prison, but even in the prison it wants to possess the whole world, because it has been possessing the whole; it cannot give up its old habits. If you wish this ambitious spirit, the avarice should be shaken off, if you desire that the people in this world should give up this ambitious nature, could you preach to them to give it up? Impossible!

MORAL: People are ambitious because they cannot go against the all possessing nature of the soul or true self.

The Cause of Greed (The Snares of 99)

A man with his wife used to live very happily in their small hut. Very happy they were.

The man used to work all day long and get a pittance to make the two ends meet. He had no other worldly ambition, no other desire, no feeling of envy or hatred, a good honest worker he was. He had a neighbour who was a very wealthy man. This wealthy man was always immersed in anxiety, he was never happy. A Vedantin monk once visited the houses of the rich man and his poor neighbour, and told the rich man that the cause of his worry and anxiety was his possessions. His possessions possessed him and kept him down, his mind wandering from this object to that. The monk pointing to the poor neighbour said "Look at him, he owns nothing, but on his face you find the bloom of happiness, and you find his muscles so strong and his arms so well built. He goes about in such a happy, cheerful, jolly mood, humming tunes of joy." This happiness the rich man could never enjoy. He had his property fashioned and moulded in the way other people liked it. Then the rich man wanted to test the truth of the monk's remarks. According to the advice of the monk, the rich man stealthily threw into the house of the poor man Rs. 99. The next day they saw that no fire was lit in the house of the poor man. In the house of the poor man there used to be a good fire and they used to cook certain things purchased with the money earned by dint of the poor man's labour. That night they found no fire in the house, they did not cook anything;, they starved that night. The next morning the monk taking the rich man with him went to the poor man and enquired as to the cause of his not lighting fire in his house. The poor man could make no excuse in the presence of the monk; he had to tell the truth. He said that before that he used to earn a few annas, and with those few annas they used to purchase some flour and vegetables, and cook and eat them but on that day when they lit no fire, they received a little box containing Rs.99. When they saw these Rs. 99, the idea came into their mind that there was only one rupee wanting to make them full Rs. 100. Now, in order to make up that Re. 1, they found that they might forego food on alternate day, and thus they might scrape up some annas and in a week or so would save up Re. 1, and thus they would have Rs.100. Hence they were to starve. This is the secret of the niggardliness of the rich people.

The more they get the poorer they become. When they get Rs. 99, they want more, if they have Rs. 99,000, they want Rs. 1,00,000.

MORAL: The more you get, the more you become greedy, niggardly and less happy. Happiness lies not in accumulation of wealth but in content only.

CHAPTER TWO

Desires

The Forecast of Coming Events (A Lady and a Photographer)

A lady went to a first class photographer to have her picture taken. The operator put his camera in good order, using a highly sensitized plate. When he examined the negative, he found on the lady's face indications of small‘ pox. He was astonished. What does this mean? Her face is clean, but there are unmistakable signs of that dreaded disease. After repeated attempts to secure a picture of the lady without indications of small-pox on the face, he gave up in disgust, and asked the lady to call some other day when conditions were better; he would succeed in taking a good photograph of her. The lady went home and after a few hours she got small-pox. What was the cause? She afterwards recalled having received a letter from her sister who was down with the small-pox, and she had wetted the envelope with her lips and closed it with her fingers. When the lady opened the letter, she became infected with the disease, and in due time became ill. The camera detected it by the refined materials used by the photographer, although the naked eye was deceived and could not see the small-pox already at work in the skin.

We, so are desires: in fact the small-pox marks seen in the camera, which have not made their appearance on the face. Desires are in fact a guarantee of their fulfillment. Desires are simply the index of the events which are sure to come to pass.

MORAL: Desires forecast the coming events.

The Secret of Fulfillment of Desires

There was a man, writing a letter to a friend whom he was pining for and longing to see. He had been separated from his friend for a long time. The letter he was writing was a long, long letter and he wrote page after page. So intent was he on his writing that he did not stop or look up for a second. About three quarters of an hour he spent on the letter, not raising his head during the whole time. When the letter was finished and signed he raised his head and lo! His beloved friend stood before him. He jumped to his feet, and going to his friend embraced him, expressing his love. Then he remonstrated. "Are you here?" The friend answered; "I have been here for more than half-an-hour." Then the man said, "If you have been here so long why did you not tell me?" The friend said, "You were too busy, I did not like to interfere with your work." So it is, so it is. Your desires are like writing the letter. You are craving, willing and washing, hungering, thirsting, worrying, all this is writing the letter, and you go on writing. He whom you are addressing the letter, the objects that you desire are according to the secret Law of Karma, already before you. But why do you not feel them, find them before you? Because you desire, you are writing the letter. That is the reason.

The very moment you cease desiring, you give up writing the letter, you will find all the desired objects before you.

MORAL: Desires are fulfilled the moment you cease desiring.

The Result of Begging (The Prime Minister and Lakshmi)

There was a prime minister of a king who underwent all the ascetic practices, which are necessary, to see the Goddess of Fortune in flesh and blood before him. Well, he practised all those mantrams, incantations and charms. A million times he repeated sacred mantrams that were calculated to make him realise the presence of goddess Lakshmi. She did not appear. Three million times he underwent all the ascetic practices; still the goddess was not visible.

He lost all faith in these things and renounced everything in the world, took up Sannyasa (monk life) and became a monk. The very moment that he embraced Sannyasa (monk life) and left the palace and retired into the forests he found the goddess before him. He cried, 'Go away, goddess, why are you here now? I want you no more I am a monk. What has a monk to do with luxury, with riches, with wealth and worldly enjoyments? When I wanted you, you came not; now that I do not desire you, you came before me." The goddess replied,

"You yourself stood in the way. So long as you desired, you were asserting duality, you were making a beggar of yourself, and that kind of being can have nothing. The moment you rise above desires and spurn them, you are a god, and to gods belongs the glory." That is the secret.

MORAL: Rise above desires and they are fulfilled; beg and their fulfillment recedes further from you.

Purifying the mind (Krishna's dance on the heads of the Dragon)

There is beautiful story in the Puranas. It speaks of Krishna jumping into the river Jumna while his father, mother, friends and relatives stood by, struck dumb with amazement. In their very presence he jumped into the torrent. They thought that he was gone, that he would never rise again. The story says that he went to the bottom of the river and there was a thousand-headed dragon. Krishna began to blow his flute, he began to play the man tram OM, he began to kick down the heads of the dragon, he began to crush down the heads of the dragon one by one, but as he crushed the many heads of the dragon one by one, other heads sprang up and thus it was very hard for him. Krishna went on jumping and dancing upon the crested head of the dragon: he went on playing the man-tram on his flute, he went on chanting his man tram and still jumping and crushing down 'the heads of the dragon. In half-an-hour the dragon was dead; with the charming note of the flute and the crushing of the dragon by his heels, the dragon was dead. The waters of the river were turned to blood and the blood of the dragon mixed with the water of the river. All the wives of the dragon came up to pay homage to Krishna, they wanted to drink the nectar of his sweet presence. Krishna came up from the river, the amazed relatives and friends were beside themselves, their joy knew no bounds, so happy were they to find their beloved Krishna, their beloved one, in their midst again. This story has a double meaning. It is an object lesson, so to say, for those who want to gain an insight of reality into their own Divinity.

That lake or river represents the mind or rather the lake of the mind, and whoever wants to become Krishna (the word Krishna means or stands for Deity, God), whoever wants to regain the paradise lost, he has to enter deep into the lake of his own mind, to dive deep into himself. He has to plunge deep into his own nature, reaching the bottom he has to fight; the venomous dragon,, the poisonous: snake of passion, desire, the venomous dragon of the worldly mind. He has to crush it down, he has to destroy its crests he has to kick down its many heads, he has to charm and destroy it. He must make clear the lake of his mind; he must clear his mind this way. The process is the same as that followed by Krishna. He is to take up his flute and play the man-tram OM through it. He has to sing that divine, blessed song through it.

What is this flute? It is simply a symbol for you. Look at the flute. Indian poets attach great importance to it. What great deed was it that the flute performed, that it was raised to such a dignity? By virtue of what great Karma was it elevated to such a position? Why was it that Krishna who was the object of worship, who was loved by mighty monarchs, who was worshipped by thousands of fairy maidens in broad India; how was it that Krishna, the beloved-one, the powerful one, the love personified, that Krishna who did not condescend to look at kings or monarchs, why gave he this flute kisses? What raised it to such a. position? The flute's answer was, "I have one virtue, one good point I have. I have made myself void of all matter." The flute is empty from head to foot, "I emptied myself of non-self." Just so applying, the flute to the lips means purifying; the heart,: turning the mind unto God - throwing every things at the feet of God, the beloved one. Just give up from your heart of hearts. Give up all claims upon the body, give up all selfishness, all selfish connections, all thoughts of mine and thine - rise above it. Wooing God, wooing Him as no worldly lover woes his lady love; hungering and thirsting after the realization of the true Self, just as a man of the world hungers and thirsts for what he has not had for a long time; hungering and thirsting for the Divine; yearning for the Truth; craving after a taste of the supreme reality of Self, putting yourself in that state of mind is applying the flute to the lips. In this state of mind, in this peace of mind, with such a pure soul begin to chant the man tram OM; begin to sing the sacred syllable OM. This is putting the breath of music into the flute. Make your whole life a flute. Make your whole body a flute. Empty it of selfishness and. fill it with divine breath.

Chant OM and while doing it begin that search within the lake of your mind. Search out the poisonous snake with its many tongues. These heads, tongues, and fangs of the poisonous snake are the innumerable wants, the worldly tendencies and the selfish propensities. Crush them one by one, trample them under your feet, single them out, overcome them and destroy them while singing the syllable OM.

Build up a character, make firm resolutions, make strong determinations and take solemn vows so that when you came out of the lake or river of the mind, you may not find the waters poisoned:; so that the waters will not; poison those who drink from them. Come out of the lake having purified it altogether. Let people differ from you, let them subject you to all sorts of difficulties, let them revile you, but despite their favours and frowns, their threats and promises from the lake of your mind, there should flow nothing but divine, infinitely pure, fresh water. Nectar should flow out of you so that it may become as impossible for you to think evil as for the pure fresh spring to poison those who drink from it. Purify the heart, sing the syllable OM, pick out all points of weakness, and eradicate them. Come out victorious having formed a beautiful character. When the dragon of passion is destroyed, you will find the objects of desire worshipping you, just as the wives of the dragon under the river paid homage unto Krishna after he had killed the snake.

MORAL: Mind can be purified by killing, one by one, all selfish desires or wants, and singing the syllable OM.

Diffusion of Good Spontaneously (The Holy Shadow)

Long, long ago, there lived a saint so good that the astonished angels came down from the Heaven to see how a mortal could be so godly. He simply went about his daily life, diffusing virtue, as the star diffuses light and the flower perfume, without even being aware of it.

Two words summed up his day:—he gave, he forgave. Yet these words never fell from his lips. They were expressed in his ready smile, his kindness, forbearance, and charity.

The angels said to God: "O Lord, grant him the gift of miracles."

God replied: "I consent; ask what he wishes."

So they said to the saint: "Should you like the touch of your hands to heal the sick?"

"No," answered the saint, "I would like rather God should do that."

"Should you like to convert guilty souls and bring back wandering hearts to the right path?"

"No: that is the mission of angels. I pray, I do not convert,"

"Should you like to become a model of patience attracting men by the lustre of your virtues, and thus glorifying God?"

"No" replied the saint, "if men should be attracted to me, they would become estranged from God. The Lord has other means of glorifying himself."

"What do you desire then?" cried the angels.

"What can I wish for?" asked the saint smiling, "That God gives me His grace; with that, should I not have everything?"

But the angels wished: "You must ask for a miracle, or one will be forced upon you."

"Very well", said the saint, "that I may do a great deal of good without ever knowing it."

The angels were greatly perplexed. They took counsel together and resolved upon the following plan: Every time the saint's should fall behind him, or at either side, so that he could not see it, it should have the power to cure disease, soothe pain, and comfort sorrow. And so it came to pass: when the saint walked along, his shadow, thrown on the ground on either-side or behind him, made arid paths green, caused withered plants to bloom, give clear water to dried up brooks, fresh colour to pale little children, and joy to unhappy mothers.

But the saint simply went about his daily life, diffusing virtue as the star diffuses light and the flower perfume, without even being aware of it. And the people respecting his humility, followed him silently, never speaking to him about his miracles. Little by little, they came even to forget his name, and called him only "The Holy Shadow".

MORAL: One who rises above all desires is always diffusing good as spontaneously and naturally as a flower gives perfume, or a star diffuses light, without even being aware of it.

The Real Poverty (King, the Poorest Man)

A monk had some copper pices[1] and was about to give them away to some boys. Many poor people came to him to get them, but he would not give them. Finally, there came before the monk a king seated on an elephant. The monk threw the copper pices into the howdah on the top of the elephant where the king was seated. The king was astonished at this unexpected act of the monk. The monk said the money was for him, the poorest man. The king enquired how he could be the poorest man. The monk said he was the poorest man, because of his possessions and of his continual hunger and thirst for more kingdoms. Hence he was the poorest man.

MORAL: The real poverty does not consist in want of riches but in an unsatiated want or greed for more and more.

The Law of Karma (A Poet Who Feigned Blindness)

There was a Mohammedan poet in India, a very good man, rather a very clever and witty man. He was living at the court of one of the native princes, who was highly interested in him. One night the native prince kept him long in his company, and this poet amused the prince with all sorts of poems, witty stories, and most amusing tales. The prince went to bed very late. He was amused by the witty poet to such a degree that he forgot all about his sleep. The queen asked the prince what was the cause of his delay, of his unusual delay in retiring to his room. The prince replied "Oh, we had a wonderful man with us this evening; he was so good, so splendid, so witty and amusing." Then the queen enquired more about him, and her curiosity made the king expatiate upon the capability and attainment of the poet to such a degree that they had to sit until a late hour, so that it was near dawn when they retired. Now the curiosity of the queen being excited to the highest pitch, she asked the prince to bring this witty poet before her some day. Well, the next day this witty poet was brought before the queen.

This poet was brought by the king into the harem[2], the private apartments of the ladies. There he sang his poems and recited his stories; the ladies were highly amused. Then the poet gave out that he was blind, he was suffering from a disease of the eyes; but he was not blind in reality. Now the wicked intention of this poet was to be allowed to live in the private apartments of the ladies, so that they might not mistrust him, and the ladies thinking him to be blind might be free in their walks, and talks, in going from room to room and might not keep any veils on their countenances when passing by him. Now believing him to be blind, the prince allowed him to remain in the apartments of the ladies. But truth cannot be concealed. It will be out one day.

"Truth crushed to earth shall rise again. The eternal years of God are hers."

One day this poet asked one of the maid servants to bring something to him.

This poet, when he got an honourable position in the house of the prince, thought it beneath his dignity to leave his seat and bring a chair to where he wanted it. So he ordered one of the maid-servants to do it, -but she replied harshly, bluntly that she was very busy, she had no leisure, she could not spare the time. After that there appeared another servant, and he beckoned to her to come forward to him and asked her to move the chair, but she said that there was no chair in the room. He said "Bring that basin of water to me" She said, "There is none this in room; I will go into the other room and bring it to you." He said "Bring it, there is one in the room, do you not see it? There it is." In his anxiety to get the thing done, he forgot himself. That is what happens. This is how Truth plays a joke with liars. This is the Law of Nature. When this poet said, "Here it is, do you not see it?" the maid at once, instead of doing that job for him, ran straight to the queen and divulged the secret, and said, "Lo, the man is not blind, he is a wicked man, he ought to be turned out of the house."

He was turned out of the house; but about three days after he was turned out of the house of the prince, he became actually blind. How is that? Why?

The Law of Karma comes and tells you that the man becomes blind by his own will. He is the master of his own destiny. Blindness is brought on himself by his own self, nobody else makes him blind: his own desires, his own cravings make him blind. Afterwards when blindness comes he begins to weep and cry, he begins to gnash his teeth and bite his lips and beat his breast.

MORAL: Everybody reaps the fruit of his own desires. This is the Law of Karma.

1 An Indian coin out of circulation

2 In India females live in separate apartments, the harem, and do not mix much with males, with gentlemen. They live apart: especially Mohammedan women, not Hindus, wear heavy veils and they do not let anybody see them excepting their husbands or those who are very pure, noble and pious.

The Consequences of Desires (The Man Who Invited Death)

There was a man carrying a heavy weight upon his shoulders; he was old, weak, and feverish, and lived in a hot country, India. He sat down under the shade of a tree and threw off his burden from his shoulders and rested a while, and cried, "Oh Death! Death!! Death!!! come, Oh Death! Relieve me, relive me." The story says that there appeared the God of Death unto him on the spot, when he looked at Him, he was astonished, he was surprised. He trembled, what is that hideous figure, that monstrous something? He asked the God of Death, "Who are you"? The God of Death said, "I am he whom you called; you have called me just now and I have come to satisfy your wish." Then the old man began to v tremble and said, "I did not call you to put me to death, I called you simply to help, me to lift this burden and put it on my shoulders."

That is what the people do. All your, difficulties, all your troubles and sorrows, what are called sorrows, are brought about by your own self; you are the master of your own destiny, but when the thing comes, you begin to cry and weep; you invite Death, and when Death comes, you begin to cry. But that cannot be. When once you bid the highest price in an auction, you will have to take the thing. When you make the horse run, the carriage follows the horse. So, when once you desire, you will have to take the consequences.

MORAL: Troubles and sorrows are the inevitable consequences of your desires.

The Result of Conflicting Desires (A Professor in a Sectarian College)

There was a bright young man working as a professor in one of the sectarian colleges in India. In one of the public meetings, he declared his life to be given to that cause, he dedicated himself to that cause. He worked there most zealously for a time and then his opinion changed, his thoughts expanded his mind broadened, his views enlarged and he could no longer work with these sectarians, and these sectarians could not sympathize with him in their heart of hearts, yet he had to pull on with them, because he had committed himself, because he had bound himself to their cause; there was no escape for this young man. His heart was somewhere, and his body was somewhere else, the heart and the body were disunited. This could not be. This could not go on. The man died; he could not change the circumstances by any other means but death; by death were the circumstances changed.

You are the master of your circumstances; you are the master of your destiny. But how is it that people are made miserable? How is it that difficulties are brought about? By the conflict of desires. You have one kind of desires which want you to do this kind of act, and then you have other desires which want you to do differently. Here are conflicting desires which cannot go together. What happens? Both must be fulfilled. While one is being fulfilled, the other suffers and you are in pain. While the other one is being fulfilled, the first one suffers, and you are in pain. This is how people bring about suffering on themselves.

MORAL: Conflicting desires bring about difficulties, sorrows, and misery.

The Result of Discordant Desires (A Man with Two Wives)

A man in India had two wives. Hindus generally do not believe in polygamy, but the Mohammedans do. It was a Mohammedan who had two wives. One of the wives used to live upstairs and the other on the lower storey. One day a thief broke into the house. He wanted to steal away all the property, but the members of the house were wide awake and the thief could not get an opportunity of stealing anything. Near dawn the members of the house saw the thief, and they caught him and took him before a Magistrate, or to the police magistrate. There was nothing stolen, yet the thief had broken into the house. That was a crime. The Magistrate put some cross questions to the thief, who at once admitted that he had broken into the house with the intention of stealing something The Magistrate was going to inflict some punishment upon him. The man said, "Sir, you may do whatever you please, you may throw me into a dungeon, you may cast me before dogs, you may burn my body, but do not inflict one punishment upon me." The Magistrate being astonished asked, "What is that?" The man said, "Never make me the husband of two wives. Never inflict this punishment upon me." Why is that? Then the thief began to explain how he was caught, how he had no opportunity to steal anything. He said that all night long this master of the house had to stand upon the stairs because one wife was pulling him up-stairs and the other was dragging him down-stairs. The hair of his head were pulled out and the stockings on his feet were torn off; he was shivering with cold all night long, and thus it was that I was caught, that I had no opportunity to steal anything.

So it is, all your sufferings come through your conflicting desires, and your desires are not in harmony, but are at war with each other, and you know a house divided against itself must fall. If you have singleness of aim and unity of purpose, you will have no trouble, you will have no suffering, but if there is conflict and discord, you must suffer.

MORAL: Discordant desires produce suffering and pain; hence harmony in desires is essential for peace and happiness.

A patient's desires

A patient was lying on the cot in a room. Come! Let us enquire after his health. Two attendants were standing towards his head. Similarly two or three persons were towards his feet. Besides, a few others were also present in the room. A gentleman came to see him. He sent his visiting card, but was refused entry to the room. On his insistence, he was, however, allowed to see the ailing patient. Instead of wishing him, the patient did not even care to look at him. When the gentleman drew his attention two or three times, the patient acknowledged it in a rather indifferent way. There were thick cushions around him. The soft pillows were also there. Persons were continuously coming to enquire after his health. The apparent concern and deference had been manipulated by the patient by falling ill. Fie on such affection, earned with illness. So, too, your worldly desires are a sort of illness and their fulfillment approximates to show respect and regard, causing demoralization of the soul.

Newton's fan

Once, Sir Isaac Newton installed a fan in his room. He had arranged the levers and the pulleys in such a way that a fan could be worked by the rats. Near the end of a toothed wheel, he had put a few grains of wheat in such a way that they were not affected by the movement of the wheel. When the rat jumped from one tooth to the other, the wheel was moved, causing the fan to work, but the grains of the wheat remained, where they were. The dupe would jump again and again in its efforts to get them, causing the wheel to continue to work the fan. Poor rat was always in the hope of getting the grains at every jump, but unfortunately, he could never get them.

O dear friend! So, too, are worldly hopes and aspirations of the man. They are never fulfilled to his satisfaction. As the rat never reached the grains, so too, the man engrossed in desires, would ever be far from Truth, and the worldly fan would continue to work incessantly.

Sacrificing of worldly desires to attaining peace and godhood

When a man enters water, the water pressure presses him down. But the dead body is thrown-up, as if the water up thrust raises it to its head.

Similarly, if you become dead to world, you are helped by Nature to gain the wholesome and strength-giving life of godliness and spiritualism. So, why not willingly die the internal death by destroying your ego, now and here, so that the external death of your gross body may not be painful and grief-stricken to you and so that you may live peacefully and also die peacefully.

CHAPTER THREE

Faith

God versus Man (A Stranger in Vedantin's House)

A man came into the house of a Vedantin one day and occupied the vacant seat of honour in the absence of the master of the house. When the master of the house was coming back into the room, that intruder put this question. "O Vedantin let me know what God is, and what man is." Well, the sage did not directly answer the question. He simply called his servants and began to talk loud and use harsh language, telling them to turn him out of the house. This peculiar language did the really wise man use. When such unexpected language was employed, the intruder got frightened; he became nervous and left the seat of honour. The wise man occupied the same then calmly, serenely told him, "Here (pointing to himself) is God and there (pointing to the intruder) is man. Had you not been frightened, had you kept your place, had you preserved your balance, had you not been put out of countenance, then you were also God. But the very fact of your trembling, quivering, and losing faith in your Godhead makes you a poor vermin."

Think yourself to be Divinity, have a living faith in your Divinity, and nothing can harm you, nobody can injure you. So long as you go on relying and depending upon outside powers, failure will be the result. Trusting upon the God within, put the body in action and success is assured.

MORAL: You are God when you have a living faith in your Divinity; you are man when you depend upon outside powers.

Right Belief (Two Men in the Niagara)

Two men were being carried down by the swift current of the Niagara. One of them found a big log and caught hold of it with the desire to be saved; the other man found a tiny rope, thrown down for their rescue by the people on the bank. Happily he caught hold of this rope, which was not heavy like the log of wood, and though the rope was apparently very wavering and frail, he was saved; but the man who caught hold of the big log of wood was carried off with the log by the rapid current into the yawning grave of surging waters beneath the roaring Falls.

Similarly, you trust in these outward names, fame riches3 wealth, land, and prosperity. These seem to be big like the log of wood, but the saving principle they are not. The saving principle is like the fine thread. It is not material, you cannot feel and handle it, you cannot touch it; the subtle principle, the subtle truth is very fine, that is the rope which will save you. All these worldly things on which you depend will simply work your ruin and throw you into a deep abyss of hopelessness, anxiety and pain.

Beware, beware. Have a stronghold of the Truth. Believe more in the Truth than in outside objects. The law of nature is that whenever a man believes practically in the outside objects and wealth, he must fail. That is the law. Trust in the Divinity and you are safe.

MORAL: Trust in Divinity and not in outside objects is the right belief.

Cure of False Imagination (Child and the Ghost)

There was once a mother, not a good sensible mother, who made her child believe that the room adjoining the parlour was haunted by a ghost, terrible monster, something hideous. The child became very much terrified and was afraid to step into that room. . One evening the father returned from his office and asked the boy to go into the adjoining room and bring him something that he wanted at that time. The child was afraid, he did not dare to enter the dark room, and he ran to his father and said, "O papa, I won't go into that room, for there is a terrible big monster, a ghost, and I am afraid". The father did not like it, and said "No, no, dear boy, there is no monster there; there is nothing to hurt you in that room, so please go and bring me what I asked;" but the child would not budge. The father was very wise and so he thought of a remedy, a cure for this disease, this superstition which the child had contracted.

The father called the servant to him and whispered something into his ears. The servant left the room where the father was, and by a back door entered the adjoining room,' the supposed haunted room. He took one of the pillows, and over one corner of it he placed black cloth and projected one of the corners of the pillow, which was covered with the black cloth, through a hole in one of the windows of the room; he stuffed it out, and fixed it so that it looked hideous. The attention of the child was drawn to that and the child looked and saw something strange and terrible-looking. The father said, "That looks like an ear. (pointing to one corner of the pillow which was sticking out) and the imagination of the child, which was very active, at once made out that it was the ear of the supposed ghost, and cried, "O papa, that is the ear of the monster, did I not tell you that this house is haunted, now we know it is true." The father said, "Dear boy, you are right, but be brave and strong; get hold of this stick and we will destroy the ghost". You know, boys are very heroic, they can dare anything, they have great courage and so getting his father's beautiful cane, the boy stuck a hard blow, a noise was heard and there was heard a tiny cry, and the servant in the dark room then drew the supposed ear of the monster back into the room. That pleased the boy and with courage he cried that he was getting the better of the monster. The father cheered him up, puffed him up, praised him and said, "O may dear boy you are so brave, you are a hero." But while talking to the child there appeared the two ears of the monster in the crack or opening between the doors of the room. The child was urged on and he ran towards the monster and dealt blow upon the head of the supposed monster. He beat it and beat it repeatedly, and cries were heard from within and the father said. "Hear, child, the monster is crying in anguish, you have conquered, you have conquered." The child went on beating the supposed monster, and the father pulled out that pillow. The father cried, "O brave boy, you have beaten the monster into a pillow, you have converted him into a pillow." The child was satisfied that this was a fact; the monster, the ghost, the superstition was gone, and the child became brave and jumped and danced with joy and went about singing and then he went into the room and brought what the father wanted.

Vedanta says, in this case of the haunted room the real ghost was not driven out by the beating of the pillow by the child, the real cause of the driving out of the monster was not the beating of the pillow, it was the evolution of the Faith in the child that there was no ghost in the room. The child was made to believe there was no ghost, and there was no ghost; the ghost had come into the room through the imagination of the child. The ghost was in reality never there, it was this false imagination which put the ghost in the room, and this false imagination it was that must be cured.

MORAL: False imagination can be cured by the practice of another imagination leading to Truth.

Faith versus Creed (Crusades and the Lance)

In the Crusades during which so much blood was shed, war and struggle were brought on by the Christians in Judea. In one of the skirmishes, the Christians were beaten and repulsed. One of the fanatics in the Christian armies, who wanted to win fame for himself, gave out that he had a vision in which an angel had revealed himself and had told him about a certain lance which had once touched the body of Christ,, and which was buried under his feet, and by finding the lance the Christians would be led to victory. The people took up the story and passed it on until it appeared to the entire army, and all the people without giving any thought as to the truthfulness or falsity of the story, began to dig and dig, but could not find the lance; they dug from early morn till late at night, but still no lance was found. They became very much discouraged and were about to give up the search when all of a sudden the same fellow began to cry out at the top of his voice that he had found the spot. All went with him to the place where he said the lance was to be found, and they found the lance. It was old and rotten, it was eaten up by ants and worms, and he said, "Here is a lance, corroded by the earth, a lance which must have touched the body of Christ;" and he held it up where everybody might see it. The Christians jumped around it with joy, their happiness knew no bounds. Being inspired with the finding of the lance covered with earth, being filled with energy and strength, all attacked the enemies again and came out victorious. Afterwards when the Christians came back to Europe, all believed that it was the virtue of the lance which had brought them victory, but after a while this same man who had told the first story fell sick, and was at the point of death. He confessed to the priest who came to bless him, and told him that the lance story was a fraud. He said the lance in reality belonged to his great grandfather, who was also in the army. The lance had been wrapped in rags and kept in the house since his great-grandfather's death. It had been used not only by his great grandfather but had been handed down to him from his ancestors. Now when the Christians were going to Jerusalem, he said he took this lance with him, wrapped up as it was, but on the field he found it worthless, and when fleeing, the idea came that he might as will be popular, he might as well win a name for himself. So he gave out the story about the lance, and when the people were digging on the opposite side from him, he took the lance and threw it into the ditch, and when they came there and began to dig, they found it.

No virtue belonged to the lance, but the virtue lay in the enthusiasm and perfect Faith of the people. The victory was due not to the lance but to the power within the people; the people, they said, manufactured spiritual force within them, and that Living Faith of the people brought victory, and not the lance. Similarly, Vedanta says, "O Christians, O Mohammedans, O Vaishnavas, O ye different sects of the whole world, if you think you are being saved through the name of Christ or Buddha or Krishna or any other saint, remember, the real virtue does not lie in the Christ, or the Buddha, or the Krishna, or anybody; the real virtue lies in your own Self."

MORAL: It is Living Faith which saves and not creed.

Wonders of True Faith (The Milkmaid's Faith)

At one time a great Pandit, a great sage was reading out the sacred texts to some people. It so happened that the village milk-maids passed by the Pandit or sage who was reading out the sacred texts to the people. The maids heard from the lips of the sage these words, "The sacred name of God, the Holy Being, is the great ship which makes us cross the ocean, as if the ocean were simply a small pool." Nothing at all. A statement of that kind they heard. These maids took that statement literally. They put implicit faith in that saying. They had to cross the river every day to sell their milk. Milk-maids they were. They reflected in their minds. It is a sacred text, it cannot be wrong, it must be right. They said, "Why should we give a four anna piece to the boat-man every day? Why not cross the river by taking the holy name of God and chanting OM? Why should we pay four annas every day?" Their faith was strong as adamant. The next day they came and simply chanted OM, paid nothing to the boat-man, they began to wade the river, they crossed the river and were not drowned. Day after day they began to cross the river, they paid no money to the boatman.

After about a month or so they felt very grateful to the teacher who had recited the texts which saved their annas, saved their money. They asked the sage to be kind enough to dine at their house. Well, the request was granted the sage had to go to their house on the appointed day. One of those maids came to fetch him. While this maid was conducting the sage to their village, they came to the river, and there in a trice the maid went up to the opposite shore and the sage remained on the other bank, could not follow her. In a short while the maid came back and asked the reason of his delay. He said that he was waiting for the boatman. The boatman ought to take him to the opposite shore. The maid replied "Sir, we are so thankful to you. You have been so kind as to save us full one rupee, and not only this one rupee but all our lifelong we shall spend no money to pay the boatman. Why don't you yourself save the money and come to the opposite bank with us? We go to the opposite bank uninjured, unharmed through your advice and teaching. You yourself also can go to the opposite shore." The sage asked what piece of advice was it that saved their money. The maid reminded him of the text he once gave. That God's name was a ship that carried us across the ocean of this world. He said, alright, alright, he too must practise it. There were other companions. There was a long, long rope. He fastened that rope to his waist and asked companions to keep the remaining part of the rope to themselves, and said he would jump into the river, he would launch into the river and take the name of God and would venture to cross the river on faith, but if they felt that he was being drowned, they should draw him back. The sage jumped into the river, went on for a few steps and was found to be drowning. They drew him out. So just mark. The kind of faith, that Pandit had, this faith which gives credence to it, this is not the saving principle. This is the crookedness in your hearts. When you begin to chant OM or when you begin to take the name of God, and say "I am health, health, health," there in your heart of hearts you tremble, in your heart of hearts you have that little quaking, quivering "I". "If" I sink, draw me out, you have that small faltering "if" in your mind, there is no conviction on faith. This is a fact that all differences, all the circumstances in this world are my creation, my doing, nothing else. You are the Divinity, the Lord of lords you are; feel that. Realize in this moment.

MORAL: Faith full of conviction and devoid of the least doubt is true faith and works wonders.

CHAPTER FOUR

God-Consciousness

God-Consciousness. (The Master State)

To a man who had reached the state of perfect freedom, there came a disciple who sat at his feet for a year or so. When the disciple was going to leave the master, he began to bow down at his feet, to kneel down before him, to prostrate himself before him, as the custom in India is. The master smiling raised him and said: "Dear, you have not yet learnt all that you could learn. You lack a great many things yet; stay for some while more." A few days more he stayed in the holy presence of the master and got more of inspiration. His heart was converted into God-consciousness. He was full of Holy Ghost. He left the presence of the master knowing not whether disciple or master himself. He went away he was looking upon the whole universe, the wide world, as his real self, and the whole universe being his real self where could he, the Self, go? When the Self fills and permeates every atom, every molecule, where can It go? The idea of going and coming becomes meaningless to him.

You can go from one place to another, if you are not already at the place where you want to go. Here he found himself, he found his true Self, the God within; God everywhere, and how could he think of going and coming? The idea of going and coming became absent for him. He was in the state of self-realization. The going of the body was a sort of reflex action. He was in himself; no going or coming for him. Then was the master satisfied. Thus, did the master test him and prove him of sterling worth. The disciple paid no respects or thanks to the master and rested in unity to such a degree that he rose above all idea of gratitude. Then did the master know that he had really understood his teachings.

Here is the master-state, where, if you honour the man, he says you are belittling him. "I am not confined in this body; I am not this little body only—I am the wide world, I am you, and honour me in you." Here is the state of a man who sells not anything to you. Here is the state of a man to whom honour and disgrace for the body have become meaningless, both shame and fame are nothing.

MORAL: A man of God-consciousness realises his omnipresence and oneness with all.

Extraordinary Powers of Realized Being (Shams Tabrez and his Father)

There was one of the greatest men in the world, an Eastern saint. Shams Tabrez was his name. This man was born under peculiar circumstances. It is related about his father that he was once the poorest man in the country. That poorest man devoted his life entirely to God-consciousness. He forgot that his body was ever born; he entirely forgot that his personality ever existed in this world. For him the world had never been a world. He was God, all Divinity. And just when a man's whole being is saturated with an idea, from head to foot, every pore of his body was alive to God-consciousness. It is related that when he walked, through the streets, the people heard through the pores of his body this song "Haq, Analhaq," which means "God, I am God." The song on his lips was always, "Analhaq, Analhaq, Divinity I am. Divinity I am." The ordinary people gathered around him. They wanted to murder him. They accused him of heresy. Why is he calling himself God? He was Divinity himself, to him the body was no body, the world was no world. When the words „Analhaq" escaped his lips, he was not even conscious of that. Just as a man snores when asleep, similarly from his standpoint he was entirely lost in Divinity, and if those words „Analhaq" escaped his lips, they were like the snoring of a man who is asleep. But the people wanted to kill him.

What is that to him whom will you kill? You will kill the body, but that body from his stand-point never existed. Kill his body, what pain can it cause him? It is related that this man's body was placed upon a cross. You know that putting a body on a cross is an easy thing, but there they have something worse than a cross. It was a long iron pole with a needle-like end, and the heart of the man was placed exactly on the top of the iron pole, the sharp pointed end of the iron pole had to press through the solar plexus.

This way was the man put to death in those days. You see, this is worse than a cross even! His body was placed upon a cross of that kind and it is related that while his body was placed there, this man's face was glowing with glory, and through every hair of his body the same sweet song was all the time coming out - "Analhaq, Analhaq, I am God, I am God. Divinity I am, Divinity I am." The body dies; to him it makes no difference. Here when the man was hanging upon that pointed pole, drops of blood fell from his body, and the story says that those drops of blood were gathered by a young girl. This young girl who believed the same way as the saint, this young girl who was of the same thought as the preacher, drank up this blood, and they say that she was conceived. It may be true or false, we have nothing to do with that. According to the Vedanta, if Christ could be of Immaculate Conception, this could also be true, because here was a man who was not inferior to Christ, really superior to him in many respects. This woman gave birth to a boy who became a sage. From his beginning, from his very childhood he was all Divinity, even far exceeding his father. There is such a great book, a large work which came from the lips of this hero. This man did not take up a pen and write it, but it is said that through him always poetry came out, all that he spoke was poetry, all that he said was poetry. But what kind of poetry! Not the doggerel of the American poets. It was real poetry in the true sense of the word. It was God-consciousness and nothing else. It was sublime with divine ideas. Every word was worth its weight in gold, if it could be weighed at all.

There is a very remarkable fact related about this man. At one time there appeared to him some people who were connected with some show, you might say, a circus or some other kind of show. When they performed in the presence of the king, he was highly pleased with them, and offered them a thousand mohars (gold coins). Afterwards the king repented. The king did not think it advisable to give away a thousand of mohars every night for mere empty shows and so, in order to get back his thousand mohars he made a pretence, and asked those people to appear in the garb of a lion, and thus if the lion's performance was pleasing to the king, he might give them something enormous, something great, otherwise the king would fine them all their property. These people could not give a lion's performance; they could not put on the garb or assume the shape of a lion and please the king.

In India there are people who put on all sorts of garbs and appear in the shape of some animals and make themselves appear to all intents and purposes the animals they play, but they could not assume the garb of the lion. These people came to this man and were weeping and crying and shedding tears.

The story that this sage being in tune with the universe, in harmony with the whole nature, being one with each and all, natural sympathy overtook his heart and all of a sudden he spoke to those people to be of good cheer because he was to appear as a lion, and to give the performance of a lion himself. So the story goes that the next day when the king and his courtiers were all standing, waiting to see a man assume the shape and figure of a lion, all of a sudden, as if by magic, a real lion jumped into the pit. This lion at once roared and roared, he took up the child of the king and tore it to pieces. He took up some other boy and threw it out to the sky. You see, here was a man who was in reality Divinity and God. To this man the idea "I am this little puny body" had become a thing of the past, it had become absolutely meaningless. He was Divinity himself, and the God that appeared in the shape of a lion, the same was he, and he was in a moment's thought a lion. (Just as you think so you become, and if you have felt and realized your Divinity as God, all your thoughts and desires are bound to fructify, to be realized on the spot.) So his man's thought that he could appear as a lion was immediately realized, and a lion he was. The show was over. The sage after killing this boy went away, because he had not to become a lion and respect this body or that. He was no respecter of persons. But here the king was exasperated, the king and the courtiers were all rage personified, they wanted to wreck vengeance upon this man. They came to him and said, "Sir, sir, please bring this boy to life again. If you can kill him, you can bring him to life also. Bring him back to life, just as Christ used to bring to life the dead, by saying Qutn Bismillah - which means "Rise in the name of God, glorify God and walk, be alive, come back to life!" They asked him to make that dead boy come to life in the name of God. The sage laughed and said, "Come back to life in the name of God,", but the boy did not revive. The saint said, "The boy does not come to life in the name of God." He said again, "Come to life in the name of God." Still the boy did not come to life. He said again, "Come to life, get up and walk in the name of God, the Lord," but the boy did not come to life. The sage smiled and said "Qum Bizzini." "Come to life by my order, through my command, come to life" and the boy came to life. This is the Truth, "Qum Bizzini," "Come to life in my name," and the boy was all right. The boy came to life, but the people all around him could not bear it. They said, "Here is man, a heretic. He takes all this credit to himself. He wants to make himself equal to God. He ought to be put to death. He ought to be murdered, flayed alive." To the sage it meant nothing. The people understood him not. He is not calling the body, the little personality, God. He- had already killed and crucified his flesh. The people wanted to slay him alive, and the story says that that man immediately applied his nails to his head, and just as the skin of animals is torn and separated from the body, so with his own nails he tore his own skin, cut it off and threw it away. And there is a fine long poem written by him on that occasion. The purport of that song is "O Self, O Self," he is addressing himself, "to whom the poison of the world is nectar and O Self, to whom the nectar of the world (that is to say the sensuous enjoyments) is poison. Here are people wanting something. The world is nothing else but a dead carcass (and here dead carcass means "sensuous enjoyments"), the worldly pleasures are nothing else but a dead carcass and the people who run after them are no better than dogs. Here are these dogs. Give them this flesh to eat.

If for the sake of Truth you have to give up the body, give it up. This is the last attachment broken. What to say of giving up worldly attachments, for the sake of Truth, for the sake of Truth you have to give up not only worldly attachments, but if there be need to give up the body, give it up. This is how you have to tread the path of Truth.

In order to realize the Truth, to tread the path of righteousness, give up all attachments; rise above worldly desires and selfish clinging. If you free yourself of worldly clinging and selfish desires, Truth you are this moment.

MORAL: Whatever a Realized Being thinks that he becomes, and whatever he commands, all nature obeys.

Ghost are Bound Souls (A cave in the Himalayas)

Rama lived at one time in a cave in the Himalayas, which was noted for being haunted by ghosts. The people who lived in the neighbouring villages spoke of several monks having died by remaining inside that cave for a night. Some of the visitors were said to have been frightened to swooning. When Rama expressed a desire to live in that cave, everybody was amazed. Rama lived in that cave, for several months, and not a single ghost or shade appeared. It seems that they all fled. There were snakes and scorpions inside the cave and tigers outside it. They did not leave the neighbourhood but never did any harm to Rama's body.

It is proved by Vedanta that free souls or the jiwan-muktas never live after death as ghosts; it is only the slaves of their own phantoms that must assume the garb of ghosts or spirits. It is only the bound souls that are enchained in those shadowy shapes.

MORAL:— Ghosts are bound souls, hence they cannot withstand the presence of a free soul (jiwan-mukta) and can therefore cause him no harm.

Subtle body of the Realized Soul (King Cyrus)

It is related of King Cyrus, the Elder of Persia, that so long as he lived in this world, he lived solely for the service and good of the people. When about to die he stated in his will, "Let not my body be placed in a magnificent tomb, but let it be hacked into small bits and distributed piecemeal all over the Persian Empire to serve as manure."

This is exactly what occurs to the subtle body of the free man; his subtle body is distributed or diffused throughout the whole world. So long as he lives, his benign presence, his holy sight spreads purity and happiness. At his death, wonderfully is the world reformed.

MORAL: A Realized soul serves the world white alive, and after death his subtle body is diffused throughout the whole world uplifting it unconsciously.

Attachment versus Detachment (Raw and dry Cocoanuts)

There was this question put to a Sage, "How is it that when Christ was crucified, he did not feel the cross?" At that time the Sage had some cocoanuts around him. (In India, people visiting friends or sages always bring fruits and these cocoanuts had been brought to the sage). One of the cocoanuts was raw and the other was dried up. The sage said, "This cocoanut is raw. Now if I break the shell what will happen to the kernel?" They said, "The kernel will be cut or broken also, it will be injured." 'Well," said the sage, "here is the dried cocoanut, and if I break this shell, what will happen to the kernel." They said, "If the shell of this cocoanut is broken, the kernel will not be injured, it will be unharmed." He said, "Why?" They said, "In the dried cocoanut, the kernel separates itself from the shell, and in the raw cocoanut the kernel attaches itself to the shell." Then the sage said, "When Christ was crucified what was crucified?" They said, "The body." "Well," said the sage, "here was a man whose body or outer shell was injured or crucified, but here was a man who had separated the immutable Self, the true kernel, from the outer shell; the outside shell was broken but the inside was intact; so why feel sorry, why weep or cry over it? In the case of other men, as in the raw cocoanut, the kernel attaches itself to the shell and so when the shell or body is disturbed, the kernel or inside is disturbed or injured also, and that is the difference."

The weakness or disease in you is this attachment to the shell, this clinging, this slavery so the shell. Thus, giving up this clinging, this bondage to the shell is death from the stand-point of worldly men. From the standpoint of your present vision, that is death, and unless you suffer this death and detach yourself from this shell and the concerns of the shell, you cannot conquer death, you cannot rise above anguish; misery, or pain. Let the body become as if it never existed. A man of liberation, a free man, is one who lives in Divinity, in Godhead, in such a way that the body was never born.

MORAL: All the miseries, pains and sufferings exist only so long as there is the attachment with the body; but they cease to exist as soon as detachment takes place.

State of death of God-Consciousness (The death of Rama's son)

At one time there came a man to a meeting where we all had God consciousness, and on entering he began to cry and weep and beat his breast; no body attended to him. He was grieving over the death of Rama's son, who was related to this man. Well, no body attended to him, and he sat down, and then he was asked quietly, calmly, plainly to hush his anxiety and to console himself; and he said he could not bear the death of this relation of his (the son of Rama). None of the audience could weep or cry or show any signs of disturbance, for there was the state of God-consciousness; there was that state where everything in the world was looked at from the standpoint of God; there was that condition where the old songs were set to the new music of Divinity. The words or remarks which escaped the lips at that time were as follows: "O brother, the fact that you are a relative, is of the same sort as somebody coming and saying 'O sir the wind is blowing', but O fellow, what if the wind does blow, what is unnatural about is to upset us? Or O sir, the river is flowing; what if the river flows, it is natural, why should it upset us; the river flows that is natural; there is nothing abnormal or extraordinary about these statements. Similarly, when you come and say that your son is dead, there is nothing extraordinary about it, it is most natural; everyone who is born, is born to die- When you enter the University, do you enter to stay but for a short time or to make it your home all the time; do you get examined and remain there all your life as a freshmen or sophomore? When you enter the fresh-man class, it is intended that you should leave that class one day and go on to the sophomore, &c.

"When you enter a staircase, it is understood that you are not to remain there always, but will leave the staircase after a short time,

"When you reincarnate, is it not understood that you must leave that reincarnation or past life?

"Similarly when you enter this body it is understood that you will leave this body. So if that boy, whom you call Rama's boy, is dead, there is nothing remarkable or curious about it. It is not strange, it should not upset you; it is like saying that you had your nails pared today. If the son is dead, all right, there is nothing unnatural about it.

This is the way to look at your worldly relations and thus keep yourself free; look from the stand-point of Reality, making Rama, the true Self, Divinity, your home, and look at all your acquaintances, connections and relations from that vantage ground.

MORAL: During the state of God-consciousness whatever (good or evil) happens in the world, appears as natural and hence affects not the least. Even the death of the nearest relation fails to disturb the peace of mind.

The Highest Standpoint (Rama and the Prince)

Once came a man and said to Rama, "O sir, a great prince is coming to pay his respects to you." Now here is an important, a critical point, where people usually feel these flattering, puffing remarks of friends. Well the man, said, "Here is a very wealthy man coming to pay his respects to you." There was Rama looking at everything from the stand-point of Divinity, and these words escaped the lips of Rama "What is that to Rama?" The man said, "O sir, he is going to purchase such magnificent, beautiful costly things to bring to you." Rama said, "What is that to me? What is a prince to me? Let me have Reality only. Trifles and frivolities, these unreal phenomena, have no interest for me; my Truth, my Divinity, my joy, my Atman is enough to keep me busy. These vain talks, these frivolous, worldly things do not concern me. This prince or these wealthy people come to the body of Rama, and if Rama become interested in these bodies, he would become a veritable interrogation point; but when the point of view is changed and when the old songs have been set to new music, when the observation is taken from the highest stand-point, then what interest can a Lord or Mayor or an Emperor excite in me? None whatever,"

So let the stand-point be changed. When newspapers have no attraction for you, when they cease to interest you then that day you have risen above the body, and have come nearer to God. This gives you one way of applying this Truth in your practice. When that crucifixion is attained, then the True Life in you will manifest itself in ways like that.

MORAL:—No worldly objects attract one who looks at them from the highest stand-point, for they cease to interest him whose interests are all absorbed in the Divinity or Atman.

True Knowledge of God-head (Swami Rama's Servant)

There was a boy who used to serve in the house in which Swami Rama used to live in India. That boy remaining all the while in contact with Rama; was one day walking on the top of the high mansion, and was shouting aloud, "I am God, I am God, I am God." There were some people in the other houses next door to the house on the top of which he was roaring. They spoke to him, "What are you raving, what are you saying? Do you say you are God? If you are God, do jump down from the roof and let us see whether you are hurt or not. If you are not hurt, then we shall believe in you as God; if you are hurt, we shall kill you, we shall persecute you. Why are you speaking that way? This profane language you have no right to employ."

The boy, full of Divine madness, spoke out, "O My own Self, I am ready to jump down; I am ready to take a leap into any abyss that you may point out; I am ready to jump into any ocean that you may indicate, but kindly let me know the place where I am not present already, because in order to jump down, we ought to have some spot where we can jump down and where we are not present already, Let me know the place which is void of Me; where I am not present already. I am the God of gods. Do point out to me the place where I am not present already, and I will jump. How can He jump who already permeates the whole? He alone can jump who is limited, who is present here and not there. He alone can take a leap."

Then the gentlemen who had asked him to jump down said, "Oh, are you that God, are you that God? You are the body." The boy said, "This body is made by your imagination: this body I am not. Your questions and objections cannot reach Me; they reach only your imagination. Similarly, how can He jump, or how can He do such things? Who is already all-permeating? There is not a single spot where He is not present already. The same am I. The same am I.

If I be present only in this body and not in that, then of course I ought to work worldly miracles through this body in order to make good my claim to Godhead. All the bodies are mine; readymade they are mine. I have simply to make possession; I have to make nothing, everything is made by me."

MORAL: One, who has true knowledge of Godhead, believes himself to be everywhere.

How the Infinite can be perceived (The Blind-men and Color Perception)

Once there were four man taken to a hospital because of cataract of the eye, which they hoped to be operated on there. Now naturally all these men suffering from cataract were stone-blind and had only the four senses left to them. One day they began to dispute as to the colour of the window glass. One said, "My son who is a student at the University was here and told me 'The glass is yellow.' It must be yellow." Another said, "My uncle who is a municipal commissioner was here the other day and told me 'the glass is red.' He is very smart and he knows." Then the third said that a cousin of his who was professor at the University had called on him, and while visiting him told him the glass was green. Of course he ought to know. Thus they quarreled as to the colour of the glass. Then they began to try and find out for themselves, what the colour of the glass was. First they put their tongues on it and tried to taste it, but colour was not to be known that way. Then they tapped it and listened to the sound, but colour could not be distinguished even that way. They tried to smell it and they felt it not. But alas! Their sense of touch, smell, taste, and hearing could not tell them what the colour of the glass was.

Similarly, we cannot know the Infinite through the senses. Now see, how impossible that would be; if you could know the Infinite through the senses, the Infinite would necessarily have to be smaller than the finite. Absurd. It is only through the Cosmic-consciousness, the God-consciousness that we know the Infinite. Suppose, I take a match-stick in my hand. Now the match-stick is smaller than the hand in which it is held. Do you see how the finite could not perceive the Infinite? The senses cannot perceive that which is beyond them. Do not depend upon anything outside of you to reveal the Self to you like the blind men who were told the colour of the glass, but did not know for themselves what the colour of the glass was, and were taking for granted that it was red because the cousin said so, that it was yellow because the son said so, and so on.

MORAL:—The Infinite cannot be perceived by the senses, because It is beyond them. It can only be perceived by the cosmic or God-Consciousness.

Effect of Heaven or Hell on a Realised Soul (A Woman carrying Fire and Water)

There was a woman who possessed the knowledge of Vedanta. She was going through the streets with fire in one hand and cool water in the other. People came up to her and asked, "What do you mean by carrying cool water in one hand and fire in the other? The man who put this question was a great Missionary. She said, "With this fire I am going to set your paradise and heaven on fire, and with this water I am going to cool down your hell."

To a man who possesses this knowledge that he himself is hell or he himself is heaven; to him all your heaven and hell lose all their attractions and fears. He stands above them.

MORAL: A Realised Soul is above all attractions of Heaven or fears of Hell, for he himself is all.

CHAPTER FIVE

Happiness

The Real Abode of Happiness (A Distressing Message)

A gentleman who has been blessed with a child is sitting in his office. He is busy with his official duties, and all of a sudden he hears the ring of the bell. What bell? The telephone bell. He jumps up to his feet and goes to the telephone, but when he is about to hear what the message, may be, his heart beats. They say, coming calamities cast their shadows before. His heart beats, never was it so with him before. He reaches up to the telephone and hears a message. Oh, what a distressing message it must have been!

The gentleman was panting and sobbing; he lost all presence of mind; his cheeks lost all colour; with a pallid, cadaverous face he came rapidly to his seat, put on his cloak and hat, and went out from the office as if he were shot with something like a ball from a gun. He did not even ask the consent of the chief officer, the head of the Department. He did not even exchange a word with the servants in the room.

He did not even look up the papers that were lying on the desk; he lost all presence of mind and went straight out of the office, and his fellow-officials were astounded. He reached the streets and saw a car running before him, he ran up to the car and there he meets a postman who gives him a letter. This letter brought to him the happy news, if it can be called happy news from the worldly point of view, the happy news of a large fortune having fallen to his lot. The man had bought a share in a lottery, and about Rs. 10,000 had fallen to his lot. This news ought to have cheered him up, ought to have filled him with joy, but it didn't, it didn't. The message he had received over the telephone was weighing heavily on his heart. This news brought him no pleasure. He found in the same car one of the greatest officials in the State sitting just in front of him. This was an official to have an interview with whom had been the one dream of his life. But look here! This gentleman did not exchange glances with the official; he turned his head away. He also noticed the sweet face of a lady friend. It had been the ambition of his gentleman's life to meet her and exchange words with her, but now he was insensible to her sunny smiles. He reached the street where his house was located, and a great noise and tumult was there, and he saw clouds of smoke rising to the sky and veiling the sun. He saw tongues of fire going up to the heavens; he saw his wife, grandmother, mother and other friends weeping and bewailing the conflagration which was consuming their house. He saw all his friends there but missed one thing; he missed the then metropolis of his happiness; he missed the dear little baby, he missed the sweet little child. That was not there. He asked about the child, and the wife could make no answer. She simply answered by sobbing and crying; she could make no articulate answer. He found out the truth. He came to know that the child had been left in the house. The child was with the nurse at the time when fire began; the nurse had placed the child in the cradle, the child was asleep and the nurse had left the room. Now the inmates of the house being panic stricken at the sight of the fire consuming the house, had quitted the house in haste, each thinking that the child must be with some other inmate of the house. All of them came out and now they found that the child was left in the room which was then being enveloped by fire. There was crying and gnashing of teeth, cutting of lips, beating of breasts, but no help.

Here this gentleman, his wife, his mother and friends, and the nurse were crying aloud to the people, to the by-standers, to the policemen, and asking them to save their child, to rescue their dear, little baby. "Save our little dear child any way you can. We will give away all our property, we shall give away all the wealth that we may accumulate within ten years from today, we will give up all; save our child.'

They are willing to give up everything for the sake of the child. Indeed, the child is a very sweet thing, the dear little baby is a very sweet thing, and it is worthwhile to sacrifice all the property, all our wealth and all our interest for the sake of the child. But Rama asks one thing, 'Is the child the source of happiness, the sweetest thing in the world, or is the source of happiness somewhere else? Mark here! Everything is being sacrificed for the child, but is not the child itself being sacrificed for something higher, or for something else? Wealth is given away, riches are given away, property is given away for the child, but the child is being given away for something else. Even the lives of those people who may venture to jump into the fire, may be lost. ,But even that dear little child is being sacrificed for something else, for something higher, and that something else must of necessity be sweeter than the child, that something else must be the real Centre of Happiness, must be the real Source of Happiness, and what is that something? Just see. They did not jump into the fire themselves. That something is the Self. If they jump into the fire themselves, they sacrifice themselves and that they are not prepared to do. On the child is everything else sacrificed, and on that Self is the child sacrificed.

MORAL: The Self is the real Abode of Happiness.

The Source of Joy (A Young Man at the Point of Death)

Rama once saw a young man at the point of death. He was suffering from a very bad disease. There was excruciating pain in his body. The pain began in the toes of the feet. At first it was not so great, but after a while it kept coming up, and then his body was undergoing a hysterical movement. Gradually the pain came up to the knees, and then rose higher, until that dreadful pain reached the stomach, and when the pain reached the heart the man died. The last words this young man uttered were these: "Oh, when shall this life leave me, when shall these pranas leave me?" These were the words of that youth.

Here is something higher even than life; something superior to prana, something which says, "My life," something which says "My prana" something which possesses the prana and is above the prana and life, and that something is sweeter by far than the individual, personal life or prana. Here we see something which is superior to the prana or life for which the life is sacrificed. That must be the home of Anand or pleasure; that must be the source, the origin of our joy. That is the Higher Self, the real home of happiness, for which even life is sacrificed.

MORAL: Self is the source of Joy.

Vain Search (A Lost Needle)

There was a woman, who lost her needle in the house. She was too poor to afford a light in her house, so she went out of the house and was searching in the streets. Somebody asked her what she was searching for in the streets. She said that she was searching for her needle. The gentleman asked,

"Where did you lose the needle?" She said, "In the house." He said," "How unreasonable it is to search in the street for a thing which was lost in the house!" She said that she could riot afford a light in the house and there was a lantern in the street. She could not hunt in the house; she had to do something, so she must hunt in the street.

This is exactly the way with people. You have the Heaven within you, the paradise; the home of bliss within you; and yet you are searching for pleasure in the objects, in the streets, searching for that thing outside, outside, in the objects of the senses. How strange!

MORAL: Searching for pleasure in the worldly objects is vain. The Home of Bliss is within you.

Worldly Blessing a Curse (The Woman and the Mendicant)

There was a woman in India who had nine sons. One day a mendicant passed her house and she gave him some alms. The mendicant was so highly pleased that he invoked a blessing upon her. He said, "O blessed Lord! Make this gracious lady the mother of seven children." When the well-meaning mendicant asked God to make her the mother of seven children, she was offended, for she had already nine children, and that meant a loss to her. She begged the mendicant to bless her again, and the mendicant again asked God to make her the mother of seven children. The lady became enraged and the people were attracted to the scene and inquired as to the cause of excitement. They were of course amused to know that the blessing was not a blessing but a curse.

Similarly, there is indescribable joy within you, and let that be enjoyed by you. That will make you free of all worldly things in this world.

Let the body, the personality, like the lily on Himalayan glaciers, bloom unknown, unnoticed by anybody. Let this body be crucified, let it be put into prison, let it be swallowed by the waves of the ocean, let it be scorched by the heat of Torrid Zone, let anything come to it, that joy cannot be abated. Feel that happiness, that joy supreme within, and rise above all worldly vanity, worldly tomfooleries, and all gloom.

But the Lord of lords, the God of gods. That ye are! That ye are!!

MORAL: A blessing of the worldly pleasures is a curse as compared with the indescribable joy within.

CHAPTER SIX

Ignorance

Crazy man's Feast (Lest there be a Real Feast)

A crazy man once came up to the boys of the street and told them that the Mayor of the city was preparing a grand, royal feast, and had invited all the children to partake of the feast. You know, children like candies and sweets. The children being assured by the crazy man of the feast arranged by the Mayor, ran to the house of the Mayor; but there was no feast at all, nothing of the kind. The children were baffled; but they were put out of countenance for a while and there was *hansi* (laughing), and the children said to him "How is it Mr.—that you too came when you knew that this story which you told was wrong?" He said, "Lest there be a real feast, lest the story be true and I miss it." For this reason because he did not wish to miss it, he also followed the boys.

Exactly the same is the case of those who by their imagination, by their own benediction make flowers beautiful, make every object in this world attractive, make everything desirable by their own imagination, like the crazy man, and then they want to run after it, so that they may not miss it.

MORAL: By our own imagination you make things attractive and then run after them.

The World, a Mirror-House (A Dog in a Mirror-House)

Once there came into a mirror-house (a house whose walls and roof are bedecked with mirrors) a dog. The dog finds armies of dogs, on his right, coming up to him, and you know that dogs are very jealous; dogs do not wish some rival dog to be present beside them. They are very jealous. When this dog saw thousands of dogs approaching him from the right, be turned to the left hand side, and again on that wall were fixed thousands of mirror and there he finds an army of dogs coming up to him about to devour him, tear him to pieces. He turned to the third wall and there he found again dogs of the same sort. He turned to fourth wall and thre the same thing. He turned his head upward to heaven and there from heaven he saw thousands of dogs coming down upon him to devour him and tear him to pieces He was frightened. He jumped up, all the dogs jumped on all sides; he was barking and he found all the dogs barking and opening their mouths at him. The sound reechoed from the four walls, and he was afraid. He jumped and ran this way and that way. The poor fellow died exhausted on the spot.

Exactly the same way, Vedanta tells you this world is like a mirror-house, and all these bodies are like different mirrors, and your true Atma or real Self is reflected on all sides, just as the dog saw his figure reflected from the four walls. Just so does the One Infinite Atma, the One Infinite Divinity, the Infinite Power, reflect itself in the different mirrors. It is the One Infinite Rama that is being reflected through all these bodies.

Ignorant people come like dogs in this world and say: "That man will eat me up, that man will tear me to pieces, destroy me." Oh, how much of jealousy and fear in this world! To what are this jealousy and fear due? To the ignorance of the dog, to dog-like ignorance is all this jealousy and fear of the world due.

Please turn the tables. Come into this world like the master of the house, of the looking-glass and mirror-house. Come into the world not as d-o-g, but as g-o-d, and you will be the master of the mirror-house, you will be the owner of the whole universe; it will give you pleasure when you see your rivals and your brothers and your enemies advance; it will give you joy when you find any glory anywhere. You will make a heaven of this world.

MORAL: Ignorance of Reality is the Cause of all Jealousy and Fear.

Foolish Rejoicing (A Man distributing Sweets)

In India, in a certain temple, a man was seen distributing sweets. The way with Indians is that on occasions of great joy and prosperity, they distribute sweets or other things among the poor. Somebody came and asked what the cause of this rejoicing was. The man said that he had lost his horse. That was the cause of his rejoicing. The people were astonished and surprised. They said, "Well, you have lost a horse and you are rejoicing?" He said, "Misunderstand me not. I have lost a horse but saved the rider. My horse was stolen by a band of robbers. I was not riding the horse at the time the horse was taken. Had I been mounted on the horse, I might also have been stolen. I am thankful that I was not stolen with the horse and that it was only the horse that was stolen." The people laughed heartily. What a simple man!

The story seems to be ridiculous. But everyone has to apply it to himself and examine, whether he or she is not behaving worse than that man He lost the horse but saved himself, the rider. But thousands, nay, millions of people are trying to save the horse and loose the rider. That is the worst of it. So he had high occasion to rejoice when he saved the rider and lost the horse. Everybody knows that the real spirit, or the seal Self, ego or soul, is related to the astral body as a rider or horseman is related to the horse. But let us go to any body and ask about his whereabouts and his real nature. "What is your self, what does it do?" The answer will be, "I am Mr. so and so. I work in such and such an office." All these signs and all these answers relate to the gross body only. That is to say, these are answers which are not to the point. We ask, "Who are you—what are you?" and his answer does not let us know what he is in reality. It is wide of the mark, not to the point.. We ask about himself, and he is telling us about the horse, the body. We want to know about the rider, he evades the question and tells us things not asked at all. Is it not that we are taking the horse to be the rider? The horse is lost; it is high time to raise the cry, lost! Lost!! Lost!!! The thing lost is the rider, the soul, the spirit, the Atman, the true Self.

MORAL:—People rejoice in caring for the body, while they have lost the soul, or Self. This is ridiculous and foolish.

Cause of Religious Quarrels (Water-melon, Hindwana and Tarbooz)

Three boys were given a four anna piece by their master to share equally among themselves. They decided to purchase something with the money. One of the boys was an Englishman, one a Hindu, and the third a Persian. None of them fully understood the language of the other, so they had some difficulty in deciding what, to buy. The English boy insisted on purchasing a watermelon. The Hindu boy said, "No, no, I would like to have a Hindwana" The third boy, the Persian, said, "No, no, we must have a Tarbooz" Thus they could not decide what to buy. Each insisted upon purchasing the thing which he preferred, disregarding the inclinations of the other. There was quite a wrangle among them. They were quarrelling and walking through the streets. They happened to pass a man who understood these three languages - English, Hindustani and Persian. That man was amused over their quarrel. He said he could decide the matter for them. All the three referred to him and were willing to abide by his decision. This man took the four anna piece from them and asked them to wait at the corner. He himself went out to the shop of a fruit-seller and purchased one big watermelon for the four anna piece. He kept it concealed from them and called them one by one. He asked first the English boy to come, and not allowing the young boy to know what he was doing, he cut the watermelon into three equal slices, took out one part, handed it to the English and said, "Is not that what you wanted?" The boy was highly pleased; he accepted it cheerfully, gratefully, and went away frisking and jumping, saying that, that was what he wanted. Then the gentleman called the Persian boy to approach him, and handed him the second piece and asked him if that was what he desired. Oh, the Persian boy was highly elated and said. "This is my Tvrbooz! This is what I wanted." He went away very merry. Then the Hindu boy was called, the third piece was handed to him and he was asked if that was the object of his desire. The Hindu boy was well satisfied. He said, "This is what I wanted; this is my Hindwana."

Why was the quarrel or quibble caused? What is it that brought about the misunderstanding between the lads? The mere names! The mere names! Nothing else! Take off the names; see behind the veil of names. Oh! There you find that the three contradictory names - watermelon, Tarbooz and Hindwana - imply one and the same thing. It is one object which underlies them all. It may be that the Persian Tarbooz, the watermelon that grows in Persia, is slightly different from the watermelons they have in England, and it may be that the watermelons of India are slightly different from the watermelons of England, but in reality the fruit is the same. It is one and the same thing. Slight differences can be ignored.

Just so are the quibbles, quarrels, misunderstandings and controversies between different religions; Christians fighting Jews, Jews conflicting with Mohammedans, Mohammedans combating Brahmans, Brahmans finding fault with Buddhists, and Buddhists returning the compliment in a similar manner. It is highly amusing to see such quarrel. The cause of these quarrels and misunderstandings is chiefly in names. Take off the veil of names, strike out the curtain of names, see behind them, look at what they imply, and there you will not find much difference.

MORAL:—Misunderstanding, chiefly in names, is the cause of religious quibbles and quarrels, whereas realizing the Reality underlying the names leads to Peace.

Superstition (Grand Mamma and the clock)

In a village in India, a boy became quite a scholar. He had studied in the University, and while living in the university town he got some of the European ways. He purchased a clock in the university town, and during the three months' vacation he lived where his grandmamma was and he felt the need of this clock, and so he took it with him to his grandmother's house. Now the grandmamma was naturally averse to this intrusion in the house. The young man brought no English clothing with him, but he felt that this clock was indispensable for him in his study. He dared not bring any English chairs or tables for they were regarded as awful, but he brought the clock at all hazards. The whole family was against it and especially the grandmamma. She could not bear this intrusion, it was something terrible, "Oh" said she, "It is all the time giving forth tick, tick, such an odious sound; break it up, destroy it, throw it out, it is a bad omen, it will engender something awful, it will be the cause of some disaster." She would not be reconciled. The young man did his best to explain, but she would not be pleased. The boy kept the clock in his study despite his grand mamma"s remonstrance.

It happened that thieves broke into the house and some jewellery and money were stolen, and the grandmamma got additional evidence in her favour, and exclaimed, "Did I not tell you. that this clock would bring disaster? Thieves came and have stolen our jewellery and money, but the clock is not stolen. They knew if they took the clock they would be ruined. O, why do you keep this dreadful thing in the house? The boy was very headstrong, and all her ravings were of no avail. The boy kept the clock in his study, and not long after, the father of the boy died, and then the grandmamma became fearful. She cried, "O audacious boy, throw away this terrible omen from the house. How can you dare keep it longer? The boy still kept the clock; and again after a short time the mother of the boy died, and then the grandmamma could not tolerate the clock in the house any longer. Like so many other people, she thought the clock to contain a worm, for they had never seen anything run by machinery. So she thought there must be a worm in the clock to make it move, she could not conceive of its ticking and running of itself. She thought the clock to be the cause of all the troubles in the family; so she caught hold of the clock and took it into her private parlour and put a stone under it, and by the aid of another stone she broke the clock into pieces, she wrecked vengeance on the clock.

Just so the people very often put this and that together and jump at wrong conclusions.

MORAL: Superstition leads to wrong conclusions.

A Terrible Absurdity (The Crazy Man)

There was a man in India, who was half crazy, and just as in the month of April, people make April fools in America and elsewhere, in the mouth of March in India people play all sorts of jokes with their friends. The merry-making young man of the village thought it high time to have some Fun with this man. So they made him drink some wine, and made him tipsy, and then sent to him his most intimate and most trusted friend and companion. When this trusted friend came up to this man, the friend began to cry, to weep and wail and shed crocodile tears, and said, "O, I have just come from your house and found your wife widowed, I found your wife a widow." And the crazy fellow also began to cry and shed tears; he also began to bewail the widowhood of his own wife. Finally, others came and said, "Why do you weep?" The crazy man said, "O, I weep because my wife is a widow." They said to him, "How that can be? You say your wife is a widow. You are not dead. How can your wife become widowed, unless you, her husband, die? You are not dead; you are bewailing the widowhood of your own wife that is self contradictory."

The crazy fellow said,

तुम् तो कहते हो सच् मेरे भाई ।

पर घर से आया है मोतबर नाई ॥

"O, go away, you don't know, you don't understand, this my most trusted friend told me, he had just come from my house, and said that my wife was widowed. He was an eyewitness to that fact, he saw her widowed.'5 They said, "Look here, what a terrible absurdity is this!"

This terrible absurdity is being perpetrated by all the sects and religions of this world and by all the vain, proud, fashionable people of the world. They don't look with their own eyes, they don't think with their own brain. Here is your own Atman, your true Self, the Light of lights, Pure, Immutable. The Heaven of heavens within you. Your real Self, your own Atman is ever alive, ever present, never dead, and yet you cry and weep and shed tears and say, "O, when will happiness come to me," and you invoke the gods to come and help you out of your difficulty. There you prostrate yourselves, adopt sneaking habits, look down upon yourselves. Because such a writer, such a divine or saint, called 'himself a sinner, because he calls you worms, therefore you must do that, your salvation lies in thinking yourselves dead. This is the way people look at matters; but it won't do.

MORAL: Man though himself the source of all happiness yet cries for happiness and. thinks himself sinner or miserable, because others call him so,—a terrible absurdity.

The Darkness of Ignorance (A Man in a Dark Room)

In some of the poor huts in India, the people are so poor that they cannot afford light in the houses, and Rama once observed in passing along the streets that upon entering the house during the darkness of the night, the master of the house found fault with the wife and others of the household. He exclaimed, "O, why did you keep this table here, I broke my knee over it? Why did you put that chair there, I nearly broke my hand over it?" Was there any remedy? No, none; for if the wife removed the table or chair to another corner or part of the room, then the man would have to go to some other place in the dark and would get hurt. So long as there was darkness, the knee, the arm, the neck or shoulders must be broken; the head must knock against the cornice or wall. It could not be helped. If you simply light the room, let things be where they are, you will not have to bother; you will then be able to walk unhurt from place to place.

So it is in the world. In order that your suffering may be remedied, you should not rely on the adjustment of your surroundings or on your position in life for the remedy, but depend upon the remedy which deals only with the adjustment of the Sun within. All people are trying to get rid of suffering by placing or adjusting as it were the furniture, by placing this and that different in the world, or by accumulating money, or by building grand houses or by acquiring certain land which somebody else owns. By adjusting your surroundings, or by placing your furniture in this order or that, you can never escape suffering. Suffering may be shunned, removed and got rid of only by bringing light into your room, by having Light, by having knowledge in the closet of your heart. Let darkness go and nothing will harm you.

MORAL: Sufferings or the darkness of ignorance can be removed not by adjusting the outer surroundings but by the knowledge of Self, the Light within.

Knowledge, the Remover of Darkness (Savages and the Cave-Monster)

There was a community of savages that lived in a certain part of the Himalayas, savages who never lighted any fire. The old savages of the world did not light fires, they knew not how to make a fire. They used to live on dried fish, and never cooked their food except by the heat of the sun, or dried it in the sun- Before the evening came they went to bed, and got up with the sun, and thus they had no occasion to mix with material darkness. There was a big cave near the place where they used to live. These savages thought that some of their most revered ancestors were living in this cave. In fact some of their ancestors had entered the dark cave and had died in it by being stuck in the mud, or probably striking their heads against the jagged walls of the cave. The savages looked upon this cave as very holy, but these people, not being accustomed to associate with darkness, the darkness in the cave was to them a giant monster which they wanted to get rid of. (This looks as an absurdity, but the people of to-day are committing greater absurdities.) Well, someone told them that the monster in the cave would leave if they approached the cave in a worshipful mood. So they went and prostrated themselves in front of the cave for years, but the monster did not leave the cave by this reverence. Afterwards someone told them that the monster would leave the cave if they bullied him, if they fought him. So they got all sorts of arrows and sticks and rocks, all kinds of weapons that they could find, and began to shoot arrows into the cave and strike the darkness with stick; but the darkness did not move, it did not leave. Another said, "Fast, fast. The darkness will leave the cave by your fasting. All these years you have not been doing the right thing. Fasting is what is needed." The poor fellows fasted and fasted. They sacrificed by fasting, but the darkness left not, the monster still did not leave the cave. Then somebody said the darkness would be dispelled if they distributed alms. So they began to distribute all that they had, but the monster did not leave the cave. At last there came a man who said the monster would leave the cave if they followed his advice. They asked him what his advice was, and he said, "Bring me some long sticks of bamboo, and some grass to fasten the bamboo-sticks together, and some fish oil." Then he asked them to bring him some straw or rags or something to burn. This man applied them to the long end of the bamboo, and by striking a stone against a piece of flint; he struck fire and lighted the straw at the end of the bamboo-stick.

Fire was made and this was a queer sight to these people, for this was the first time they had seen fire. This man then told them to take hold of the bamboo-stick and run it into the cave, and with it catch hold of the ears of the monster and drag him out of the cave, if they met the monster, darkness. At first they did not believe in his theory and said that could not be right, since their great-grandfathers had told them that the monster would leave the cave if they prostrated themselves before it, or if they fasted, or if they gave alms, and they had practised all these things for many years, and the monster had not left the cave. "And now,5' they said, "here is a stranger; he surely cannot advise us aright; his advice is worth nothing. O, we will not listen to it." So they put out the fire. But there were some who were not so prejudiced. They took up the light and went into the cave, and lo! the monster was not there. They went on and on into the cave, for it was a very long cave, and still found no monster; then they thought the monster must be hidden in the holes in the cave, and so they thrust the light into all the holes in the cave, but there was no monster anywhere, it was as if it had never been there.

Just so, ignorance is the monster, darkness, which has entered the cave of your hearts and is making havoc there, and turning it into a hell. All anxiety, all suffering, all pain lies in yourself, never outside.

MORAL: Ignorance or darkness can be removed by Gyana, or knowledge of the Self and not by penances, fasting or other ceremonies.

Wrong Reasoning (A Crazy Woman and her Cock)

There was once a crazy woman living in a small village. She had a cock with her. The people of the village used to tease her, and called her names and caused her much annoyance and trouble. She said to the people of the village living near her. "You tease me; you worry and bother me so much.

Now, look here, I'll wreak vengeance on you." At first the people paid no heed to her. She cried, "Beware O villagers! Beware! I shall be very hard on you." They asked her what she was going to do, and she said, "I will not allow the sun to rise in this village." They asked her how she would do that, and she replied. "The sun rises when my cock crows. If you go on troubling me, I shall take my cock to another village and then the sun will not rise on this village."

It is true that, when the cock crew, the sun rose, but the crowing of the cock was not the cause of rising of the sun. O, no. Well, she left the village and went to another; she was very much troubled. The cock crew in the village where she went and the sun rose on that village; but it also rose on the village which had been forsaken by her.

Similarly, the crowing of the cock is the craving and yearning nature of your desires. Your desires are, like the crowing of the cock and the coming up of the objects of desires before you is like the rising of the sun. The cravings and yearnings for the objects of desires are brought about, governed, controlled, and ruled by the One Sun or the Infinite or the Self. It is the true Self, the governing Sun, which is bringing about morning or evening, day or night. All worldly affairs are governed and controlled by this true Self, Infinity. It penetrates the senses. The wire puller is controlled by the Sun of suns, that Light of lights. Remember that.

People usually attribute all this to the little, craving, hungering, selfish self. Do not make that mistake; please be free from it.

MORAL: To attribute the qualities of the Higher Self to the lower self is wrong reasoning.

Misinterpretation of Scriptures (The son of a Wine Merchant)

There was a body, the son of a wine merchant, in India. He was put to school and began to learn English.

In India, specially in the Missionary Schools, it is the Bible that is taught first. The English reading was concerned with the Bible. Well, when the boy came to this passage "The Spirit of God brooded over the waters," he was puzzled. The boy knew the word Spirit, and he knew the word brooded and the word water, but he did not know the word of God; and he said. "The Spirit of God brooded." Does God mean barley, corn, or grapes? I know spirits come from barley and corn, or grapes &c, and he thought here was a queer kind of wine put in the ocean. His father used to mix alcoholic spirits with water, and he was acquainted with, that kind of spirits, but here was a queer kind of mixture.

This is the way people misinterpret the Scriptures, because they live in wine shops too much, because they live in materiality too much, and those sublime and sacred Scriptures are taken in the gross sense and materialized.

MORAL: Scriptures are very often misinterpreted, because the people do not raise themselves to the level of the author.

Search due to Ignorance (The Forgotten Necklace Regained)

There was a man who wore round his neck a most precious and long necklace in invaluable garland. It slipped down the back of his body by some means, and he forgot it. Not finding it dangling on his breast, he began to search for it. The search was all in vain. He shed tears and bewailed the loss of his priceless necklace. He asked someone to find it for him, if possible. Well, said someone to him, "Can I find the necklace for you, what will you give me? The man answered, "I will give you anything you ask," The man reaching his hand to the neck of his friend and touching the necklace said, "Here it is, here is the necklace. It was not lost, it was still around your neck, but you had forgotten it." What a pleasant surprise!

Similarly, your Godhead is not outside yourself, you are already God, you are the same.

It is strange oblivion that makes you forgetful of your real Self, your real Godhead. Remove this ignorance, dispel this darkness, away with it and you are God already. By your nature you are free; you have forgotten yourself in your state of slavery. A king may fall asleep and find himself a beggar, he may dream that he is beggar, but that can in no way interfere with his real sovereignty!

MORAL: It is due to ignorance that we search for the Atman which is already with us, nay, our own Self.

Weakness Within (Finding Fault with Gravity)

A man fell down and hurt his legs, and he began to find fault with Gravity and cried, "O wretched Law of Gravity, you made me fall." Well, it is better for millions of men to fall and break their legs than for the Law of Gravity to be eliminated. Fight not with Gravity; take your steps cautiously and you will have no falls. All your falls, al) your injuries, all your hurts, all your anxieties and troubles are due to some weakness within you. Remove that and fight not with circumstances, do not blame your fellow men, throw not the blame on the shoulders of others, but remove your own weakness.

Bear in mind that whenever you fall or suffer or are troubled, it is due to some weakness within you. Remember this and fight not with Gravity.

What is this weakness within? It is the dark pitch of ignorance which makes you look upon the body, the senses, as you. Get rid of it, discard it, and then Power itself you become.

MORAL: Anxieties, miseries, sufferings and troubles cannot be removed by fighting with the circumstances but by removing one's own weakness within to which they are really due.

Ignorance, the Cause of Ruin (The Three Intoxicated Men)

Once there were three men sitting together and drinking a great deal; they all became very intoxicated. One of them said, "Let us have a little picnic,*' and so they sent one of the party for meat and other things that they might all have a good time of it. While he was gone, one of the two remaining began to feel peculiar and said to his partner, "The breath is going out of me." The other said, "No, no, the breath must not go out of you," and he held the one of the sick men that the breath might not escape; he stopped up his ears and held his mouth shut, thinking thereby to keep the breath in the body, but we know fully well what he could accomplish thereby.

They did not realize the truth and the inefficacy of such a performance.

MORAL: Ignorance shrouds knowledge and is thus the cause of ruin.

The Result of Dogmatism (The Rev. Doctor's Book)

A few years ago, when Rama was in India, a book by a Reverend Doctor, an American gentleman, a professor in a University in India, came into Rama's hands. The subject of this book was "After Death." By a very beautiful allegory it was shown that this world is like one station and the other world is like another station, beyond: the bay, beyond the seas, and all those who have to go beyond this bay have to purchase tickets. Those who do not possess the right kind of tickets will be thrown overboard into the deep abyss. Those who have the right kind of tickets will be allowed to pass on to the goal, to the destination. Tickets are of several kinds, first class, second class, third class, etc. Then there are some counterfeit tickets. They are white, black, yellow, green etc., but the real genuine tickets, the right kind of tickets, which have to take you to the destination are red, besmeared with the blood of Jesus, the Christ. Those alone who have such tickets, will be allowed to reach the destination successfully; others never, never. The white, black, yellow and other kinds of tickets were the tickets of other religions, so to say, and the red tickets bore the blood of Christ; they were the Christian tickets. This was the subject of the book, and it was very beautifully brought out. The reverend doctor had lavished all his ingenuity and English literature in writing that book.

Something like this is the belief, not only of Christians but of all other religions. Mohammedans say that after death, the ticket-collector, or say the great station master, or the examiner of accounts, is Mohammed, and those who do not bear the sign of Mohammed will be cast down Into hell. Other religions also have ideas of the same sort, and they say that all the dead, whether they died in America. Europe, Africa, Australia, or Asia, all these people will be subjected to the disposal of a single man, let it be Christ, Mohammed, Buddha, Zoroaster, Krishna, or anybody; and this is the cause of all the warfare, strife, and struggle between religions. This superstition, this dogmatic view is the cause of most of the bloodshed in this world, the bloodshed that was carried out in the name of religion.

MORAL:—Dogmatism in the name of religion brings about warfare, bloodshed, strife and struggle in this world.

Effect of Maya or Ignorance (Milton's Wife)

In Milton"s life there is very beautiful story told about a lady, who was his wife. In her dream she saw her husband, her lord, and her heart was leaping in her bosom for her lord, for her husband. She embraced her husband. and said, "My lord, I am wholly yours." Just at that moment she woke up and found that a dog that had been sleeping in the same bed with her had been pressing its body to her; that dog leaped out of the bed to the floor, and in reality it was the pressure of the dog that appeared to her in her dream to be her lord, her husband. Had the dog pressed its body more and more, she would have felt a mighty Himalaya on her breast.

And Vedanta says, so long as the dog of ignorance, the dog of Maya remains pressing you down, your dreams are continually changing from good to bad, and from bad to good, sometimes a husband and sometimes a mighty Himalaya presses on you. You will be always like a pendulum oscillating between a tear and a smile; the world will weigh heavily upon your heart, there will be no rest for you. Vedanta says, "Get rid of this dog of ignorance, make yourself God Almighty, make yourself That, realize That, and you are free.

MORAL: It is Maya or Ignorance which makes you weep or smile and keeps you in bondage. If you get rid of it, you rise above sorrow and pleasure. Realise God-head and be free.

True Imitation (Imitating Majnun)

There was a man who was reading a love poem, a beautiful poem, which described the love of Laila and Majnun. He admired the hero of the poem, Majnun, so much that he attempted to become Majnun. In order to become Majnun, he took a picture which somebody told him was the picture of the heroine of the poem he had been reading. He took up that picture, hugged it, shed tears over it, placed it on his heart, and never parted with it. But you know, artificial love cannot exist long. Here is artificial love. Natural love cannot be imitated and he was trying to imitate love.

There came up to him a man, and told him, "Brother, what are you doing? That is not the way to become Majnun. If you want to become Majnun, you need not take up his lady love; you ought to have the real internal love of Majnun. You do not want the same object of love; you require the same intensity of love. You may have your own object of love, you may choose your own heroine, you may choose your own lady love, but you ought to have the same intensity of feeling and loving which Majnun had. That is the way to become a genuine Majnun."

Similarly, if you want to become a Christ, a Buddha, a Mohammed, or a Krishna, you need not imitate the things that they did, you need not imitate the acts of their lives, you need not become a slave of the way themselves behaved. You need not sell your liberty to their deeds and their statements, you will have to realize their character, you will have to realize the intensity of their feelings, you will have to realize the depth of their realization, you will have to realize the deep spirit, the genuine power that they had.

MORAL: True imitation of a great person lies in imitating not his external] deeds but his internal intensity and depth of feeling.

The story of an ignorant child

If you show to a child a piece of sweet in one hand and a gold sovereign in the other, innocent and ignorant as he is, he would like to have the sweet, instead of the sovereign, because the sweet will immediately give him the pleasant taste, even though it is only short lived. Poor chap does not know that the sovereign can get him a huge quantity of sweets.

This is exactly how the world people behave. They give up True Freedom to accept the transitory pleasures of this world.

The prince and the painted plate

The young child of a king was fond of a small painted plate. Whenever some edible was served, he would insist on taking it in this very plate. Even when food was served in a bigger and more beautiful tray, he would kick it off. He would become wild by crying aloud. If someone asked him as to who else was the owner of the variety of the beautiful dishes of gold and silver, he would not listen to any one and would continue to insist on his demand most obstinately.

Like-wise, O true sons of Almighty, you are the owners of unlimited wealth, but whatever little is contained in your intellect (the small plate, as in the above case) is accepted by you as your own At man - you own self. You spurn it unknowingly. Even when it is suggested that the unbounded and unlimited legacy is all yours, instead of appreciating it, you get annoyed at it.

A fool's joy at the theft of his horse

One day a man was distributing the edible offerings (Prasad) in a temple, as a token of gratitude to" the gods and was very much rejoicing. Someone enquired of him the reason of his unusual happiness. He replied: 'I have gained a second life. I have been spared from the clutches of the thieves. They have stolen away my horse, but, thank God, I was not there at that moment on the horse, or else they would have stolen me as well. I am happy, because I have been saved.

You might be laughing at the reply of this fool. He could not understand that had he been on the horse it could not have been stolen at all, nothing to say about his own theft by the thieves.

O dear friends! If you ask any one 'Who are you?' he would not say a word about the rider; he would only talk about the horse; he would give you the address and introduction of his body only. He would say that he is employed in such and such office and that he is earning this much of salary. He would give you his caste, his parentage, residence and his age. He may also let you know his qualities or the distinctive phases of his life etc. This is the description of the body, the horse. But you are not the body or the horse. You are the master of the body or the rider of the horse. Do you know who you are? Why don't you reply? Why are you silent? Lost, lost, lost!! What is lost? Why this hue and cry? Have you lost your horse? No. The horse is already there, but rider (soul) is lost. What strange is it! What a joke!!

I would like you to peep into your own inner Self to see what is going on there. Is the horse missing or the rider?

The lion and other animals

When the lion comes out in search of his food he roars in the jungle. Hearing him, the deers, stags and other animals get apprehensive, come out of their dens and run about hither and thither in jungle. The lion thus notices them easily and attacks them. These animals leave their dens and bushes, because they, on hearing the thunderous roar, think that the lion has come near them or entered their dens, and, in order to save themselves, they run out. But their effort to save themselves proves fatal to them.

So, too, is the Case of frightened and dismayed persons, who waste their time and energy in devising ways and means to save themselves from their imagined troubles.

The imagery of the hunter and his game

There is a picture lying in front of Rama. In this, there is a hunter aiming his arrow at his game. He is taking his aim at a deer, in the long grass among the beautiful flowers with soft red petals under shady trees. Alas! The hunter will now kill the deer in no time. But no. Don't be afraid. Come and realise what the facts are. Is it a deer? No. Those who call it a deer are wrong. It is only paper and nothing but paper. As a paper, it looks a hunter here and fatal arrow and the deer there. Who should, then, be afraid of whom? There is no danger, no fear and no peril.

Why should one be afraid, when there is nothing to be afraid of? Nothing can harm an immortal, unchangeable and immutable Being. One who knows this secret can never be gloomy or sad.

Please dive deep into the reality of your name and form and discover your real Self. Don't be afraid of your own glory. Is fire ever afraid of its own heat? Everything is your own manifestation. Do not mind anything. Be fearless.

Story of Nawab – afflicted with false sense of vanity

During the days of mutiny in India in 1857, the soldiers attacked the residence of a Nawab. The main gate of the house was bolted from inside, but the back door in a narrow lane was open. The bed of the Nawab was close to this back door. Seeing that soldiers had started breaking open the main gate, he wanted to escape through the back door. How could do so without putting on the shoes? The Nawab was given to luxurious pomp and show. He would never sit in his buggy without the support of his servants. How could he think of running away all by himself? He regarded walking on foot against his culture. How could he then escape without an escort? He called out his personal attendant, "Alim, Alim, look sharp. Make haste, quick, quick. Help me put on the shoes."

When a man is in danger, he first thinks of saving his own life. Alim was terribly afraid of the soldiers. Their shining swords and pointed spears were before his mental eyes. When he saw the back door open, he jumped out and ran away to save his own life. The Nawab could only abuse him for his disobedience. He then called out other servant, "Kalim, Kalim, shoe, shoe." Kalim did come but instead of carrying out his orders, he, too jumped out of the back-door and fled away. The Nawab then called out the third servant, "Salim, Salim." He implored Salim in an apologetic tone to make him put on the shoes. But by this time the main gate was nearly broken. Salim was awfully nervous. He could not even listen to the orders of the Nawab. He also ran out of the back door. The soldiers were by this time inside the house. Poor Nawab! His life was no more safe.

This sort of slavery makes one dependent upon others. Is it richness? No. The Nawab was not the Master. He was in fact dependent upon his own servants. He was slave of his slaves. Fie on such a mastery. Fie on this freedom-looking imprisonment.

The man, who falls prey to the freaks of ignorance, is ultimately deluded. He does not deserve to be called free.

CHAPTER SEVEN

Knowledge

Turning the Fearful into useful (Moses and the Snake)

When Moses heard a voice in the bush, he found a. hissing snake beside him. Moses was frightened out of his wits; he trembled; his breast was throbbing; all the blood almost curdled in his veins; he was undone. A voice cried unto him - "Fear not, O Moses; catch the snake; hold it fast; dare, dare catch hold of it." Moses trembled still and again the voice cried unto him, "Moses, come forth, catch hold of the snake". Moses caught hold of it and lo, it was a beautiful and most splendid staff.

The snake (sanp) stands for truth (sanch). You know, according to the Hindus and the other Orientals, Truth or Final Reality is represented by the snake (Shesh). The snake coils up itself in a spiral form, making circles within circles, and puts its tail back into its mouth. And so we see in this world; we have circles within circles; everything repeating itself by going round and round and extremes meeting. This is a universal law or principle which runs through the whole universe.

To catch hold of the snake means to put yourself boldly into the position of the wielder of Divine Law, or Ruler of the Universe. Put yourself boldly in that position and realize your oneness with Divinity.

MORAL: The world is a dreadful dragon to one who fears it, but it serves him faithfully who faces it boldly with the knowledge of self.

Divine Knowledge (The King and the Qazi)

Once upon a time a Qazi or Governor happened to come to a certain Emperor, under the Mohammedan rule. The Emperor, who honoured the Qazi so much because of his religious pretensions, wanted to examine his capabilities. He was no scholar himself, but the following questions which he was going to put to the Qazi were suggested to him by somebody else who wanted to get the Governorship. This Qazi came before the Emperor and he was asked: "Where does God sit?" "In which direction does God keep his face?" "What does He do?" The King told him if he could answer the questions to the king's satisfaction, he would be promoted. The Qazi thought that the questions coming from the king must be very difficult. He knew how to humour and flatter the king by praising him, and then asked him for an interval of eight days to answer these questions.

For eight days the Qazi went on thinking and thinking but could come to no conclusion. How could he answer to the King's satisfaction! Finally, the eighth day came, but the answers to the questions did not come to the Qazi. He then pretended to be sick in order to gain time. The Qazi's servant Paji approached him and wanted to know what the matter was. He said, "Off with you, don't bother me, I am about to die." The servant said, "Please let me know what the matter is. I will die rather than you should be subjected to any pain." The difficulty was then explained to him. This servant occupied a very lowly position, one that was not considered at all respectable, that of slacking lime or mortar. But in reality he was a pupil of the Qazi and a learned man. He knew the answers to the questions and he said he would go and answer them, and the Qazi should write on a piece of paper ordering him to go, and if his answers were not to the satisfaction of the king he would die and not his master. The Qazi hesitated to do this, but just at this moment a messenger of the king approached him and he trembled and trembled. So he told the servant to go. He put on his best clothes which consisted of mere rags. He was a Vedantic brother. In India, the kings always go to the Swamis and learn a great deal of wisdom and knowledge. This servant Paji fearlessly approached the king and said, "Sir, what do you want? What do you wish to ask?"

The king said, *"Gould you answer the questions given to your master?" The Paji said, "I will answer them, but you know he who answers them is a teacher and he who asks them is a pupil. We expect you to be a true Mohammedan and to conform to the laws of the sacred Scriptures, According to the law, I must have the seat of honour and you must sit lower down than myself". So the king gave him some beautiful clothes to put on and he sat on the king's throne, and the king sat down on the steps. But the king said, "There is one thing more, if your answers are not satisfactory to me, I will kill you." The Paji said, "Of course, that was understood."

Now the first question, which was put, was "Where does God sit?" If he answered it literally, the king would not have understood, it so he said, "Bring a cow." A cow was brought. He said, "Does the cow have any milk?*' The Icing said, ''Yes, of course" "Where does the milk sit?" "In the udder," answered the king. "That is wrong," said the Paji "the milk pervades the whole cow. Let the cow go." Then some milk was brought. "Where is the butter? Is the butter present in the milk?" They said, "It is." "But where is it?" said the Paji, "let me know." They could not tell. Then he said, "If you cannot tell where the butter sits, still you have to believe it is there, in fact, the butter is everywhere. Similarly, God is everywhere throughout the whole universe. Just as the butter is everywhere present, in the milk, the milk is everywhere present in the cow. In. order to get the milk, you have to milk the cow, so in order to get God, you have to milk your own heart."

The Paji said, "Are you answered, O king," and the ting said, "Yes, that is right." Now all these people, who said God was living in the seventh or eighth heaven, fell in the estimation of the king. They were nothing to him, their position was not correct.

Then came the next question. "In which; direction does God look—to the East, West, North; or South?" This was also very queer, but these people looked upon God as a personality. He said, "All right, bring a light." A candle was brought and lit. He showed them that the candle did not face the North, South, East or West, but was every-where equal. The king was satisfied. Similarly, God is the candle in your heart which faces in all directions.

Now came the question, "What does God do? He said, "All right,' and told the king to go and bring the Qazi. When his master came, he was astonished to find the servant seated on the king's throne. Then he told the Qazi to sit at the place that the Paji was to occupy, and the king to sit in the Qazi's place, and he himself on the king's throne. "This," he said, "is the way - God does constantly keep things moving, changing Paji into king, king into Qazi and Qazi into Paji."

This is what is being continually done in the world, one family rising into ascendency, then becoming unknown and another taking its place. For a time one man is highly honoured, then another takes his place, and so on, day after day and year after year. And so on, in this world change is going on all the time. From that day the Paji was made a Qazi.

MORAL: God is all pervading facing all directions and bringing about continual rise and fall in the world.

Cure of Ignorance

When a good looking baby has an attack of smallpox, his life is endangered. To safeguard against this dreaded disease, the Vaccination prepared from the udder of the cow is necessary. In the same way, the Hindu nation has contracted the contagion of small-pox of ignorance. Her blooming face has become ugly. She, therefore, stands in need of vaccination. But whence will the lymph come for her vaccination? It will also be taken from cow's udder (*go-dhan)* 'Go' also means Upanishad. It is, therefore, necessary to learn Brahma Vidya (knowledge of Self) through Upanishad and, by practising its teaching, this small-pox of ignorance is sure to be cured soon.

The forgetful barber

In the Punjab the barbers also work as domestic servants. It is an old story that once a village Patwari ordered his barber to go to his Samdhi's (a close relative) village at a distance of about seven miles with an important message.

The poor barber did all haste to comply with the orders of the village Patwari. He first went to his own house, took a piece of bread and tied it to his towel, so that he may eat it somewhere in the way, and hurried towards the Samdhi's village.

The poor barber, however, forgot to take the message from his master, the village Patwari, to be delivered to his Samdhi. He forgot to do so in haste. On reaching his destination, he met the person concerned but could not deliver any message. The Samdhi was very much surprised. He threatened and scolded the barber but he could not extract any message from him. An idea struck him and he said to the barber *I have understood your message. Well done. Now you take my reply back to yout master. But please see that you go back with the same haste with which you came here.'

The barber was very happy. The Samdhi showed him a heavy log of wood and said to the barber, 'Take this small log and tell you master that this is my reply to his message.' The poor barber performed all his duties very faithfully with hard labour. But since he initially committed a mistake, he was punished to carry a heavy load on his shoulder which made him breathless due to tiredness.

So, too, scientists are making rapid progress. On, on, on, go on, go on. Well done. Bravo. Go on, go on. But unfortunately, they do not know what for they are progressing. They should have met Him whose message they are supposed to be carrying. O you scientists, you have mistakenly taken the scientific research, the Railway, Telegraph, Telephones, balloons etc., as your destination of life, the Samdhi of Atman, the source of existence, knowledge and bliss. You are running post haste. But please listen attentively. 'You will not get peace and happiness in these worldly achievements. Sooner or later you will have to come back with the heavy log of the so-called civilization to your original Self, Atman.'

CHAPTER EIGHT

Logic

Want of Time, A groundless Complaint (Dr. Johnson and an Enquirer)

Once a man came to Dr. Johnson, and said, "Doctor, I am undone, undone. I am unfit for any work; I cannot do anything. What can a man do in this world?" Dr. Johnson inquired what the matter with him was. He ought to lay down reasons for his complaint, and this man began to state his argument in this way. "Man lives in this world for a period of hundred years at the utmost, and what are a hundred years compared with infinity, eternity. Half of this age is passed in sleep. You know we sleep every day, and our period of childhood is one long sleep, and our period of old age is also a time of debility and helplessness, when we can do nothing; again our period of youth is misspent in evil thoughts, in all sorts of temptations. Again what is left to us is spent in sporting about. We play a great deal, and what is left out of that is wasted away in attending to nature's calls, and in eating, drinking, etc.; and what is left out of that goes in anger, envy, anxiety, troubles, and worries. These are also natural for every man. What remains still, what little is left to us, is taken up by attending to our children, to our friends and relatives. What can a man do in this world? We must weep for those that die, and we must rejoice at the birth of new arrivals. All our time must be wasted in this way. How can a man do anything solid, anything real? How can a man spare time for realizing his God-head? We cannot.

Away with these churches, away with these religious teachers and preachers, Tell them that people in this world cannot spare time for religion, they have no time for realizing their God-head. That is too much for us." Dr. Johnson did not smile at these words, he did not reproach this man, but only began to weep and to sympathise with him. He said, "Men ought to commit suicide, because they have no time for godly professions. Brother! To this complaint of yours, I have another complaint to add, I have a worse complaint to add". This man then asked Dr. Johnson to state his complaint. Dr. Johnson began to cry a mock cry, and said, "Look here! There is left no soil or earth for me; there is left no soil or earth which will grow corn enough to feed me, I am undone, undone." "Well", he said, "Doctor, how could that be? I admit that you eat too much, you eat as much as ten men do, yet there is soil enough on the earth to produce food for your stomach; there is earth enough to produce corn or vegetable for your body. Why do you complain?" Dr. Johnson said. "Look here, what is this Earth of yours? This Earth is nothing, this Earth is looked upon as a mathematical point in astronomical calculations. When we are calculating the distance of stars and suns, we regard this Earth as nil, as a cipher, and three-fourths of this cipher or world is occupied by water, and what is occupied by water, and what is left out of that? Mark?

A great deal is taken up by barren sands and a considerable part is taken up by barren hills and stones and a considerable part is taken up by lakes and rivers; again a considerable part of this Earth is occupied by sites of big cities like London; again roads, railroads, streets take up a great deal of this Earth. What is there in this Earth left for man? We will suppose that there is something left for man out of all that. But how many living beings are there, who want to take advantage of the insignificant part of the soil that is left? There are many birds, so many ants, so many horses, so many elephants, all of these want to keep themselves on the Earth that is left and is capable of producing anything; very little falls to the lot of man. How many men are there in this world? Look at London, full of millions and millions of men. Look at this enormous population, all this wants to feed upon the insignificant part of this big cipher or this world. How can the Earth produce food enough for my satisfaction? My logic leads me to this desperation, to this sad conclusion that I should die, because I can find no Earth which can produce food to feed me." Now the man said, "Doctor, your argument is not right; your logic seems to be right but still despite this logic of yours, this Earth can keep you." And Dr. Johnson said, "Sir, if this complaint of mine is groundless, your complaint that you have got no time to supply yourself with spiritual food is also groundless. If the earth is sufficient to supply me with material food, time also is sufficient for your purpose; it can also supply you with spiritual food."

MORAL: Want of time for spirituality is a groundless complaint. There is enough time under any circumstances, if one makes a proper use of it and will to do a thing.

A Mistaken way of Arguing (The Oil-Vender and his Parrot)

There was an oil-vender in India. He kept in his house a very beautiful parrot. One day this oil-vender left his shop and went out to some place. His servant also went out on some other errand. The parrot was there in the shop. In the absence of the oil-vender, there came up a big cat. At the sight of the cat the parrot got frightened; the parrot was in the cage but it got frightened and jumped up; the parrot fluttered his wings and jumped this way and that way until the cage' which was hanging on the wall, slipped down, and fell upon ajar full of very precious oil. The jar was broken and all the oil was spilt. After a while came up the oil-vender, and being very angry, he lost his temper, seeing that his precious oil was spilt. He got annoyed with the parrot; he thought that the parrot had done some mischief, he was beyond himself with rage and could not keep his temper because the parrot had thrown down the cage upon the jar and had cost him a loss of about Rs. 50/- He opened the door of the cage and just snatched all the plumes from the head of the parrot. The parrot was made bald; no crest was left on its head; the head of the parrot was bleeding. The parrot did neither speak nor entertain the master for two weeks. The master was very sorry for what he had done. After two weeks there came a customer to the oil-vender's shop. This customer was bare-headed at that time, and this man, this customer, was also baldheaded. The parrot laughed a hearty laugh; the parrot laughed; the parrot was very happy to see another companion. Then the master asked the parrot what was the cause of his hilarity, what made him full of joy, and the parrot said, "Oh, I thank God, I am not the only servant of an oil-vender. This man also must have been servant of an oil-vender, otherwise how could he lose the hair on his head, and how could he become bald if he had not been the servant of an oil-vender?"

Exactly the same is the kind of reasoning some people employ. They think that all the works they perform, all the duties they discharge, everything they do is with some kind of motive or other. They do with some kind of selfish desire or premeditation or other. They say that God created the world; He also must have done that with some kind of motive or other;

He must also have done with some kind of desire or other; He also must have done that with some kind of premeditation or other. This is a mistaken way of arguing.

MORAL: Because people do things generally with a selfish motive, so they impute a selfish motive to God also in creating the world. This is a mistaken way of argument.

Unfair and Untrue (An Anglo-Indian)

A man of India, an Anglo-Indian who lived in India for some time, on coming back to England, was boasting to his wife about his valour and strength, about his prowess. They were living at their country house, and there appeared a bear on the scene. This Anglo-Indian climbed up to the top of an adjoining tree, while his wife took up a weapon and killed the bear, and then he came down. Some other people came to where they were and asked, "Who killed the bear?" He said, "I and my wife have killed the bear." Oh, it was not so. Similarly, when the thing is done by others, to say that it is done by me, or it is done through Christianity, is not true.

MORAL: Taking credit of what is good for one's own self and throwing blame of what is evil on others is unfair and untrue.

False Reasoning (Theories about the Origin of a River)

There was a river flowing, on the banks of which, some people were standing and philosophizing as to its origin.

One of them said, "This River comes from rocks, from stones, hills. Out of hills, water gushes in spring fall, and that is the cause of this river." Another man said, "Oh, no impossible. Stones are so hard, so tough and so rigid and water is liquid, and so soft. How can soft water come out of hard stones? Impossible, impossible! Reason cannot believe that hard stones are giving out soft water. If stones could give out water, then let me take up this piece of stone and squeeze it. Out of this no water flows. Thus the statement that this river flowed from those mountains is absurd. I have a very good theory. This river flows from the perspiration of a big giant somewhere. We see every day that when a person perspires, water flows out of his body. Here is water flowing; it must have flowed from the body of some person who is perspiring; that is reasonable, our intellects can accept it. That seems to be plausible; that is all right." Another man said, "No, no, it is somebody standing somewhere, who is spitting and this is the spit." Another man said, "No, no. There is somebody there who is vacating his water, making water, and this is the cause of the river."

Now these people said, "Look here, look here, all these theories of ours are feasible, all these theories of the origin of water are practical. Every day we see such things". These theories about the origin of the river are very plausible, are very feasible, seem to be good and grand, but the theory that water flows from stones, the ordinary intellect of a man who has never seen water gushing out from stones, who has never been on the mountains will not accept; and yet it is true. And on what does the truth of this theory rest? On experience, on experiment, on direct observation.

Similarly, the origin of the world, why this world, and whence this world, the origin of the stream of this world, the origin of the stream of universe, the river of life» the origin of this is described differently by different people. The origin of the world according to people of that kind of intellect which ascribed the origin of the river to spittle, to perspiration, is taken to be something of the same sort as they observe every day round them. They say, "Here is a man who makes boots, the boots could not be made without somebody with some intention or design of making. Here is a man who makes a watch. Now the watch could not be made without somebody with some intention or plan or design of making it. Here is a house. The house cannot be made without somebody having the plan and design. They see that every day, and then they say, 'Here is the world. The world could not have been made without some kind of person of the same sort as the shoemaker, the watch maker, the house maker, and so there must be a world maker, who makes this world." And thus they say that there is a personal God, standing upon the clouds, not taking pity upon the poor fellow that he might catch cold. They jay some personal God must have made this world.

This argument seems to be very feasible, seems to be very plausible, seems to be very reasonable, seems to be of the same sort as the arguments of those people who said that the river flows from perspiration of somebody, who look upon the origin of the river to be of the same sort as the water coming out 'the bodies. The world also must have been made by somebody.

Vedanta does not propose any theory of that kind. No, no, it does not. Vedanta says, see it, make an experiment, and observe it, through direct realization you see that the world is not what it appears to be. How is that? Vedanta says so far I can explain to you that the water is coming out of those stones. How the water comes out of the stones, I may or may not be able to tell you, but I know the water comes out of the stones. Follow me to that place and you will see the water gushing out of the stones. If I cannot tell why the water comes out of the stones, do not blame me; blame the water, it is coming out of the stones. I am unable to tell you how the water comes out of the stones, but it remains a fact, you can verify it yourself.

Similarly, Vedanta says whether or not I am able to tell you why this Maya or Ignorance is, it remains a fact. Why it came I may not be able to tell you. This is a fact, an experimental fact. The Vedantic attitude is merely experimental, and scientific. It establishes no hypothesis, it puts forth no theory. It does not claim to be able to explain the origin of the world; this is beyond the sphere of intellect or comprehension. This is the position of Vedanta. This is called Maya. "Why does the world appear?" Vedanta says, because you see it. "Why is the world there?" Vedanta simply says, because you see it. You do not see, there is no world. "How do you know that the world is there?" Because you see it. Do not see and where is the world?. Close your eyes, a fifth of the world is gone; that part of the world which you perceive through your eyes is no longer there. Close your ears and another fifth is gone; close your nose and another fifth is gone. Do not put any of your senses into activity, and there is no world. You see the world and you ought to explain why the world is there. You make it there. You should answer yourself. Why do you ask me? You make the world there.

MORAL: Reasons ascribed to that which is beyond reason is false reasoning.

Queer Reasoning (A Swami's Quaint Orders)

Once a Swami went to a goldsmith and said to him, "Bring out your best ring and put it on the finger of God." Then he went to the shoemaker and said to him, "Bring your best shoes and put them on the feet of God." Then he proceeded to the tailor and to him he said, "Put your best suit on the body of God," thereby meaning his body. When the people heard this, they called him a blasphemer and said, "Away with him, he must be put in prison." Before they took him away, the Swami asked for an audi¬ence, saying that he wanted to tell them something before he was thrown into prison. He said to them, "Whose world is this?" They answered, "God''s". "Whose are the stars and the sun?" "God's." "Whose are are the fields and all they contain?" "God's." "Do you believe this?" They answered "Most certainly, that is the truth." He then said, "Whose body is this?" and they said, "God's"—"Whose feet?" "God's". "Whose finger?" "God's." It was God's indeed. Since by their own reasoning he brought them to see that what he had said was right, of course nothing could be done to him.

They were ignorant ones and had not looked as deeply as had the Swami.

MORAL: Because everything is God's, therefore the body of every individual is also God's.

Practice of Half Truth (Al Koran Practised in Part)

A Mohammedan gentleman was seen drinking wine and running after the pleasures of the flesh, enjoying carnal desires. A Mohammedan priest came up to him, and admonishing him told him not to do so because he was infringing the rules laid down by their prophet; and then this man, this drunkard, at once recited the first of the verse in the Al Koran, and said, "Look here. The Al Koran says *Drink ye and make merry and give ye yourselves up to sensuality.' Here is the exact reading in the Al Koran, our Scriptures, our Bible. The Al Koran, holy Scriptures enjoined drinking and sensuality. Why should they not?"

Then the priest said, "Brother, brother, what are you going to do? Read the succeeding part also, 'Ye shall work your own ruin.' (This was the second part of the verse). Read the second part too." The drunkard replied, "There is not a man on the face of the earth who could put into practice the whole of the Al Koran. Let me put into practice this part. Nobody is expected or supposed to put in practice all the teachings in the Bible. Some can put into practice only a small fraction, and some a larger fraction; that is all. The whole of it nobody puts into practice, so why do you expect me to put into practice the whole of the verse? Let me enjoy the first part of the verse."

The logic or philosophy of that Mohammedan drunkard ought not to be employed; the whole of the verse should be read, then the conclusion drawn, not before that.

MORAL: Practice of half truth is misleading and ruinous.

CHAPTER NINE

Love

Why Things are dear to us? (A Monkey with her Children in a Flood)

There was a great flood, a great inundation of the river Ganges, and the river went on rising. On the branches of a tree were sitting several monkeys; there was a female monkey and some children of this female monkey. All these children came up to the monkey. The water rose up to the place where the monkey was seated. Then the she-monkey jumped up to a higher branch; the water came up to that place. The female-monkey came up to the highest top branch, and the water rose up even to that place. All the children were clinging to the body of this female monkey. The water reached her feet; then she just took hold of one child, one baby-monkey, and placed it underneath her feet. The water rose still higher, and then this female-monkey took hold of another child and placed it under her feet. The water still rose, and the third child she also took up and mercilessly placed under her feet to save herself.

Just so it is with us. People and things are dear to us as long as they serve our interest, our purpose. The very moment that our interests are at stake, we sacrifice everything.

MORAL: Things are dear to us for the sake of Self.

The Secret of Love (Laila Majnun)

There was a lover, Majnun, who pined for his beloved Laila. All his body was reduced to a veritable skeleton; all his flesh was dried up, so to say. The king of the country in which this young man lived brought him into his court one day, and he also brought the lady-love of the young man into his presence.

The king saw that the woman was very ugly. The king then brought before this lover all the fair damsels that adorned his court and then he asked this lover to choose one of these. This man said, "O Shah! O king! O king!! Don't make a fool of yourself. O king! You know, Love makes a man very blind. O king! You have no eyes to see. Look at her with my eyes, and then say whether she is fair or ugly. Look at her with my eyes".

This is the secret of all charms in this world, the secret of all the fascination of the attractive objects in the world.

O man! You yourself make all objects attractive by your looks. Looking at it with those eyes you yourself shed your lustre upon the subject, and then you fall in love with it.

MORAL: The objects are lovely because of the reflection of Self in them.

Law of love (A King's change of Mind)

A king went into a forest on a hunting expedition. In the heat of the chase the king became separated from his companions. Under the scorching rays of burning sun he felt very thirsty. He found in the woods a small garden. He went into the garden, but being in this sportsman"s dress the gardener could not recognise him, the poor village gardener having not seen the king's person before. The king asked the gardener to bring something to drink, because he felt so very thirsty. The gardener went straight into the garden, took some pomegranates, squeezed out the juice, and brought a big cup full of it to the king. The king gulped it down, but it did not quench his parching thirst entirely. The king asked him to bring another cup of pomegranate juice. The gardener went for it. When the gardener had left the king's presence, the latter began to reflect within himself, "This garden seems to be very rich; in half a minute the man could bring me a large cup full of the fresh juice; a heavy income-tax ought to be levied on the owner of such a flourishing concern," etc., etc. On the other hand, the gardener delayed and delayed, did not return to the king even in an hour. The king began to wonder, "How is it that when I first asked him to bring me something to drink, he brought that pomegranate juice in less than a minute, and now he has been squeezing out the juice of pomegranates for about an hour and the cup is not full yet. How is that?" After one hour the cup was brought to the king, but not brimful. The king asked the reason why the cup was somewhat empty, whereas he filled the cup so soon at first. The gardener who was a sage replied, ''Our king had very good intentions when

I went out to bring you the first cup of pomegranate juice, and when I went out to bring you the second cup, our king's kind, benevolent nature must have changed. I can give no other explanation for such a sudden change in the rich nature of my pomegranates." The king reflected within himself, and lo! the statement was perfectly right. When the king had first stepped into the garden, he was very charitably disposed to and full of love for the people there, thinking in his mind that they were very poor and needed help; but when the old man had brought him one cup of pomegranate juice in so short a time, the king's mind had changed and views altered. The falling out of tune with Nature on the king's part affected the pomegranates in the garden. The moment the Law of Love was violated by the king that very moment the trees held back the juice from him.

So long as you are in perfect harmony with nature, so long as your mind is in tune with the universe and you are feeling and realizing your oneness with each and all, all the circumstances and surroundings, even winds and waves, will be in your favour. The very moment you are at discord with the All, that very moment your friends and relatives will turn against you, that very moment you will make the whole world stand up in arms against you.

MORAL: Love brings harmony and help, hatred produces discord and division.

Intensity of Love (Majnun's reply to God)

There was a man called Majnun. He was called the prince of lovers. Nobody ever loved as he did, but his love was for the personality, the body of his lady, and it was thus that he could not see her. This poor fellow did not possess the secret; yet he was the ideal lover of the whole world. He became crazy and went mad over his great disappointment and the poor crazy prince left the father's house and roamed about in the forest. If he saw a rose, he would rush to it thinking it to be his beloved one; the cypress tree he kissed it thinking it to be his beloved one; he came up to a deer and thought it to be his beloved one. That was his feeling; he had transformed these little bodies into the body of his beloved one, seeing that everywhere. His object of love was material and he suffered through it. This poor fellow knew not where to find true Happiness or God. Blessed is he who realizes the Truth like that Majnun, who realized his lady-love in the trees, in the animals and in the flowers. The poor fellow at last fell senseless in the forest, and his father searching for him came upon the spot where he was lying.

He picked up the poor boy, wiped his face and said, "O my beloved son, do you recognise me? Majnun was staring vacantly, and he looked and looked, but to him there was nothing left in the universe. Majnun's whole frame was saying "What is father, what is father?" The father said, "My beloved son! I am your father, do you not recognize me?" He said, "What is father!" Meaning - is there anything in this world but my beloved one?

So long as Majnun was alive, he could not see his beloved one. But Majnun was brought into the presence of God, and God said, "O fool, why did you love so much a material, a worldly object? Had you loved me with a millionth part of the intensity of love which you wasted upon your lady-love, I would have made you the Archangel of Heaven." It is related that Majnun answered God in this way: "O God, I excuse you for this; but, if you were really so anxious to be loved by me, why did you not come as my beloved lady? If you had the desire to be worshipped you should have become the object, the lady-love."

You must have the same intense love of Truth. You must love your Atman; you must think It, the beloved one. Love It; feel, feel It, as Majnun did, and nothing else must come to you except It be presented to you as the beloved Truth. You must see the beloved Divinity in It, nothing else.

Realization means the same love of Truth as this fellow had for his material object, for the flesh and skin. When you rise to that height of Divine love, when you rise to such a degree that in your father, in your mother, in everybody you see nothing but God, when you see in the wife no wife but the Beloved one, God; then, indeed you do become God; then, indeed you are in the presence of God.

MORAL: Intensity of love means forgetfulness of everything else except the Beloved one. Such intensity of love with Divinity of Truth leads to Self realization.

Why things are dear (Yajnavalkya and Maitreyi)

Yajnavalkya had two wives, Maitreyi and Katyayani. He was a very rich man; he was the preceptor of one of the richest princes of India. At that time he wanted to divide his property between the two wives, and retire to the forest. Maitreyi declined to accept her portion, saying if this led to immortality, her husband would not give it up.

You see that in the heart of Maitreyi the idea arose how it was that her beloved husband, one of the richest men in all India, was going to give up all this wealth and adopt another kind of life. Surely no one ever leaves one kind of life for another unless there is more joy, more pleasure in the new life than in the old one. This showed that for her husband the kind of life he wanted to adopt was more pleasant and enjoyable than the kind of life he then lived. She reflected and asked her husband, "Is there more joy in spiritual wealth than in worldly wealth, or is it otherwise?"

Yajnavalkya replied, "The life of rich people is what it is, but in such life there is no real joy, no real happiness, no true freedom." Then Maitreyi said, "What is it the possession of which makes you altogether free, which makes you free from worldly greed and avarice? Explain to me this nectar of life, I want it"

All his wealth and property were made over to Katyayani, and this wife. Maitreyi got all his spiritual wealth. What was that spiritual wealth?

न वा अरे पत्युः कामाय पतिः प्रियो भवति ।

आत्मनस्तु कामाय पतिः प्रियो भवति ॥

न वा अरे जायायै कामाय जाया प्रिया भवति ।

आत्मनस्तु कामाय जाया प्रिया भवति ॥

(Brihadaranyaka Upanishad)

This passage has many meanings. Max Muller translates it one way and many Hindus another way. Both the translations are right.

According to one interpretation, "The cause of the husband being dear is not that he has some good attributes, or that there is anything particularly lovely in him, but he is dear because he serves as a mirror to the lady. As we see our own selves reflected in the mirror of her husband, and that is why she loves her husband, and that is why her husband is dear."

The other meaning is that, "The wife loves the husband not for the husband's sake, but for her own sake. She ought to see God, the true Divinity in the husband."

You know that if love is not reciprocated, then nobody loves. This shows that we love only ourselves as reflected in others. We want to see our true Self, the God within, and we never love anything for its own sake.

MORAL: Things are dear not for the sake of things but for the sake of Self, the Atman.

The Result of Worldly Love (Lord Krishna and the Dragon)

Lord Krishna, the famous God of India, the Christ of India, was about to be devoured by a big demon. He took a dagger in his hand. He was devoured and swallowed up. Finding himself in the stomach of the dragon, he pierced the heart of the dragon; the heart broke, the dragon bled to death, and Lord Krishna came out. That is exactly the case. What is Love? Love is Krishna; that means Love is God. Love is God and it enters the heart, it enters the inner mind of a man of sensual desires. It enters the heart and just when it has got a seat, when it has a place in the very core of the heart, it deals a thrust, and what is the result? The heart breaks. Agony and sorrow is the result; weeping and gnashing of teeth comes about in all the cases of worldly love? That is the way. That is what happens. That is the law.

Attach yourself to any worldly object, begin to love any worldly object for its own sake, and there the God Krishna gets into you and then stabs you. The heart breaks, you are sorrow stricken, and you murmur and cry, "Oh, this love is very cruel, it has ruined me."

MORAL: Love for the worldly objects puts you in troubles and sorrows.

Oneness through Love (Love's Union)

There was a girl very deeply in love, her whole being transformed into love. At one time she was seriously ill, and the doctors were called. They said that the only way to cure her was to take out some of her blood. They applied their lancets to the flesh of her arms, but no blood came out of her body. But at the same time curiously enough blood was observed gushing from the skin of her lover. What a wonderful union! You will call that a tradition, a false story, but it can be true. Often do those people who experience love though of a lower degree, verify something, like that in their own lives.

The girl had forgotten her own personality and had made herself one with her. lover and the lover had merged himself in the lady's love. Such a union with God is religion. Let my body become His body and let His Self become my Self.

MORAL: The feeling of oneness conies through love, hence love is essential for union with God, or Self realization.

No Trace of Separation (Sivoham in Tiger's Fangs)

Some time ago a Hindu monk was sitting on the bank of the Ganges, in the deep Himalayan forests. On the opposite bank some other monks were observing him while he was chanting to himself Sivoham! Sivoham! Sivoham! Which means, I am God, I am God. There appeared a tiger on the scene. The tiger came and got him in his claws and though in the fangs of the tiger, same chant was coming out from him in the same tone, in the same fearless strain, Sivoham! Sivoham! Sivoham! The tiger tore off his hands and legs, and there was the same sound, unabated in intensity.

Embracing Him, accepting Him, wedding Him, become one with Him, to such a degree and so intensely that there may be left no trace of separation.

MORAL: To realize Unity, love should be raised to such a degree of intensity that no trace of separation be left.

The Primary Stage of Love, "I am His" (While counting _Terhan')

A highly revered saint (Guru Nanak) in India was in his early youth working in a place where it was his duty to give away alms, to distribute food and treasure to the people. Some poor men were brought before him, with an order from his Master to give unto them thirteen bushels of flour. He gave them one bushel; he gave the second, the third, the fourth, the fifth, the sixth, until he came to the number thirteen. He was counting the number of bushels audibly while dealing out the flour. The number thirteen is called Terhan in the Indian Punjabee language. This is a very remarkable world. It has two meanings; one is thirteen, ten plus three; and the other meaning of the word is "I am Thine; I am Thine! I am God's! I am part of Him! I am His!" Well, he counted 12 and then came the turn of the number Terhan. When he had given the thirteen bushels and was pronouncing Terhan, such holy associations were aroused in him that he actually gave up his body and all to God. He forgot everything about the world; he was beyond himself; no, he was in himself. In this state of ecstasy he went on saying Terhan, Terhan, Terhan, Terhan, and went on unconsciously giving to the people bushel after bushel saying Terhan, Terhan,- until he fell down in a state of super-consciousness, in a state of transcendental bliss.

Thus we see that the people who are in the elementary stages can often rise to the greatest heights, if they are as good as their word; if they are sincere and earnest; if they do not want to throw dust into the eyes of God; if they do not want to make promises with God and them break them.

When once in the temple or church, they say, "I am Thine". Let them feel it. Let them realize it. This is true religion, the primary stage of spiritual development, "I am His! I am His! I am God's!"

Different sects throughout the world can be classed under these three heads—"I am His", "I am Thine", "I am He". So far as the forms are concerned, the second form, "I am Thine", is higher than the first, "I am His", and the third from, "I am He" is the highest. When this state of "I am He" or "I am Thou" is reached, there are no more births. The man is free, free, free! Man is God, God! He has reached the end! OM!

MORAL: The primary stage of love is that in which the lover entirely surrenders himself unto God, the beloved.

The Middle Stage of Love, —I am Thine (The Angelic Face in the Museum of Naples)

In a grand museum in Naples, there is a beautiful angelic face on the roof, and at whatever part of the museum you may happen to be, whatever part you may happen to visit, you may go to the roof, you may go to the basement, wherever you may be, the bright, dazzling, pure eyes of the angel look you straight in the eyes.

People who are in the middle state of spiritual development, if true to themselves, live constantly under the eye of the Master. They feel and realize that where ever they may go, in the innermost chamber of the house, in the most secluded caves of the forest, they find themselves under the eyes of God, seen by Him, fed by light, nourished by His grace.

MORAL: The middle stage of love is that in which God's presence is felt and realized everywhere.

The Final Stage of Love, "I am He" (A maiden's Ardent Love with Krishna)

In India, long ago, the Hindus used clay lamps, and when one family got their lamps lit, the people of the adjoining houses would go into their neghbour's house to light theirs. One evening a maiden, who was ardently in love with Krishna, went to the house of his father on the pretext of lighting her lamp. It need not be said that it was in reality a desire to get herself singed like a moth at the light of Krishna's face that led her to this house of Krishna rather than to any other house with lighted lamps. She really went to see him; the lighting of the lamp was only the excuse she gave her mother. She had to apply the wick of her lamp to that of the burning lamp; but her eyes were not on the lamps, they were on the face of the dear little Krishna. She was looking at that charming, bewitching face of Krishna; she was looking at him so intently that she did not notice that instead of the wick of her lamp being in contact with the burning lamp, her fingers were burning in it. The flame continued to burn her fingers, but she noticed it not. Time passed on and she did not return home. Her mother became impatient and could bear the delay no longer. She went to her neighbour's house and there she saw her daughter's hand burning and the daughter unconscious of it; the fingers were singed and shriveling, and the bones were charred. The mother panted for breath, gasped and wept and cried, aloud, "Oh, my child, my child, what are you doing? In the name of goodness, what are you doing?" Then was the girl brought to her senses, or, you may say, she was brought from her senses.

In such a state of Divine love, in this stage of perfect love, the beloved and the lover become one. "I am He," "I am Thou."

This is final state, and beyond that comes the state where even these expressions cannot be used.

MORAL: The final stage of love is that in which the lover and beloved become one, but beyond that comes a state where is left no sense of love, lover or beloved, and which is, therefore beyond expression.

The True Worship of God (Shaikh, the worshipper of man)

There was a certain Shaikh. He saw in one of his visions an angel writing the names of people in a book. The Shaikh asked, "What are you doing, Sir?" The angel replied, "I am writing out the names of those who are the nearest, dearest and greatest worshippers of God." And then Shaikh put down his head and was dejected, and he said, "I wish I had been a worshipper of God as others have; I never pray, I never fast, I never attend church, I shall be debarred. I shall not be able to enter the Kingdom of Heaven." The angel said, "Can't help!" Then Shaikh put another question to the angel and said, "Will you ever put down a list of those who love man and the whole world and not God?" The Shaikh said, "Put down my name as a worshipper of man." The angel disappeared. The Shaikh had a second vision, and in the second vision the angel reappeared with the same book; and when he was turning over the leaves of the book and had revised it all, the Shaikh inquired what he was doing, and the angel said he had written down the worshippers of God in order of merit, and the Shaikh asked if the angel would allow him to look at the register, and lol to his great surprise, the Shaik, who had given his name as a worshipper of man, found his name at the top of the list of worshippers or devotees of God. Is not this strange? It is a fact.

If you worship man, or in other words, if you look upon man not as man but as the Divine, if you approach everything as God, as the Divinity and then worship man then you worship God. To worship God in the best way is to worship the Divinity arid God in your friend. If you find faults in your friends, try and keep yourself away from those faults, but hate not. They are God, recognise the Godhead in them.

MORAL: To love all humanity, to see Divinity in every being, and to serve all as God is the true worship of God.

Mad in Love (Aziz, the School-master)

Ganimat of Punjab in his Nairang-i-Ishq tells us of Aziz, the school-master, poor school-master! madly in love with one of his pupils, Shahid. While correcting the calligraphy exercises of his students, the senseless teacher guides himself. by the blurred and slurred scribble works of his pupil-master who was just a beginner in school. Well done! How true! Defects are visible only where our eyes are jaundiced with lack of love.

MORAL: A person mad in love sees no defect in his beloved.

Owning Other's Beloved (Falling in love with Laila's Picture)

A man on reading Nizami's Laila and Majnun, cut out the picture of Laila from the book, was hugging it to his breast and kissing it ever so fondly. Why? "I have fallen in love with Laila," he replies. Fool! It is not worthwhile to take away poor Majnun's sweetheart! You may have Majnun's burning love, but as to lady love, have a living one of your own.

MORAL: To have burning love like others is wise but to own other's beloved is foolish.

Universal Love (A Woman's loss of her Child)

A woman complained about the loss of her only child. Rama asked, "Gould you adopt Negro baby and caress it as your own? Are you ready for it?" She said, "No." "Then that is why you lost your child." Inclusive love, not exclusive attachment, is the unfoldment of Heaven.

MORAL: Universal Love, not personal attachment, is the door to Heaven.

Transformation of Sensual Love (Tulsi Das and his Wife)

In India, there was a saint Tulsi Das by name, an ancestor of Swami Rama, who was very fond of his wife; he loved his wife as no man ever loved before. At one time it happened that his wife had to go here father's house which was located in another village, some seven or eight miles distant from the village in which the saint lived. The saint could not bear the separation, and so he left his house and went in search of his wife. It was about eleven o'clock at night when he learnt of her departure, and in his desperation he ran from his own house like a mad man. A river separated the two villages and at the time at night, it was very difficult to cross owing to the very rapid current of the river, and besides, there was nobody available at that hour of the night. On the bank of the river he found a rotten corpse and through his mad love, through his desperation to reach his wife he clasped the corpse tightly and swam across the river, safely reaching the other side. He ran on and on and when he reached the house where his wife was, he found all the doors closed, he could not gain entrance, neither could he arouse any of the servants, nor inmates, for they were all sleeping in some of the innermost rooms. Now what was he to do? You know they say if a river is in the way, love crosses it; if mountains are in the way, love climbs them. So, on the wings of love he had to reach his wife. While puzzling his brain, he found something dangling alongside the house and he thought it was a rope; he thought his wife loved him so dearly that she had placed this rope alongside the house for him to climb up. He was overjoyed. Now, this rope was not a rope but a long snake. He caught hold of the snake and it did not bite him, and by that means he climbed to the upper storey of the house and gained entrance to the room in which his wife was lying. The wife got up and was astonished, and exclaimed, "How did you get here, it is very strange." He shed tears of joy and said, "It was you yourself, O blessed one, who made my passage here so easy. Did you not place a kind of canoe by river for me to cross over, and did you not place that rope upon the wall for me to climb up? He was crazy, love had made him mad. The wife began to shed tears of pity and joy. She was a learned woman, she was a goddess of Divine wisdom, and she then said, "O Divine one! Sweet one! had you really entertained the same intense love for the Reality, the Divinity, which keeps up and supports and is embodied in this apparent self, in this physique of mine, you would have been God; you would have been the greatest prophet in the world, you would have been the grandest sage on the earth; you would have been the worshipped sire of the whole universe."

When the wife was inculcating the idea of Divinity in him, and was teaching him that she was one with the Divinity, she said, "O dear husband, you love this body of mine; this body is only transitory; it left your house and came to this house; in the same way, body may leave this earth today or tomorrow; this body may become sick to-day and all its beauty be gone in a second. Now see, what is it that gives bloom to my cheeks, what is it that lends lustre to my eyes, what is it that lends glory to my person, what is it that shines through my eyes, what is it that gives this golden colour to my hair, what is it that lends life, light and activity to my senses and my physique? See, that which has fascinated you is not this skin, is not this body of mine. Mark please, see please, what is it? It is the true Self, the Atman which charms and fascinates and bewitches you.

It is the Divinity in me and nothing, else; it is God, nothing else; it is that Divinity, that God within me, nothing else. Feel that Divinity, see that Divinity everywhere. That same Divinity, God, is it not present in the stars, does is not look you in the face, in the moon?"

This saint rose above sensuality, rose above carnal desires, and worldly attachments. This saint as he was originally extraordinarily in love with one wife, he realized that Beloved one, that Divinity everywhere in the world; so much so that this saint, a lover of God, this holy man drunk in Divinity, this pious man was one day walking through the woods, and he approached a man who held hatchet in his hand, and who was about to cut down a beautiful cypress tree. When the blows of the hatchet fell upon the roots of the beautiful cypress tree, there was the saint about to faint away. He ran up to the man and cried. 'These blows of yours hurt me, they are piercing my bosom; please refrain from doing this." "How is that, saint," asked the man.

The saint said, "O sir, this cypress, this beautiful tree is my beloved one; in it I see my true Divinity, in it I see God."

Now, Divinity, God became his bird, his wife, his husband, his child, his father, his mother, his sister, and everything to him. All his energy, all his love was thrown at the feet of Divinity, was given to Divinity, the Truth, and thus the saint said to the man, "I see my beloved one there, I cannot bear blows on my beloved Divinity,"

One day a man was about to kill a stag or deer, and the holy saint was observing this. He came up and threw his body at the feet of the man who was about to kill the stag. "How is this saint," asked man. He exclaimed, "O, please spare the deer, behold my beloved one penetrating those beautiful eyes. Oh! Kill this body of mine, sacrifice this body in the name of Divinity, in the name of God, sacrifice my body I perish not, but spare, O, spare the beloved one."

All the attractiveness you see in this world is nothing else but the true Divinity; the same which appears to you in the body of a beloved one, puts on a different dress in trees, in mountains and hills. Realize this please, this is how you can rise above all worldly passions and desires. This is the way to make spiritual use of worldly desires and make use of them for their own sake. You are making spiritual wrecks of yourself, you are becoming sinners. But if you are raising these worldly desires, by using them properly then these same acts become virtuous.

MORAL: Intense love, even though it be sensual if diverted into proper channel, can be transformed into Love for Divinity and thus be a means of Realization.

The Result of Intense Love (Laila and Majnun)

One day the sweetheart of Majnun said that she did not feel well and nothing seemed to do her any good. So the Doctor was sent for. As was the old custom, he immediately proceeded to Laila to draw out a little blood, that is, he cut a little gash in the arm thinking thereby to draw out blood, but no blood came from Laila. From Majnun however it streamed forth.

Such was the oneness of these lovers.

MORAL;—Intense love results in the oneness of lover and beloved to such a degree that any impact on the one is reproduced in the other.

CHAPTER TEN

Maya

Infinity (A Mirror Creation)

There was a small child that was never shown a looking glass. (In India small children are not shown looking glasses). This small baby once happened to crawl into the room of his father, and there was a looking glass lying on the floor, with one end of it leaning against the wall and the other end resting upon the ground. This little baby crawled up to the looking glass, and lo! There he sees a baby, little child dear little baby. (You know, children are always attracted by children. If you have a child and you go to your friend's house with it, when you go to talk with your friend, the child will at once make friends with the other children of the house). So this child saw in the looking glass a child of its own size. He went up to him and when he was moving up to the child in the mirror, the latter moved up to him also. He was delighted. He found that the child in the mirror was on friendly terms, liked him just as much as he liked the child in the mirror. Their noses met. He put his nose against the mirror and the child in the mirror also drew his nose up to his nose; their noses touched each other. Their lips touched. He put his hands on the mirror and the child in the mirror also extended his hands to him, as if he was going to shake hands with him; but when the hands of this baby-were on those in the mirror, the mirror fell flat on the ground, and broke into two pieces. Now the child saw that instead of one child there were two children in the mirror. His mother, in the other room, heard this noise and came running to the room of her husband, and there seeing that the husband was not there, but the child was making havoc with the articles in the room, and had broken the mirror, she came up to him menacingly, in a threatening manner as if she was about to strike him. But you know, children know better, they know threats, frowns and browbeating of their mothers mean nothing. They know it through experience. The child, instead of being frightened at the words of the mother, which were "What have you done, what have you done, what aie you doing here?", took these words not in the sense of threat or frown, but in good sense. He said, "O, I have created two, I have made two." The child created two children out of one child. There was originally one child only that was talking to the one child in the mirror, and now this child made two children. A small child became the father of two children even before he was of age. He said, "I have made two; I have made two." The mother smiled and took the child up in her arms, took him to her own room.

Take up these two pieces of looking glass, break them, spare them not, you will get more looking glasses; break these pieces into four pieces and you will get four children. Now the small child by breaking these four pieces of glass into eight pieces could create eight children. Any number of children might by created that way. But we ask, "Does that real Divinity, does that real child increase or decrease by the breakage of the mirrors?" It neither increases nor decreases. The increase and decrease take place only with looking glasses. There is no increase in the child that you see in the looking glass, that remains the same. How can the infinite be increased? If the infinity increases, it is not infinity. How can infinity decrease? If it decreases, it is not infinity.

MORAL: Infinity neither increases nor decreases. It is beyond all change. The form may increase or decrease but the Substratum, the Divinity remains the same.

The Cause of Bondage (How a Monkey is caught?)

A monkey is caught in India in a very queer manner.

A narrow-necked basin is fixed in the ground, and in that basin are put some nuts and other eatables which the monkeys like. The monkeys come up and thrust their hands into the narrow-necked basin and fill their hands with the nuts. The fist becomes thick and it cannot be taken out, i There the monkey is caught; he cannot come out. Queerly, strangely is the monkey caught.

We ask what it is that binds you first. You yourself have brought under thralldom and bondage. Here is the whole wide world; a grand magnificent forest; and in this grand magnificent wood of the whole universe, there is a narrow necked vessel found. What is that narrow-necked vessel? It is your brain, this little brain, narrow-necked. Herein are some nuts, and people have got hold of these nuts, and all that is done through the agency of the brain or through the medium of this intellect, is owned as one's own, "I am the mind," is that everybody says; everybody has practically identified himself with the mind, "I am the mind," "I am the intellect," and he takes a strong grip of these nuts of the narrow-necked vessel. That is what makes you slaves, that is what makes you slaves to anxieties, slaves to fear, slaves to temptations, slaves to all sorts of troubles. That is what binds you; that is the cause of all the suffering in this world. If you want salvation, if you want freedom, only let go the hold, free your hand. The whole forest is yours, you can jump from tree to tree and eat all the nuts and eat all the walnuts and all the fruits in the woods, all being yours. The whole world is yours; just rid of this selfish ignorance, and you are free, you are your own savior.

MORAL: Identification with the mind is the cause of bondage. Get rid of it and your are free.

World a Play (Hide and Seek)

A prince in his childhood was playing hide and seek with the children of noblemen. He had much ado to search out the boys. A by-stander remarked, "What is the use of making so much fuss to discover the play-fellows who could be collected immediately it he exercised his princely authority to call them out?" The answer to such a question is that in that case the play would lose its relish. There would remain no interest in the game.

Just, so, in reality you are the supreme Ruler and all-knowing omniscient Divinity, but as you have in fun opened the quest of your own subject (all sorts of ideas and so-called knowledge) in the great hide-and-seek labyrinth of the world, it would not be fair play to give up the trail of thought and to exercise in the game the authority which checkmates the whole play.

MORAL: The play of the world lasts only so long as we do not assert our authority and give up attachment, because the attachment makes the world real and not a play, whereas the assertion of authority brings the play to an end.

Why and Wherefore of the World (The Child and the Mirror)

There was a child; the child saw in a mirror the image of a little boy, his own image, and somebody told the child that in the mirror was a very beautiful, dear little child, and when he looked into the mirror, he saw a dear little boy, but the child did not know that it was his own reflection, the child took it to be some strange boy in the mirror. Afterwards the mother of the child wanted to persuade him that the boy in the mirror was only his own reflection, not a real boy, but the boy could not be persuaded, the boy could not understand that in the mirror there was not really another boy. When the mother said, 'Look here, here is a mirror, there is no boy in it,' the child came up to it and said, 'O mamma, O mamma, here is the boy! Why, the boy is here?' When the boy was saying, 'here is the boy,' in the very act of saying 'here is the boy,' he cast his own reflection in the mirror. Again the mother wanted to persuade him that there was not a real boy in the mirror, then again the boy wanted to have a proof or demonstration. The boy went up to the mirror and said, 'Look here, here is the boy,' but by the very act of proving that there was no object in the mirror, the boy put the object in the mirror.

Similarly, when you come up and say, 'why the world,' 'whence the world,' how the world,' the very moment you begin to investigate the origin and the why and wherefore of the world, that very moment you put in the world there, you create the world there.

MORAL: The very question about the why and wherefore of the world posits the idea, of the world where there is really no world.

A Logical Fallacy (The Boys and the Inspector)

There came an inspector into a school, and he put this question to the boys, "if a piece of chalk is allowed to fall in air, when will it reach the earth?" A boy answered, "In so many seconds." 'If a piece of stone is allowed to fall from such and such a height, in what time will it fall?" The boy answered, "In this time." Then the inspector said, 'If this thing is allowed to fall, what time will it take?" The boy answered. Then the examiner put a catch question, "If the earth falls." The boys were confounded. One smart boy answered, "First let me know where the earth will fall?"

Similarly, we can put the question, when was this lamp lighted, when was this house built, when was this floor set, etc. But when we ask the question, 'When was the earth created, when was the world created,' this catch question is ' of the same sort as the question, 'During what time will the earth fall?' 'Where will the earth fall?' Why, when, and wherefore are themselves a part of the world, and when we are speaking of this why, when, and wherefore of the whole world, then we are arguing in a circle, making a logical fallacy. Could you jump out of yourself? No. Similarly, why, when and wherefore being themselves the world, are part of the world, they cannot explain the world, the whole Universe. This is what Vedanta says.

MORAL: Why, when, and wherefore are themselves part of the world; so arguing about them is reasoning in a circle and hence a logical fallacy.

The Illusion of the Why, When and Where (A Picture Boat and Boat-man)

Here is a beautiful boat, and here is the picture of a boatman, a man who ferries the boat across the river. The boatman is a very good man and he is the master of the boat, only so long as the boat is looked upon to be real; the master of the boat is master in the same sense as the boat is a boat. In reality the boat is nowhere and the master of the boat is nowhere. Both are unreal. But when we point out to a child, "Come along, come along, what a beautiful master of the boat," both the master of the boat and the boat are of the same sort. We have no right to call the master of the boat more real than the boat itself.

Similarly, according to Vedanta, the Controller, Governor, Master of the world, or God, the idea of God or Creator, is related to this world as in that picture the boat-driver, or I say, the boat-man is related to the boat. So long as the boat is there, the boatman is also there. When you realise the unreality of the boat, the boatman also disappears.

Similarly, the idea of a Controller, Governor, Creator, Maker, is real unto you so long as the world appears to you to be real. Let the world go, and that idea also goes. The idea of the Creator implies creation, why, when and wherefore.

The question of the why, when, and wherefore of the world is related to this world like the boatman to the boat; both of them are parts of one whole picture. If they are both of the same value, both are illusions. The question „the why, when, and wherefore" also is an illusion. The question—why, when, and wherefore—is the driver, the boatman, or the leader of this world. When you wake up and realize the truth, the whole world becomes to you like the boat drawn upon canvas, and the question why, when, and wherefore, which was the driver of the boatman, disappears. There is no why, when, and wherefore in the Reality which is beyond Time, beyond Space, beyond Causation.

MORAL: The appearance of the creation (world) creates the idea of its creator. Hence when the world is illusion, the idea of its creator must also be illusion.

The Intrinsic and the Extrinsic Illusion (The Boy and the Snake)

A boy comes to his father and says, "Papa, papa, I am frightened; there is a snake there." He asks, "Child, how long was the snake?" and the boy says "The snake was about two yards long". "Well, how thick was the snake?" And the child says, "It was very thick. It was as thick as the cable I saw the other day in the ship which was leaving San Francisco." Well, we ask, "What was the snake doing?" He said, "The snake had coiled itself round." You know that the snake was not there; the snake was unreal, only the rope was lying there. The rope was about two yards long, and was as thick as the cable which he saw the other day when the ship was leaving San Francisco. The rope was coiled around on the floor, and there the properties of the rope, its thickness, length, and position have, as it were, mirrored themselves in the illusory serpent. There the rope casts its thickness, its width, and its position into the illusory serpent. The serpent was not so long, the length only applied to the rope; the serpent was not of that thickness, the thickness only applied to the rope; the serpent was not in that position, the position only applied to the rope. So you mark that originally we had the serpent as the result of intrinsic illusion, and subsequently we have in the serpent created another kind of illusion, which we might call extrinsic illusion, the properties of one attributed to the other.

This is the second kind of illusion. In order to remove these illusions, what process is to be adopted? We shall remove one illusion first and then the other. The extrinsic illusion will be removed first, and then the intrinsic illusion.

According to Vedanta, all this universe, this entire world, is in reality nothing else but one indivisible, indescribable Reality, which we cannot even call reality, which transcends all languages, which is beyond Time, Space, and Causation which is beyond everything. In this rope of a reality, in this underlying substratum, substance, or whatever you might call it, appear names, forms, and differentiations, or you might call it energy, activity, or vibrations. These are like serpents. There we see that after this intrinsic illusion is completed, the extrinsic illusion comes up, and on account of the extrinsic illusion, we look upon these names and forms, these personalities and these individualities as having a reality of their own as subsisting by themselves, as existing by themselves, as real on their own account. There is the second illusion put forth, there is the extrinsic illusion put forth.

MORAL: The appearance of names and forms in the one underlying Substratum or Reality is the Intrinsic Illusion, and the subsequent belief that they have their own separate existence is the Extrinsic Illusion. Hence, the removal of the Extrinsic Illusion helps in removing the Intrinsic Illusion also.

Where lies the Charm? (A Dancing Girl's Song)

A very wealthy merchant in India was at one time going to give a grand feast to the people living in his city. To the grand feast is often invited a bevy of dancing girls. This custom is now being given up in India, but at one time it was prevalent in full force.

One of the girls began to dance and sing. She sang a song which was awfully lewd awfully bad, a song which nobody would have enjoyed, and still on that particular occasion, the song sank deep into the hearts of the whole audience. What was the reason? You know, learned men and young gentlemen in India never like such bad songs, vulgar songs;. but on that occasion the song so much insinuated itself into the hearts and souls of the audience that they were enraptured by it. Months and months after that occasion, most of the learned scholars, who had heard that song once were seen walking through the streets humming it by themselves, and gentlemen were whistling it to themselves. And all of them, who had once heard it, were loving the song and liking it, were cherishing it, and nourishing it in their hearts.

Here the question is, in what lay the charm? Ask any one of those people who heard the song, in what lies the charm, and what is it that makes the song so dear to you? All these will say, the song is so beautiful, oh, the song is so sweet, oh, the song is so ennobling, so elevating, and the song is very good. But it is not so. The same song was abominable to them before they heard it sung by this dancing girl, but now they like it. This is a mistake. The real charm lay in the tone, the face, the looks, the appearance and the manner of singing employed by the girl. The real charm lay in the girl, and that real charm was transferred to the song.

That is what happens in the world. There comes a teacher who has a very sweet face, who has got very sweet eyes, who has a beautiful nose. His voice is very clear, and he can throw himself this way and that way. Oh, whatever he says is beautiful, is most attractive, oh, it is so good. It is so charming. That is the mistake made by the world. Nobody examines the truth by itself. Nobody thinks anything of the song. It is the acting or the way of putting things, or it is the manner of speaking, the delivery, it is the charm in the outward things which makes the teaching so attractive, so dear, so lovely to the audience.

MORAL: Although the charm really lies within, yet people deceive themselves believing it to the outside.

The delusion of Duryodhana

After the end of Rajsuya Yajna (The Royal Festival of charity) and the farewell of all the other guests, Pandavas affectionately detained Duryodhana for some time more at Indraprasth and entertained him lavishly. One day, they showed him their beautiful palace, designed and constructed by skilful and experienced engineers. At a place the mosaic floor was so beautifully made out of precious and transparent quartz that it looked like running water. Duryodhana was, therefore, deluded by this deceptive flooring. He began undressing himself to cross it by swimming. Seeing this, Bhima, Draupadi and others laughed heartily.

So, too, dear readers! This world is made of Maya, the illusion. It looks different from what it actually is. It has been very beautifully decorated, so as to appear charming and attractive. There are also mirage-like circumstances which bewilder you. You think that you are drowned and start raising hue and cry, due to extreme nervousness. But when your ignorance is gone, you find yourself absolutely safe, as if nothing had happened.

My dear! Do not forget that all the things in this world are for your own good, though they may appear to you to be harmful, damaging or unnerving. Why should you be afraid of them? It is your own ignorance which is deluding you; otherwise there is none to harm you.

The story of a self-realized ascetic

There was a young ascetic who used to go out every day to beg alms. One day he went towards the mansion of a rich man. The lady of the house saw the charming face of this young ascetic and got enamored of his attractive personality. She came down and, while offering alms to him, said that his eyes were really very bewitching. The Sadhu (hermit) took the offering, but did not use it. He threw it into the river. The next day, the sadhu took out his both the eyeballs with the help of a knife, put them in a handkerchief and somehow went tottering to the mansion of the lady with the help of a stick. The lady wanted to take him to the inside of the house. But when she approached him, the sadhu handed over to her the handkerchief, containing his eyeballs, and said, 'Madam you are enamored of my eyes, they are here, as my present to you. I do not mind losing my eye sight, but I cannot afford to lose the light of my soul. I would only request you not to tarnish my conscience.' The lady on hearing this, was stunned and did not know what to say. Rama need not elaborate this story any further.

They, who have moved this world, had a strong determination like that of this Sadhu or hermit. They could not be won over by any temptation.

CHAPTER ELEVEN

Mind

Concentration and Character (The Cold Stricken Snake)

A boy while walking over snow came across a cold stricken snake, lying coiled up. The boy handled it, and thinking it to be dead carried it home. But while sitting before the fire of the hearth, the snake got warmed. It stretched itself and bit the very boy. The venom had not really gone from the snake and so the boy died on account of the poison.

In the case of most people concentration is simply the snake of the mind coiled around; the poisonous fangs of this snake are the desires which apparently die out for a time. This little mind sleeps, or in other words, is thrown into a state of Samadhi. The snake is practically dead, cold-stricken, but not really dead. The snake might be handled in another way. We might take up a musical instrument and blow mantrams until the snake is charmed; then by skill on our part we can get hold of the snake, and take out its fangs and teeth. The snake is then fangless and toothless, the poison being taken out of it.

This is the Vedantic way of controlling the mind.

Spiritualists usually put their minds in a state comparable to that of the cold-stricken snake and are in a state of bliss; but in this work-a-day life their relatives, friends, brothers, sisters and enemies, all of them come and warm up the snake of the passions and desires, they heat up this snake and then the snake of passions and desires is roused, the mind within is up to mischief again. The fangs of the snake were not taken out and are poisonous as before. No character is built, no true spirituality is gained.

Concentration of mind is all right, but make the snake poison less, pick out the fangs of the snake, rise above all temptation; build your character. These things are to be looked after and must be remembered. When all the points of weakness are cured, you are the snake without the fangs, without the teeth, and even then you can be cold-stricken, but there is no necessity of remaining in that state, there is no venom in your stings You have character now, and in the busy work-a-day life you are unharmed, undamaged, you are beyond it.

MORAL: In simple concentration, caused by ordinary Vairagya or Hatha Yoga, the desires do not really die out but are capable of rising up and stinging the mind again under favourable worldly impact.

In concentration with character, caused by the practice of self-knowledge, the desires are permanently rooted out, and hence no worldly contact, whatsoever, can make them grow again.

How to Acquire All Knowledge (The Two Artists)

Two men came before a king and asked him to employ them in ornamenting and painting the walls of his palace. These two rival artists applied to the king in order to get the monopoly of the whole business. The king wanted to examine their work before engaging them, and accordingly they were asked to paint two opposite walls.

Screens were placed before the walls so that the artists could work independently of each other. They worked for about a month and at the end of that time, one of the artists came to the king and told him that he had finished his work and would like him to come and see what he had done. The king then asked the other artists how long it would take him to finish; and he replied, "Your Majesty, I also have finished." The day was appointed and the king together with his entire retinue and other visitors came to see which of the artists had outrivaled the other. The screen before the wall of the first artists was taken, down. The king and his retinue and all the visitors pronounced the work as marvellous, splendid; they fell into raptures over the work, thought it great and sublime.

The courtiers whispered to the king that nothing better could be expected; that there was no use to look at the work of other artist, because this painter had far surpassed all their expectations, they thought the entire work ought to be given to this man. The king was, however, wiser than his courtiers, and accordingly ordered the screen to be taken off from before the other wall, and lo! the people were astonished, they opened their mouths and raised their hands and held their breath in amazement. O wonder of wonders, it is marvellous. Do you know what they have discovered? Now the second painter had painted nothing on the wall during the whole month. He had worked to make the wall transparent as far as possible; he rubbed and scrubbed and beautified this wall; he succeeded in making this wall perfectly transparent. Upon examining the wall, all that was painted on the opposite wall by his rival was perfectly reflected in this wall. Besides, this wall was more smooth, more even and beautiful, while the other wall appeared to be rough, uneven and ugly. All the painting or that wall was reflected in this beautiful, smooth wall, and consequently the second wall had all the beauty of the first wall added to it.

Now the kings and people of those days were not acquainted with mirrors, and they did not examine very closely, but exclaimed, 'Your Majesty, this man has entered .deep into the wall; he has dug two or three yards and has painted everything."

The images appeared in the mirror the same distance as the paintings were from the mirror.

Now as this painter rubbed and scrubbed the wall with sand and worked with it until it became a mirror, so Rama tells you that people, who are busy reading books, gain superficial knowledge; while painting outside, let them paint the walls so as to make them beautiful by the process of gaining all knowledge.

This process is trying to make the walls of your mind or intellect transparent, smooth, thin, by rubbing and scrubbing them as it were; by purifying your hearts, by making your hearts transparent; then all the knowledge of the world will be reflected in your mind; you will be inspired with the whole universe.

MORAL: If you make your mind a mirror by purifying your heart, all knowledge of the universe will be reflected in it.

Idealism and Realism (Mr. Axe and Mr. Wood)

Once two men in India were quarrelling. They were Darveshes. One went by the name of Mr. Wood, and the other by the name of Mr. Axe. Mr. Axe was enraged and said to Mr. Wood, *I will slash you to pieces!' and Mr. Wood replied 'But my dear sir, you must have me behind you, otherwise you can do nothing.* You see the handle of the Axe is made of wood, and so it is that Idealism and Realism go hand in hand, they are interdependent.

. . Just so, strike a match on the sand paper and a flame is produced. Now the flame was not in the match, neither was it in the sand-paper, but the coming together of the two produced the flame. Similarly, strike the hands together and there is a sound produced. The sound is neither in the right hand nor in the left, but is the result of the two coming together.

MORAL:—Idealism and Realism are not independent of each other but are interdependent.

Two ways of Acquiring Knowledge (The Two Painters)

They say, at one time a prince was going to get one of his most glorious palaces painted in a marvellous way. Many painters came hoping that he would select the very best painter for the job. He gave them an examination. Two walls stood side by side parallel to each other, and two painters were employed to paint these walls. Curtains were hanging on these walls so that the work of one painter could not be seen by the other. About two weeks were allowed to them to finish their work. One of the painters reproduced on the wall all the scenes of the Mahabharata, the grand book of the world, and his work was most marvellous and glorious indeed. As to the other painter, I will not tell you yet what he was doing. Two weeks passed, and the king with his retinue came to the scene, arid the curtain was lifted from the work of the first painter, and there were thousands and thousands of pictures upon the wall. Everybody who looked at the wall was wonder-struck. They stood, all surprised, in a most wonder struck mood. How glorious was the work! All the spectators cried out. "Give him the reward, select him for the highest work which you want to be done! Let him be the victor, let him be rewarded." Then the king ordered the other man to lift up his curtain, and when the curtain was lifted, all the people stood there with bated breath, their lips half open, their breathing suspended, and their eyes wide open with amazement. They could not utter a word; they were pictures of .amazement and surprise. Why? What had this second man done? Everything on the wall of the first man was inscribed on the wall of the second man, with this difference that while the first man's paintings were relatively rough and rugged*and uncouth, the second man's paintings were so smooth, neat and clean, and so soft and polished, that even a fly in its attempt to sit upon the wall would slip away. So beautiful was the work! and further, they saw that in the second man's paintings there was a curious beauty of the paintings, which were inscribed three yards within the wall. How had this work been done? The second man had been polishing, purifying and smoothing his wall to such an extent that he made it transparent, and it became a veritable mirror, a looking-glass. Like a looking-glass, it took in all that the first man had done, but everything was painted within it. You know that the picture within a mirror is reflected within it as far away as the object is without it.

Thus, there are two ways of acquiring knowledge. One is the cramming and outside painting work, taking in picture after picture, and idea after idea, and pumping into the brain thoughts and ideas of all varieties, Geology, Astrology Theology, Philology and all sorts of Ontologies and nonpracticologies. This is one way of acquiring knowledge. You can acquire superficial knowledge, just as that man painted the wall by all sorts of colours used on the surface. But there is another way of mastering the knowledge of the world. It is a purifying process. It is not stuffing in, but taking away. This process in trying to make the walls of your mind or intellect transparent, smooth, thin, by rubbing and scrubbing them as it were; by purifying your hearts, by making your hearts transparent; then all the knowledge of the world will be reflected in your mind; you will be inspired with the whole universe.

MORAL: Cramming or stuffing in is one way of acquiring knowledge, while the other way is to purify the mind as a mirror, so that the knowledge of the whole universe is reflected in it.

CHAPTER TWELVE

Obstacles

Difficulties Unavoidable (A Horseman and a Persian Wheel)

There was a man on horse-back going to distant place. He happened to pass by a Persian wheel in India. When water is pumped out of a well by Persian-wheel, there is a noise. Now this man brought his mare or horse to brink of the water that was coming out of the well by the Persian-wheel, The horse not being accustomed to hear that kind of noise, was startled a little and did not drink that water. The horseman asked the peasants, who were working that Persian-wheel, to stop that noise. The peasants stopped that noise by stopping the Persian-wheel; the noise was stopped, but with the stopping of the noise the coming of the water also stopped. Now the horse had no water to drink; the horse advanced towards the cistern, where the water was to be found; but there was no water at all' Now this horse-man turned to the farmers and complained to them, "O queer farmers! I asked you to stop the noise; I did not ask you to stop the water, strange fellows you are; you will not show kindness to a stranger to allow his horse a drink of water." The farmers said, "Sir we wish from the bottom of our heart to serve you, to treat you and to serve your horse with water, but your request is beyond our power to comply with. We cannot comply with your request. If you want to have water, if you want to water your horse, you ought to coax him to drink when the noise is going on: because when we stop the noise, no water will be supplied; water comes always a long-side of this noise."

If you want to realize Vedanta, realize it even in the midst of ail sorts of noise, even in the heart of all sorts of troubles. In this world you can never get yourself in a state where there twill be no noise or no botherations from without. Live on the heights of the Himalayas; there also you will have troubles around. Live as savages, there also you will have botherations around you. Go wherever you please, botherations and troubles will never leave you; they are always with you. If you want to realize Vedanta, realize it when the noise of the Persian wheel is going on all around you. All the great men have been produced despite discouraging environments and circumstances; in fact the harder these circumstances, the more trying the environments, the stronger are the men, who come out of those circumstances. So, welcome all these outside troubles and anxieties. Live Vedanta even in these surroundings; and when you live Vedanta, you will see that the surroundings and circumstances will succumb to you, will yield to you, they will become subservient to you; you will become their master.

MORAL: Vedanta can be realized even in the midst of all sorts of troubles and botherations, for they cannot be avoided, wherever you be.

Obstacles as Source of Strength (A Good Man and His Wicked Servant)

There was very good man who kept a very naughty and wicked servant. He used to do everything in a wrong way; he used to carry out the commands of his master in a curious way; in fact his way of doing things was such as to upset even the most serious man. This faithful master was never annoyed, but always treated the servant in a most charming manner. At one time, one of the guests remonstrated against the servant; he was very much annoyed and displeased with his actions and asked the master to dismiss him. The master said, "Your advice is very good, and it is given with the best intention; I know that you wish me well; I know that you want my work and business to prosper, and it is on this account that you give me this advice; but I know better, I know that my work is being spoiled, I know that my business suffers. But I keep this servant on the very ground or from the very fact of his being so unfaithful; it is his bad conduct and his wicked habits which make him so dear to me. I love him the more because he is a sinner, a wicked and unfaithful servant." This was a very strange way of speaking.

The master said, "This servant is the only person in the world, or with whom I come in contact, that disobeys me; he is the only person who does things which are uncomplimentary, derogatory or detrimental to me. All others with whom I come in contact are so gentle, so pleasant, so loving that they dare not offend me, and so this man is out of the ordinary; he is a kind of dumb-bells, a kind of special training to my spiritual self. Just as many people use dumbbells, pulleys, or heavy weights, to exercise the muscles in order to develop their physical strength, so this servant serves as a kind of weight or dumb-bells by which my spiritual body is strengthened. Through this servant I get strength. I am compelled to do a kind of wrestling with this servant, which brings strength."

If you think your family ties are a hindrance and a stumbling block, you need not get annoyed. Just follow the example of the faithful master; make difficulties and differences an additional source of strength and power.

MORAL: Obstacles and hindrances, properly used, can be turned into a source of strength and power.

Family Ties no Obstacles (Socrates and his Unruly Wife)

Socrates had a wife, the most undesirable in the world. One day he was thinking very deeply, was philosophizing; and his wife, as was her wont, approached him and spoke in very harsh, rough, language; she reviled and insulted him and called him names: she demanded his attention; she asked him to attend to her, to do this and that thing; but Socrates went on philosophizing. His method was never to leave a problem until it was solved.

The wife roared and stormed at him, and still he did not listen. Then getting enraged, she took up a basin filled with dirty water and poured it upon his head. Was Socrates ruffled or annoyed? Not in the least. He smiled and laughed and said, "Today is proved the saying, „Oft-times when it roars it rains"."

Always when she roared, it did not rain, but today she roared and stormed, and at the same time there came rain also. After that remark, he continued his philosophizing.

This shows that people must not become despondent about their capability of overcoming their temper. If one man, Socrates, could get such complete control of his temper, then all can. Even today are there not people who have control over their temper, and over their habits? Most certainly there are such people, and you can do this also by trying.

The way to realize the truth, or to realize your oneness with the Divinity, the way to realize the union with the All, or your sameness with the whole world, the way to this Divine realization of the Self can be made smoother through your family ties if you will.

MORAL: Family ties instead of being obstacles, can be utilized as means to self-control and self-realization.

Removal of Obstacles Essential (The Saint Who Poked out His Eyes)

It is related of a Hindu Saint that he was once going through the streets hungry. In India saints or sages come down from the mountains and walk through the streets when they are hungry, and beg food for their bodies. On very rare occasions they visit the streets. Usually they live outside the cities in the forests, devoting their time entirely to God-consciousness. The hungry saint was fed. A lady brought to him dainty food to eat. He just took that loaf of bread in his handkerchief, left the house, went out into the forest, as is the way with monks in India. There he put it in water and making it wet ate it. The next day he came again to the streets at the usual time. Again the girl approached him, and gave him something very rich to eat. He went back. The third day also that girl brought him something very good to eat but while she was giving him this dainty food, she made the remark, "I keep waiting for you. My eyes have become sore in waiting for you, in keeping watch at the door, your eyes have bewitched me." These were the words that escaped the lips of that lady. The sage went away. He went to some other door and there he got some food and eating that food he went out to the forests and threw into the river the food which was offered him by the first lady who had expressed her love to him, and the other food that was presented to him by the second lady he ate. The next day, he got very hot irons, poked out his eyes, tied them in the hand kerchief, and- with the aid of a stick, with great difficulty walking along the streets felt his way to the house of the lady who had expressed her Jove to him. There he found that the lady was waiting for him very anxiously. His eyes were fixed on the ground. The lady did not notice that he had poked out his eyes, and when she brought something very rich for him to eat he presented his eye-balls to her saying, "Mother, mother, take up these eyes because the eyes had bewitched you, and had caused you so much trouble. You have every right to possess these eyes. Mother, you wanted these eyes. Have them, keep them, love and enjoy them, do with these eye-balls whatever you wish, but for heaven's sake, for mercy's sake do not retard my progress onward. Make me not stumble in the path of Truth."

Now, O people, if your eyes are the stumbling block in your way, cast them out. It is better for your body to be without light than for your whole being to perish in darkness. This is the way.

If your eyes stand in the way of your realising the Truth, poke them out. If your ears tempt you and keep you backward, cut them out. If your wife, money, property, wealth or anything stands in the way, away with it.

Gould you love Truth with the same love as you have for your wife and relatives, could you love Divinity and Atman or realisation with the same zest or zeal with which you love your wife, could you love God with even half the love that you show your wife, you would realise the Truth this second.

MORAL: Howsoever dear a thing may be, if it proves an obstacle in the way of Self realization it must be removed forthwith.

The Greatest Obstacle (Atlanta and the Gold)

There is a very beautiful story in the old mythology of Atlanta. They say that every man who wanted to wed her had to run a race with her. Nobody could get ahead of her but one person consulted his god Jupiter and asked the advice of his favourite god as to the way of outrunning Atlanta and winning her. The god gave him a very queer advice. He told this man to bestrew the path along which they had to run with gold bricks. You know the god Jupiter could not help this devotee of his to outrun Atlanta in any other way. This Atlanta had got from the highest deity a boon which made her the strongest and swiftest being in the whole Universe. But this devotee of Jupiter threw gold bricks all along the race-course, and challenged Atlanta to run a race with her. Both began to run. This man was naturally much weaker than Atlanta. She outruns him in one second, but as she had lost sight of him, she saw gold bricks lying along the path and stopped to pick them up. While she was picking up the gold bricks, that devotee went ahead of her. There after a minute or so she overtook him again and again saw to the left of the race-course another brick. She went to pick up that brick and got it. In the meantime that devotee of Jupiter went ahead of her and after a while she got him again, and there she found some more gold bricks. She stopped to pick up those; in the meantime that fellow outran her and so on. Towards the close of the race, Atlanta had got with her a very heavy load of gold. It was very difficult for her to carry it and also outrun him. Finally that man got the better of Atlanta who was won. All the gold that Atlanta had got also fell to the share of the man who outran her, it went to him and she herself went over to that man. He got everything.

Such is the way with most people who want to tread the path of Righteousness and the path of Truth. When you commence to tread the path of truth, you find all sorts of base lucre and worldly temptations around you. You stoop to pick them up, but the moment you do so and enjoy these worldly temptations and enjoyments, you find you are lagging, behind. You are losing the race, procrastinating, making your path dreary, and losing everything. Beware of worldly attachments and materiality. You cannot reach the Truth and also enjoy worldly pleasures. The saying goes that if you enjoy the Truth, you will no longer be able to enjoy worldly pleasures. Enjoy worldly pleasures, and Truth will elude your grasp, get ahead of you. Get rid of attachment, and at the same time shake off all hatred and jealousy, which is inverted attachment. Have all your attachment severed from every object, and concentrate yourself on one thing, the one fact, one truth, your Divinity. Immediately on the spot you gain realization.

MORAL: Attachment with worldly objects and pleasures is the greatest obstacle in the path of Realization, while worldly detachment with full concentration on the one Truth, the Divinity within, gives immediate Self-realization.

Impatience an obstacle (When Rama was a child)

When Rama was a child, he and several other children would get some seeds of corn and barley or rice and dig holes in the garden of the court-yard and in these holes we would place these seeds together with some water and then cover this all over, and so earnest were we in our work that we would forego our meals. We were impatient to see what the seeds would produce, we were impatient to see something come out of the place where we had but a few minutes before planted the seeds of corn, barley and rice. We could not leave the spot for one moment, fearing lest the seeds might sprout without our knowing it. We were very anxious, and about an hour after sowing we were examining the place closely to see if there were any sprouts; we could see nothing. Disappointed we were, and we removed the earth a little to see if anything had happened, but could see nothing; we removed the earth a little more and nothing had commenced to germinate; we removed the earth still more and lo, the seeds were unchanged.

Be not like those children impatient and expecting to reap fruit in less than a quarter of an hour. You can sow the seed, but you cannot reap the harvest in so short a time. It must take some time at least, but most certainly the effect will be produced.

MORAL: No purpose is served by impatience; on the other hand, it impedes progress.

CHAPTER THIRTEEN

Om : The Sacred Syllable

Om, the Source of Vedas (Shankhasur and Vedas)

It is related in the Puranas that at one time the Vedas were taken, by a demon and carried to the bottom of the sea. The word 'Veda' has two meanings. The original meaning is knowledge, the kingdom of heaven. The second meaning is the most sacred scriptures of the Hindus.

The name of this demon, said to have carried the Vedas to the bottom of the sea, was Shankhasur which etymologically means the demon of the conch-shell or the "insect dwelling in conch".

In order to redeem the Vedas, in order to bring back the treasures of knowledge, God incarnated as a fish, fought with the demon, destroyed it, and brought back the Vedas to the world. Children read that story and take it literally; common people read it and take it literally; but there is a deep, hidden meaning in the story. The story was meant to illustrate a general truth.

God incarnated as a fish to bring back the Vedas from the worm living in conch-shell. God incarnated as a fish and fought the demon or insect at the bottom of the sea, and destroyed it. What was the use of this? The fish is a maritime animal and the conch-shell is also inhabited by a creature of the sea. Now God, the All, in the shape of the fish fought the insect of the sea. The insect was driven out of the shell and the waves of the sea washed the shell ashore. People picked it up. The conch-shell was blown and there came out of it the reverberating sound OM. This is Veda. In this sense was the Veda the conch-shell, brought from the bottom of the sea. The story-teller meant to lay particular stress on the importance of the sacred Mantram OM. The object is to show that this sacred syllable Om is the end of knowledge in the entire world. It is all the Vedas, all the Kingdom of Heaven put in a conch-shell, condensed to its smallest compass. That was the object of this story.

MORAL: All knowledge or Veda is condensed in the sound of Om produced by a conch-shell, and it is the key to unlock the kingdom of Heaven within.

The Effect of Mantram Om (A Newly Married Girl)

There was a newly married girl, the very personification of simplicity, she had had no experience of confinement as a mother. During the first month of her pregnancy she felt a little change in her disposition and naively imagined that the coming months would produce no further change. In India, the bride lives at the house of the mother-in-law and it is the mother-in-law who attends to the wants of the daughter-in-law and her children. This young daughter one day quaintly addressed her mother-in-law thus: "Mother, mother, when I am in confinement, will you kindly wake me lest the child be born without my being aware of its birth." The mother replied, "Dear girl, when the time comes there will be no necessity to wake you, you will be in a state to wake up all the neighbours by your screams and cries." During the days of pregnancy a wonderful change was going on, the effect was being produced although the mother was not aware of it. When the proper time comes the effect is made manifest.

Similarly, go on feeding on the man tram OM, go on nourishing yourself, drink deep of this nourishing milk and the effect will, in due time, be brought forth, you need not get impatient.

MORAL: One need not be impatient for the effect of Mantram Om, but should go on chanting and meditating over it, and the result will surely manifest itself in due time.

CHAPTER FOURTEEN

Oneness

The Result of Perfect Union (The Invincible Union)

Once, a lady was thrown into fire. The people saw that the fire did not burn her. Her lover was thrown into the fire, but it did not burn him also. How was it? They were thrown into the river but it did not carry them off. They were thrown down from the tops of mountains and not a bone was broken. How was it? At that time they could not give any explanation, they were beyond themselves; they were in that state where no questions could reach them.

Long afterwards the reason was asked, and they said that to each of them the beloved one was all in all; the fire was no fire, it appeared to that lady her lover and to the man the same fire appeared to be his beloved one. The water was no water to them; it was all the beloved one. The stones were no stones to them;-the body was no body to them;, it was all the beloved one. How could the beloved one harm them?

MORAL: Nothing can harm one who feels himself one with all.

The Right way to Profit the Part (The Selfish Hand)

Once the hand became selfish and wanted to violate the law of brotherhood or unity and began to reason this way: — "Here am I, work all day, but all the benefit of my work is reaped by the stomach or other parts of the body, I do not eat anything. I should not allow the teeth or mouth to reap all the advantage, I will have everything myself." The hand, after advancing this argument, became willing to carry it into effect. The food that was served on the table milk, meat, all sorts of things, fruit, vegetable,—all those things the hand must now himself eat; the hand must get the benefit of it himself.

The hand took a pin, made a hole and poured that milk into it, injected that milk, so that the mouth would not get the benefit. The hand made itself sick, it could not be benefited by it. There was one other way. In order to make itself fat the hand wanted to take honey, and where from does it come? From the bee. So the hand took the bee and made it sting it. The hand got so much honey, it got life of the bee into it, you know the bee dies after it stings. The hand became very fat, all the honey was in the hand. Oh, but this made the hand bitter and painful, it tortured the hand. When the hand had suffered, after a while it came to its senses. The hand said, "All that I earn must not go to myself alone. All that I earn must go into the stomach and there it must be used by the blood, by the hands and feet, by every organ of the body, and then alone can I, the hand, be profited; there is no other way. Now the hand was forced to believe that the self of the hand was not confined within this small area.

The self of the hand will be profited when the self of the whole body is profited; the self of the hand will be profited when the self of the eyes is profited. The self of the hand is the same as the self of eyes, the self of ears and the self of the whole body. So, try to be selfish in the same way as the hand did, and you will suffer the consequences, you will suffer the same way as the poor hand did by trying to execute his selfishness. The Divine law cannot allow you to separate yourself from your own kind. The most sacred truth is violated when you consider yourself not one with your fellow-men. The merchants who do not look upon the interests of their customers as their own, or the shopkeepers who do not regard the interests of their customers as identical with their own, are shunned and avoided by the people and ruin themselves. In your life you will have to realize this, then and then alone will you prosper. O hand, your Self is the Self of the whole universe; your Self is the Self of the eyes, the feet, the teeth and every other part of the body. Feel that, realize that. If you want to keep yourself above misery and make yourself happy, realize and feel this oneness with each and all. Your practice will show, your own experience will prove that when you feel and realize this unity, when you concentrate your mind upon this truth, everybody around you is bound to come up to your help the same way as the hand comes up to help this part, when this part is itching or suffering. Here you feel an itching sensation, the hand immediately comes up there. Similarly if you realize that the Self, the Atman or the true Nature of yourself, is the same as the Self or Atman of your fellow who is related to you as true Self, when you are in need your fellows will immediately come to you and aid you.

MORAL: The right way to profit the part is to profit the whole, as they are one and not separate.

Inspired Life (A Whistling Boy)

A boy was merrily whistling in the streets. A policeman objected. The boy replies, "Do I whistle? No, sir, it whistles itself."

Let a nightingale or dove be perched on the top of a stately cypress, and full, delicious notes begin instantaneously to flow from the bird.

Let the little self be flung into Infinity, May you wake up to your oneness with Life, Light, and Love (Sat-Chit-Anand), and immediately the Central Bliss will commence springing forth from you in the shape of happy heroic work and both wisdom and virtue. This is inspired life, this is your birthright.

MORAL: The feeling of oneness with Life, Light and Love lets the inner Bliss flow freely from you and makes your life inspired.

True Feeling of Oneness (Krishna's Oneness with Radha)

Krishna was to give a feast. All the ministers were invited, but he had not invited his sweet-heart, Radha. The prime minister urged him to send her invitation, but he would not listen to him and said, "No." However, the prime minister did not heed him and went to Radha to inform her of the feast which Krishna was to give.

She said to him, "When you have a feast, you send invitations to your friends, but you do not send an invitation to yourself, do you? I know that Krishna is to have feast. We are one."

MORAL: True feeling of oneness needs no outer show of love.

The True Neighbour (Rama and the Fellow Professor)

When Rama took up the order of Sannyasa, gave up family connections, gave up worldly positions, there came some people and said, "Sir, sir, how is it that you have disregarded the claims of your wife, children, relatives and the students who were looking to you for help and aid, why have you utterly disregarded their claims? This was the question put. That man who put the question to Rama was a fellow-professor in the college. To him Rama asked "You are a professor, you lecture on philosophy in the college, In the University, and now can you tell whether your wife and children also have got the same learning as you have? Can you tell whether your auntie and your grandmamma possess the same learning as you do? Do your cousins possess the same knowledge?" He said, "No I am a professor." Rama said, "How is it that you come to the University and lecture, and you do not lecture to your little children, your wife and your servants? Why do you not lecture to your grandmamma and to your cousins and to your auntie? How is that?" And he said that they could not understand that, and then it was explained to the man as follows:

Look here. These are not your neighbours; these servants, this grandmamma, wife, children, and even your dogs, they are not your neighbours. Even though the dog is your constant companion, never leaves you, and is your greatest companion in the eyes of ignorant, still you know that the dog, the servants, and the ignorant auntie and grandmamma are not your neighbours. Who are you? You are not the body, you are the true Self, but you do not admit that, being a European philosopher. You are the mind; your neighbours are those that dwell constantly with you on the same meridian where your mind lives. All the students, the Masters of Art, the Bachelors of Art, all these in their parlour, in their reading room, pore over the same books, they keep pondering over the same subject, reading the same thing as you read. Your mind dwells upon the same subjects as theirs, and they are your neighbours. When you are in your reading room, people say that he is in the reading room. Upon your honour, say whether you are in the reading room or whether you are in your thoughts. You do not live in the reading room, even though the dog is seated on your lap, even though your children come into the room, they are nothing to you, you are there on the philosophical plane, and on that height your neighbours are the students who are reading the same subject in their own homes. These are your neighbours, your nearest neighbours, and thus can you extend your helping hand to the students more than to your auntie, grandmamma and dog and servants, who are not your neighbours. Your neighbour is he who lives nearer to your spirit, he who lives on the same plane where you live. Your neighbour is not he who lives in the same house; rats and flies live in the same house; dogs and cats live in the same house.

MORAL: The true neighbour is not he who lives in the same house with you but that who lives on the same plane of thought with you.

Clairvoyance created by Oneness (The Queen and the Lady painter)

In the Mahabharata, the greatest book of the world,. consisting of four hundred thousand verses, the story is given of a queen who, in a vision, sees the most beautiful prince and falls in love with him. She was so deep in love with him that her body under the severe passion of love, fell sick. Her father sends for all sorts of doctors and physicians, but to no avail. At last somebody discovers that her disease is the blessed disease of love. The Prime Minister of the king comes up and he puts his hand upon her pulse, and orders one of the greatest painters to come up and paint the pictures of all the beautiful kings in India. This painter was a woman. This woman-painter comes up, and, on a board against the wall, she draws picture after picture of the great kings that lived in India in those days. This Prime Minister is watching the beating of the pulse of the princess. The paintress draws the picture of Shri Krishna. Then her pulse beats faster, and the Prime Minister stops short. He thinks that here is the man perhaps whom she had seen in her vision. But he sees that the pulse did not beat fast enough, and orders the painter to go on painting pictures. Then she pain ts the picture of the youngest son of Krishna, and when that picture is painted, lo, not only to say nothing about the pulse, but her whole heart begins to heave and beat up to the very earth, as it were. Then the Prime Minister comes to the conclusion, "Here is the man who will drive away her sadness." This we believe to be no story but historical fact.

As to this paintress, what about her? Did she see all the kings and princes of the land? No! She was under what we call Divya Drishti (clairvoyance), under that higher vibration with the All, so much so that the book of Nature remained no longer sealed book, but everything was an open book to her.

MORAL: The feeling of oneness with all under higher vibrations makes one clairvoyant.

CHAPTER FIFTEEN

Renunciation

True Renunciation (A Prince prostrating before a Monk)

There came a man, a prince, to a monk in India, and he prostrated himself before him. The monk asked him as to the cause of this homage that the prince was paying him. The prince said: "O sir, O holy sir, you are a monk, and you have adopted this order by giving up your kingdom which you ruled at one time. You are a great man of renunciation, and so I look upon you as God, I worship you." The monk replied to the prince, "If that is the reason why you honour me, I must wash your feet, I must kneel down before you, because, O king, you are a greater man of renunciation than all the monks in this world put together." The king remarked, "That is very strange. How could that be?" Then the monk began to explain: "Suppose, here is a man who possesses a magnificent palace, and this man casts out the dust and dirt of the house; he throws out or renounces only the dust or dirt of the house. Is that man a man of renunciation?" The prince said, "No, no; he is not." Then the monk continued, "Here is a man who treasures up the dirt and dust of the house and gives away the whole house; the magnificent palace. What do you think of this man?" The prince said, "This man, who keeps only the dirt and dust, and resigns the palace, is a man of renunciation!" Then the monk said, "Brother prince, you are then the man of renunciation, because the Self God, the real Atman, that which is the magnificent palace, the real Home, the Paradise, the Heaven of heavens, you have renounced, and only the dust and dirt of that palace, which is this body, this little selfishness, you have retained. I have renounced nothing. I am myself the God of gods—the Lord of Universe."

MORAL:—True renunciation does not consist in renouncing anything but realising the Self as the God of gods - the Lord of Universe.

The Result of Renunciation (Alexander and the Indian Monk)

When Alexander, the Great, visited India after conquering all the other countries in the world that were known to him, he wanted to see the strange Indians of whom he had been hearing so much. He was just led to a monk or priest on the bank of the Indus river. The monk lay there on the sands, bare-headed, bare-footed, naked, wearing no clothes and not knowing where from his tomorrow's food was to come, just lying there and basking in the Sun. Alexander, the Great, with his crown shining, dazzling with brilliant diamonds and gems that he had got from Persia, stood beside him in all his glory. Beside him was the monk with no clothes on—what a contrast, what a contrast! The riches of the whole world represented by the body of Alexander on one side, and all the outward poverty represented by the saint on the other side! But you have simply to look at their faces to be convinced of the poverty or riches of their true souls-Here is the saint whose soul was rich, here is the saint who had realized the richness and glory of his Atman. Beside him stood Alexander, the Great, who wanted to hide his inner poverty. Look at the beaming countenance of the saint, the happy joyful face of the saint. Alexander, the Great, was struck by his appearance. He fell in love with him, and just asked the saint to come with him to Greece. The saint laughed, and his answer was. "The world is in Me. The world cannot contain Me. The universe, Greece and Rome are in Me. The suns and stars rise and set in Me."

Alexander, the Great, not being used to this kind of language, was surprised. He said, "I will give you riches. I will just flood you with worldly pleasures. All sorts of things that people desire, all sorts of things which captivate and charm people will be in wild profusion at your service. Please accompany me to Greece."

The saint laughed, laughed at his reply and said, "There is not a diamond, there is not a sun or star which shines, but to me is due its lustre. To me is due the glory of all the heavenly bodies. To me is due all the attractive nature, all the charms of the things desired. It would be beneath my dignity, it would be degrading on my part, first to lend glory and charm to these objects, and then go about seeking them, to go begging at the door of worldly riches, to go begging at the door of flesh and animal desires to receive pleasures, happiness. It is below my dignity. I can never stoop to that level. No, I can never go begging at their doors."

This astonished Alexander, the Great. He just drew his sword and was going to strike off the head of that saint. And again, the saint laughed a hearty laugh and said, "O Alexander, never in your life did you speak such a falsehood, such an abominable lie. Kill me, kill me, kill me! Where is the sword that can kill me? Where is the weapon that can wound me? Where is the calamity that can mar my cheerfulness? Where is the sorrow that can temper with my happiness? Everlasting, the same yesterday, to day, and forever, pure, and holy of holies the Master of the universe,—that I am, that I am. Even in your hand I am the power that makes them move, O Alexander. If your body dies, there I remain. I am the power that makes your hands move. I am the power that makes your muscles move." The sword fell down from the hands of Alexander.

The outward loss, outward renunciation, can be achieved when inward perfection, inward mastery or king-hood is attained. No other way, no other way.

MORAL: A man of true renunciation is beyond all fear and temptation.

Possession versus Renunciation (Two Monks Travelling Together)

Two monks were travelling together. One of them maintained in practice the spirit of accumulation. The other was a man of renunciation. They discussed the subject of possession versus renunciation, till they reached the bank of a river. It was late in the evening. The man who preached renunciation had no money with him, but the other had. The man of renunciation said, "What do we care for the body; we have no money to pay the boat-man; we can pass away the night even on this bank, singing the name of God." The moneyed monk replied. "If we stay on this side of the river, we can find no village, no hamlet or hut, no company; wolves will devour us, snakes will bite us, cold will chill us. We had better ferry to the other side. I have money with which to pay the boatman to ferry us over to the other bank. On that side there is a village; we will live there comfortably." Well, the boatman came over and both of them were ferried across the river to the opposite shore. At night, the man who had paid the fare remonstrated with the man of renunciation: "Do you not see the advantage of keeping money? I kept money and two lives were saved. Henceforth you should never preach renunciation. Had I also been man of renunciation like you, we would have both starved or been chilled and killed on that side of the river." But the man of renunciation answered: "Had you kept the money with you, had you not parted with the money, renounced it to the boatman, we would have died on the other bank. Thus it was the giving up of money or renunciation that brought us safety." "Again," he continued, "if I kept no money in my pocket, your pocket became my pocket. My faith kept money for me in that pocket. I never suffer. Whenever I am in need I am provided for".

So long as you keep your desires in your pocket, there is no safety or rest for you. Renounce your desires, rise above them and you find double peace—immediate rest and eventual fruition of desires. Remember, that your desires will be realised only when you rise above them into the supreme Reality. When you consciously or unconsciously lose yourself in the Divinity, then and then only will the time be ripe for the fulfilment of desires.

MORAL: Renunciation is for better than possession, for it brings double peace, immediate rest and eventual fruition of desires.

The Right Way of Renunciation (An Old Lady Wanted to Retire)

An old lady came to a saint in India and asked if it was advisable for her to leave her house and her family, and to retire to Brindaban (in India), where Krishna was born.

Was it advisable for her to break her family ties and sever all her relations with each and all and retire to that lovely city, Brindaban, the Jerusalem of India? This lady had her grandson with her. The sage replied, "See please, mark please, what is it that looks into your eyes through the eyes of your grandson? What force, what energy, what Divinity is it that looks at you from every pore of the body of this child? The lady said "It must be God. In this dear little baby there is no thought of temptation or wickedness. This dear little baby is innocent and pure. When he cries, in his wailing is the voice of God and nothing else." Again the sage said, "When you go to Brindaban, you shall have to cling to the one image of Krishna. There in the Jerusalem of India, and there in that image of Divinity, you must worship the Divinity. Is not the body of the child just as good an image of Krishna as the image you shall have to see in that Jerusalem of India?" The lady was surprised a little; and after thinking and reflecting, she came to the conclusion that she might just as well worship Krishna through the body of this child by regarding this child as the incarnation of Krishna. For God is that looks through the eyes of the child; God it is that gives the child its power; God it is that works through the ears of the child; God it is that makes the child's hair grow; God it is that works through every pore of his body; it is Divinity.

According to the direction of the saint, she must no longer regard the child as her grandson, or look upon him as related to her in any way, but must regard him as God, and thus break all family and worldly ties. The only tie should be the tie of Godliness or Godhead. This is the way to renunciation.

Renunciation does not mean asceticism. Renunciation means making everything holy. Renouncing the child does not mean giving up all connection with the child but thinking the child, the grandson, to be God. Realizing the Divinity in each and all: this is Renunciation according to Vedanta. Vedanta asks you to give up your wife or your husband and other relations. Vedanta says, "Give up the wife, as related to you, give up the wife as the wife, but realize the true Self, the Divinity within her. Give up the enemy as the enemy, see only the God in the enemy; give up the friend as a friend, but realize the Godliness or Godhead in the friend."

Renounce the selfish, personal ties; see the Godliness in each and all. See the Divinity in each and all. This is what the Hindu Scriptures enjoin upon every husband and every wife to live.

MORAL: The right way of renunciation is to give up not the persons and things themselves but the personal relations with them and to realise the Divinity or God in each and all.

False Versus True Dedication (An Intoxicated Man)

A man drinks wine until he becomes intoxicated and while in that condition, he sells his house for Rs. 500; while in this-condition he writes out a document selling his house for Rs. 500. His wife soon gives him vinegar or some sour drink and he becomes sober, he is then sorry for what he has done and the folly of selling his big house for nothing. He decides to bring a law suit against the man who bought his house hoping to gain his point on the ground of his intoxicated condition which rendered him unaccountable for his actions. He was not sober at the time.

Just so it is with some people. They are in a kind of intoxicated state, and while in that state they sell out to God, they give all their money, renounce all their possessions, give up father, mother, sister, brother, friend, all, all for God; they have lost all for God's sake. Very good, they are in concentration and after a short time worldly wants begin to tell upon them and petty cares make their existence felt. They are given vinegar, all intoxication subsides, and then they take back everything from God. The body becomes my body, the house my house, and they keep on wanting until they want even what is their neighbour's to be taken back, want everything taken back from God. This is all very well so far as it goes, but true peace and happiness you can have only when you rise to that state of perfection, when you give up everything permanently for God and when you have built your character which makes you proof against all troubles. There is no anxiety, no fear no hope of the world. You stand above all this.

MORAL: Dedication which is impulsive or emotional and is caused by the effects of external circumstances, is only temporary and false whereas that which is due to self-knowledge and is caused by complete renunciation is permanent and true dedication.

The Snake of True Renunciation (The Strange Dream-Snake)

A man was asleep, and in his sleep he found himself detected as a thief; he found himself a beggar; he was in a wretched condition. He prayed in his dream to all sorts of gods to help him, he went to this and that court, he went to this and that lawyer, he went to all his friends and sought their help, but there was no help. He was put in jail and be cried bitterly; for there was no help for him. There came a snake which bit him and he felt excruciating pain, and this pain was so great that it woke him up. He ought to have thanked the snake which bit him in his sleep. Whenever we dream sad and horrible things, whenever we have the night-mare, we are awakened. So the snake in the dream woke him up, and he found himself sitting in bed all right, he found himself surrounded by his family, and he was happy. Now, we say in the dream he was bound, and he sought release, and in the dream the snake came and bit him, and this snake was the same as the other objects in the dream with this difference that this snake woke him up, it startled him. It ate him up. We do not mean that the snake ate the man but that is ate the dreaming ego of the man; the dreaming ego of the man was as the other objects in the dream, and this snake not only destroyed the dreaming ego of the man but it destroyed ail the other objects in the dream viz., the jail, the jailor, the monkey, the soldiers and all the rest. But this serpent was a strange serpent, it did something very*extraordinary, it ate up itself, because when the man woke up, he no longer saw this strange snake. According to Vedanta, all this world that you see is but a mere dream, Maya; and what about yourself who sees the dream. You are the dreaming ego, the dreaming culprit, or the thief etc. and all your friends and the other people are the companions in prison, from whom you seek help and invoke aid, you invoke aid from all gods in heaven and hell, and they cannot release you. You go to your friends to seek aid but there is no peace, no true aid; no true or real joy comes to you until the time comes when you find yourself bitten by a snake. Now what snake is that? The snake of Renunciation. Renunciation appears to be serpent-like and it bites you. The word Renunciation seems awful to you, it stings you as it were. True Renunciation means knowledge, it means Vedanta.

When this true Renunciation comes, what we call Jnana follows. The great saying "I am Brahma, I am Divinity, I am the Lord of lords" is realized.

MORAL: As a man, bitten by a snake in the dream, wakes up and thus gets rid of ail the bondage and miseries of the dream-world, just so a man in the waking state gets rid of all the worldly bondage, troubles, and anxieties when bitten by the snake of true renunciation.

Life is too sacred to be wasted (Collecting Pebbles)

A man was collecting heaps of money in box. A monk passed by. On being invited to the house of this rich man who was hoarding this money in large boxes and steel chests, the monk asked the reason of this act. The wealthy man said, "Sir, what do you care, you are fed by the public, and even if they do not feed you, you do not care a straw for your body, but for us it is necessary to lay by some money so that it may be of use to us at the right time." The monk was silent. The next day the wealthy man had to go and see the monk in the rotten cottage where he lived. When the wealthy man came to the cottage of the monk, he found that the monk had with great labour dug a big pit and in that pit he was throwing beautiful, round stones, heaping stones upon stones in that pit, and had been laboring all day long in that manner. When the rich man came up, he said, "Swami, Swami, what are you doing here?" The monk said, "I am collecting these beautiful pieces of stone, don't you see how round they are?" The wealthy man smiled and said, "Why are you collecting them? Here is a whole mountain full of these stones. What is the use of collecting them?" The monk said, "I preserve them for the time of need, I may require them sometime and it may be that all these mountains will be washed off the surface of the earth so I will collect them and store them away." The wealthy man answered, "How is that possible? How can the stones be washed away from the earth?" Then the monk jumped upon the wealthy man and said, "You taught me this lesson, O fool, there never will come a time when your food will not be laid before you by God. What is the use of just wasting your energy and lavishing your precious time in this laying by of gold and silver? Learn a lesson from me.

Life is not for this waste, for this spendthrift purpose.

It is not to be wasted in such petty, sordid cares and anxieties."

MORAL: Life is too sacred to be wasted in hoarding money, or in petty, sordid cares and anxieties.

True Renunciation (Shikhadhwaj and Chudala)

There was in India a king called Shikhadhwaj. He was a great king, a mighty monarch. He wanted to realize his God-consciousness; and in order to do that he thought that he ought to give up this family life.

His wife was Chudala. She wanted to teach him but he would not listen to her, for he thought nothing of her.

He renounced everything, gave up his kingdom, and his wife became the ruler, and he then went to the Himalayas, and there he lived about a year or so.

In the mean time, the Empress, his wife, thought of a plan to bring him real happiness. So one day she put on the garb of a Sannyasin and walked up to the cottage where her husband then was. She found him lost in a state of meditation; she remained standing beside him, and when he came to his senses, he was filled with joy. Thinking her a great Sannyasin, he showered flowers on her.

She was in a blissful mood. He spoke, "I think God has incarnated in you to lift me up." She replied, "Yes, yes." He wanted her to teach him and she did so. She said, "O King, if you want to enjoy perfect bliss, you will have to renounce everything." He was surprised, and replied, "I have renounced my empire, my wife, my children." She said, "You have renounced nothing."

He could not understand, and asked, "Am I not a man of renunciation, have I not given up my empire, my family?"

She answered, "No, no, do you not possess something still?" "Yes," he replied, "I possess this cottage, this staff and this water-vessel." "Then you are not a man of renunciation," she replied. "So long as you possess anything, you are possessed by that thing. Action and reaction being opposites you cannot possess anything, without its possessing you." He then burnt the cottage, threw his staff into the river, and burnt his water-vessel, and exclaimed, "Now am I not a man of renunciation?" She replied, "Renunciation cannot come from renouncing these objects." She said, "O king, you have burnt the cottage, but do you not possess still three cubits and a half of clay? It was wrong for you to destroy those things, for you have gained nothing by it. What you possessed then, you still possess namely, that three cubits and a half of clay, where you lie down.*' He began to think, and determined to burn the body. He piled up wood and made a great fire, and was about to jump into the fire, but the wife prevented him and exclaimed, "O king, when your body is burnt, what will be left?" He replied, "Ashes will be left." "Whose ashes?" She asked. He replied, "My ashes." Then she replied, "You must still possess ashes. By burning the body, you have not attained renunciation." He began to think, and exclaimed, "How can I renounce, what shall I renounce".?

She asked, "Whose body is this"? He answered, "My body," "Well, renounce it." "Whose mind is this"? He answered, "My mind." "Then renounce it." The king was then made to ask questions. He said, "Who am I then? If I am not the mind, I am something else; and if I am not the body, I must be something different." He reflected and the conclusion was that the king realized, "I am the God of gods, the Lord of lords, the Infinite Being, the Supreme Excellence." He realized that, and said that this Supreme Excellence cannot be renounced, though other things may be.

The story goes that the wife of this king lived on for some time, and at one time threw off her yogic garb or powers and made the king believe that she was playing false to him in favour of a former lover of hers, and to his knowledge remained in that state for some time.

She afterwards came to the king and apologised, and said, "O king, you will please pardon me. I am wicked, and have been false to you, forgive me, I pray you." The king looked at her and said, "O girl, what is the meaning of these excuses and apologies? Your misconduct would have caused me pain, had I believed in this body, had I been prompted by ignorance, had I believed that I am the owner of this body, and that you belong to me. If I were a victim of that desire, a victim of that idea of the copy-writing spirit, if I had been subject to that malady, I would have been annoyed and deeply grieved, but as it is, I see no husband in my body; I do not hold in my hands any rope; I possess nothing and am possessed by nothing. I find myself the Infinite. Think, reflect, O girl, you may become pure, but there are other girls in this world who are impure; they are mine also. As the Light of the Universe, I am the owner of the whole world; for what shall I chafe, and for what shall I be pleased?" If a crime is committed by your neighbour, there is no grief, but if a crime is committed by your wife, oh, then you are deeply grieved. This comes through this self-appropriating, copy-writing spirit.

The queen went back to the kingdom and soon returned to the king and exclaimed, "O king, you are a veritable God. What difference does it make where you live? Are the Himalayas more yours than those palaces?" The king replied that he was present everywhere. "All bodies are mine,*' said he, "this body is not any more mine than other bodies. This body is not present in the eyes of the Jnani; it is present only in those who do not know the whole truth."

All this world is created by your own thought. This is as true as mathematical certainty. It is a bold statement, but it is literally true.

They took the king to the throne again. He was living in the midst of all the luxury, in the midst of all these uncertainties, pure, pure, no dupe of the senses, not led by his senses. He ruled for years. What was he? He was neither a king nor a monarch but God Himself. This was renunciation.

To him the pebbles and stones, the thorny roses and velvet cushions, and those silk quilts, those princely, royal magnificent houses were the same.

Renunciation is to begin with those things nearest and dearest. It is that false ego which I must give up: this idea that "I am doing this," that "I am the agent," and "I am the enjoyer," the idea which engenders in you this false personality. These must be done away with these thoughts. "My Wife," "My body," "My mind," "My children." Unless these ideas are renounced, realization is not attained, Retire into the Jungle and still you are not a man of renunciation, because the thought of making this or that belong to you, is in your mind. Hermits do not always get rid of this thought; while kings living in royal state do get rid of it sometimes. The man of renunciation is one who gets rid of this little appropriating self, this little apparent self.

MORAL: True renunciation consists, not in giving up this or that, the family or even the body, but in doing away with the idea of possession, the enjoyer, the agent, or of false personality.

CHAPTER SIXTEEN

Self-Realization

The Way to Get Anything (Shadow Hunting by the Child)

There was a little child, a small baby that had just learnt to crawl, to walk on all fours. The child saw its shadow and thought it to be something strange, something remarkable. The child wanted to catch the shadow; it began to crawl to the head of the shadow and the shadow also crawled. The child moved and the shadow also moved, The Child began to cry because he could not catch the head of the shadow. The child falls down, the shadow is with it; the child rises up and begins to hunt for the shadow. In the mean time, the mother taking mercy on the child made the child touch his own head, and Io, the head of this shadow was also caught.

Catch hold of your own head and the shadow is also caught. Heaven and Hell are within you. The source of power, joy, and life is within you. The God of men and nature and nations is within you.

MORAL: The way to get anything is not to hunt after it outside but to search within.

What is God? (A Prince's Question to Swami Rama)

Once upon a time, the son of an Indian king came to Rama in the mountains, and put this question, "Swami Swami, what is God?" This is a deep question, a very difficult problem. This is the one subject which all the theologies and all the religions propose to investigate, and you want to know all about it in a short time. He said, "Yes, sir yes, Swami. Where shall I go to have it explained? Explain it to me." The boy was asked, "Dear prince, you want to know what God is, you want to make acquaintance with God, but do you not know that the rule is when a man wants to see a great personage, he will have to send his own card first, he will have to send to the chief his own address and name? Now you want to see God. You had better send to God your card; you had better let God know what you are. Give Him your card. I will place it in the hands of God directly, and God will come to you and you will see what God is." Well, the boy said, "It is all right, it is reasonable. I will directly let you know what I am. I am the son of king so and so, living on the Himalayas in Northern India. This is my name." He wrote it out on a piece of paper. It was taken up by Rama and read. It was not put into the hands of God directly, but was given back to that prince who was told, "O prince, you do not know what you are. You are like the illiterate ignorant person who wants to see your father, the king, and cannot write his own name. Will your father, the king receive him? Prince, you cannot write your name. How will God receive you? First tell us correctly what you are and then will God come to you and receive you with open arms."

The boy reflected. He began to think and think over the subject. He said. 'Swami, Swami, now I see. I made a mistake in writing my own name I have given you the address of the body only, and I have not put upon the paper what I am."

There was another attendant of that prince standing by. The attendant could not understand it. Now the prince was asked to make his meaning clear to this attendant, and the prince asked this attendant this question; "Mr. so and so, to whom does this card belong?" The man said, "To me," and then taking up a stick from the hand of the attendant, the prince asked him, "O Mr. so and so, to whom does this stick belong?" The man said, "To me." "Well to whom does this turban of yours belong?" The man said, "To me." The prince said, "All right. If the turban belongs to you, there is a relation between the turban and you; the turban is your property, and you are the owner. Then you are not the turban, the turban is yours." He said "Indeed, that is so plain." "Well, the pencil belongs to you, the pencil is yours, and you are not the pencil". He said, I am not the pencil because the pencil is mine; that is my property, I am the owner." All right! Then the prince asked that attendant, taking hold of the ears of that attendant, "Whom do these ears belong to?"

And the attendant said, "To me." The prince said, "All right, the ears belong to you, the ears are yours, consequently you are not the ears. All right, the nose belongs to you. As the nose is yours, you are not the nose. Similarly, whose body is that?" (just beckoning to the body of the attendant). The attendant said, "The body is mine; this body is mine." "If the body is yours, Mr. Attendant, then you are not the body; you cannot be the body because you say that the body is yours; you cannot be the body. The very statement my body, my ears, my head, my hands, proves that you are something else and the body together with the ears and hands and eyes, etc., is something else. This is your property, you are the owner, the master; the body is like your, garment and you are the owner. The body is like your horse and you are the rider. Now, what are you?" The attendant understood it so far, and also concurred with the prince in saying that when the prince had put down on the paper the address of the body and had meant that this, address stood for himself, the prince had made a mistake. "You are not the body, not the ears, not the nose, not the eyes, nothing of the kind. What are you then?" "Now the prince began to reflect, and said; "Well, well, I am the mind, I am the mind; I must be the mind." "Is that so indeed?" The question was put to that prince now.

Now, can you tell me how many bones have you got in your body? Can you say where the food lies in your body that you took this morning? The prince could make no answer, and these words escaped his lips, "Well, my intellect does not reach that. I have not read that. I have not yet read anything of physiology or anatomy. My brain does not catch it, my mind cannot comprehend it."

Now the prince was asked, "Dear prince, O good boy, you say your mind cannot comprehend it, your intellect cannot reach up to that, your brain cannot understand this» By making these remarks, you confess or admit that the brain is yours, the mind is yours, the intellect is yours. Well, if the intellect is yours, you are not the intellect. If the mind is yours, you are not the mind. If the brain is your, you are not the brain. These very words of your show that you are the master of the intellect, the owner of the brain, and ruler of the mind. You are not the mind, the intellect, or the brain. What are you? Think, think, please. Be more careful and let us know correctly what you are. Then will God be just brought to you, and you will see God, you will be introduced directly into the presence of God. Please tell us what you are."

The body began to think, and thought and thought but could not go further. He said, "My intellect, my mind cannot reach further."

Oh, how true are these words! Indeed the mind or intellect cannot reach the true Divinity or God within. The real Atma, the true God is beyond the reach of words and minds.

The boy was asked to sit down for a while and meditate upon what his intellect had reached so far. "I am not the body; I am not the mind." If so, feel it, put it into practice, repeat it in the language of feeling, in the language of action; realise that you are not the body. , If you live this thought only, if you work into practice even so much of the truth, if you are above the body and the mind, you become free from all fear. Fear leaves you when you raise yourself above the level of the body or the mind. All anxiety ceases, all sorrow is gone, when you realize even so much of the truth that you are something beyond the body, beyond the mind."

After that, the boy was helped on a little to realize what he himself was, and he was asked, "Brother, prince, what have you done to-day? Will you please let us know work or deeds that you have performed this morning?"

He began to relate; "1 woke up early in the morning took bath, and did this thing and that thing, took my breakfast, read a great deal, wrote some letters, visited some friends, received some friends, and came here to pay my respects to the Swami."

Now the prince was asked, "Is that all? Have you not done a great deal more? Is that all? Just see." He thought and thought, and then mentioned a few other things of the same sort. "That is not all," said Rama. "You have done thousands of things more; you have done hundreds thousands, nay, millions of things more. Innumerable actions you have done, and you refuse to make mention of them. This is not becoming. Please let us know what you have done. Tell us everything that you have done this morning."

The prince, hearing such strange words that he had done thousands of things besides the few that he named, was startled. *'I have not done anything more than what I have told you sir; I have not done anything more." "No, you have done millions, trillions, quadrillions of things more." How is that? The boy was asked, "What is looking at the Swami?" He said, "1" "Are you seeing this face, this river Ganges that flows beside us?" He said, "Yes, indeed." "Well, you see the river and you see the face of the Swami, but who makes the six muscles in the eyes move? You know the six muscles in the eyes move, but who makes the muscles move. It cannot be anybody else; It cannot be anything extra. It must be your own self that makes the muscles in the eye move in the act of seeing."

The boy said, Oh! Indeed, it must be I; it cannot be anything else."

"Well, who is seeing just now, who is attending to this discourse?" The boy said, "I, it is I." "Well, if you are seeing, if you are attending to this discourse, who is making the oratory nerves vibrate? It must be you, it must be you. Nobody else. Who took the meals this morning?" The boy said, "I, I." "Well" if you took the meals this morning and it is you that twill go to the toilet and vacate, who is it that assimilates and digests the food? Who is it, please? Tell us if you ate and you threw it out. Then it must be you who digests, it must be yourself that assimilates, it cannot be anybody else. Those days are gone when outside causes were sought after to explain the phenomena in Nature, If a man fell down, the cause of his. fall was said to be some outside ghost. Science does not admit such solution of the problem. Science and philosophy require you to seek the cause of a phenomenon in the phenomenon itself.

Here you take the food, go into the toilet and throw it off. When it is digested, it must be digested by yourself, no outside power comes and digests it; it must be your own self- The cause of digestion also must be sought within you and not without you."

Well, the boy admitted so far. Now he was asked, "Dear Prince, just reflect, just think for a while. The process of digestion implies of hundreds of movements. In the process of digestion, in mastication, saliva is emitted from the glands in the mouth. Here is again the next process of oxidation going on. Here is blood being formed. There is the blood coursing through the veins, there is the same food being converted into carnal muscles, bones, and hair; here is the process of growth going on the body. Here are a great many processes going on, and all these processes in the body are connected with the process of assimilation and digestion.

If you take the food, it is you yourself who are the cause of digestion; you yourself make the blood course through your veins. You yourself make the hair grow; you yourself make the body develop, and here mark how many processes there are; how many works, how many deeds there are that you are performing every moment."

The boy began to think and said, "Indeed, indeed, sir, in my body, in this body, there are thousands of processes that the intellect does not know, about which the mind is unconscious, and still they are being performed, and it must be I that am performing all that, and indeed it was a mistake I made when I said that I had done a few things; a few things only, and nothing more; a few things that were done through the agency of intellect or mind." It must be made further clear. In this body of yours two kinds of functions are being discharged; there are two kinds of works being done, involuntary and voluntary. Voluntary acts are those that are performed through the agency of the intellect or mind. For instance, reading, writing, walking, and drinking. These are acts done through the agencies of the intellect or mind. Besides these, there are thousands of acts or processes being performed directly, so to say, without the agency, or without the medium of mind or intellect. For instance, respiration, the coursing of blood through the veins, the growth of hair etc.

"Well," he said, "indeed I have understood it so far that I am something beyond the intellect." At this time, the attendant of the prince asked: "Sir, make it more clear to me, I have not quite comprehended it yet." Well, that attendant was asked, "Mr. so and so, when you go to bed, do you die or live? The attendant said, "I do not die." And what about the intellect? He said, "I go on dreaming, the intellect is still there." "And when you are in the deep sleep state, (you know there is a state called the deep sleep state; in that state no dreams even are seen), where is the intellect, where is the mind?"

He began to think. "Well, it passes into nothingness; it is no longer there, the intellect is not there, the mind is not there, but are you there or not? He said, "Oh, indeed I must be there; I remain there." Well, mark here, even in the deep sleep state, where the intellect ceases, where the intellect is as it were, like a garment hoisted on a peg, hoisted on a post like an overcoat, the intellect is taken off and placed upon the post, you are still there, you do not die out. The attendant said, "The intellect is not there, and I do not die out. This I do not quite comprehend."

Well, the attendant was asked, "When you wake up after enjoying this deep sleep, when you wake up, do you not make such statements, *I enjoyed a profound sleep to-night; I had no dream to-night.'

Do you not make remarks of that kind?" He said, "Yes." Well, this point is very subtle. The readers should attend it closely. When after waking up from the deep sleep state, this remark is made, "I slept so sound that I saw no dreams, I saw no rivers, mountains, in that state there was no father, no mother, no house, no family, nothing of the kind; all was dead and gone; there was nothing, nothing, nothing there, I slept and there was nothing there." This statement is like the statement made by the man who bore witness to the desolation of a place, and said: "At the dead of night, at such and such a place, there was not a single human being present." That man was asked to write out this statement. He put it on paper. The magistrate asked him, "Well, is this statement true?" He said, "Yes, sir." Well, is this statement made on hearsay, or founded upon your evidence, are you an eye witness?"

He said, "Yes, I am an eye-witness. This is not based on hearsay." "You are an eye-witness that at the time mentioned on the paper and at the place mentioned on the paper, there was not a single human being present?" He said, "Yes" "What are you? Are you a human being or not?" He said, "Yes, I am. a human being." "Well, then, if this statement is to be true according to you, it must be wrong according to us, because, as you were present and you are a human being, the statement that there was not a single human being present is not literally true. You were present there. In order that this statement may be true according to you, it must be false according to us, because in order that there might be nobody, there must be something, must be at least yourself present at the time."

So when you wake up after enjoying the deep sleep, you make this remark, "I did not see anything in the dream." Well, we may say that you must have been present; there was no father, no mother, no husband. no wife, no house, no river, no family present in that state, but you must have been present; the very evidence that you give, the very witness that you bear, proves that you did not sleep, that you did not go to sleep; for had you been asleep, who would have told us about the nothingness of that place? You are something beyond the intellect; the intellect was asleep, the brain was at rest in a way, but you were not asleep. If you had been asleep who would have made the blood run- through the blood vessels, who would have continued the process of digestion in the stomach, who would have continued the process of the growth of your body;, if you had really fallen into the deep sleep state? So you are something which is never asleep. The intellect sleeps, but not you. You are something beyond the intellect mind, and body.

Now the attendant said, "Sir, sir, I have understood it so far, and have come to know that I am a power divine, that I am the infinite power which never sleeps, never changes. In my youth, the body was different; in my childhood, the mind was not the same as I have now, the body was not the same as I have now. In my childhood, my intellect, brain, body, and mind were entirely different from what they are now." "Doctors tell us that after seven years, the whole system undergoes a thorough change; every moment the body is changing, and every second the mind is changing, and the mental thoughts, the mental ideas which you entertained in our childhood, where are they now? In the days of childhood you looked upon the Sun as a beautiful cake which was eaten by the angels, the moon was a beautiful piece of silver; the stars were as big as diamonds. Where are these ideas gone? Your mind, your intellect has undergone a thorough, a wholesale change. But you still say, "When I was a child, when I was a boy, when I shall grow up to the age of seventy." You still make such remarks which show that you are something which was the same in childhood, which was the same in boyhood, which will be the same at the age of seventy. When you say, "I went to sleep, I went into the deep sleep state, etc.," when you make remarks of that kind, it shows that there is the true "I" in you, the real Self in you, which remains the same in the dreamland, which remains the same in the deep sleep state, which remains the same in the wakeful state. There is something within you which remains the same when you are in a swoon, which remains the same when you are bathing, when you are writing. Just think, reflect, just mark please. Are you not something which remains the same under all circumstances, unchanging in its being, the same yesterday, to-day and forever? If so, just reflect a little more, think a little more, and you will be immediately brought face to face with God. You know the promise was, know yourself, put down your right address on paper, and God will be introduced to you immediately.

Now, the boy, the prince, expected that as he knew about himself, he had come to know that he was something unchanging, something constant, something which was never asleep. Now he wanted to know what God is. The prince was asked: "Brother, mark, here are these trees growing. Is the power that makes this tree grow different from the power that makes that tree grow?" He said, "No, no, it must be the same power certainly." "Now, is the power which makes all these trees grow different from the power that makes the bodies of animals grow?" He said, "No, no, it can on t be different, it must be the same." "Now, is the power, the force which makes the stars move, different from the power which makes these rivers flow?" He said, "It cannot be different, it must be the same." "Well, now the power that makes these trees grow cannot be different from the power which makes your body or your hair grow.

The same universal power of nature, the same universal Divinity, or the Unknowable, which makes the stars shine, makes your eyes twinkle, the same power which is the cause of the growth of that body's hair which you call mine, the same power makes the blood course through the veins of each and all, indeed, and then what are you? Are you not that power, which makes your hair grow, which makes your blood flow through your veins, which makes your food get digested? Are you not that power? That power which is beyond the intellect, the mind, that indeed you are. If so, you are the same power which is governing the force of the whole Universe, you are the same Divinity, you are the same God, the same Unknowable, the same

Energy, Force, Substance, anything you may call it, the same Divinity the All which is present everywhere. The same, the same you are."

The boy was astonished and he said, "Really, really, I wanted to know God. I put the question what God is, and I find my own Self, my true Atma is God. What was I asking, what did I ask, what a silly question did I put! I had to know myself. I had to know what I am, and God was known." Thus was God known.

MORAL: God is your own Self, beyond body, mind and intellect.

Turning Water into Wine (An Essay on the Miracle of Christ)

Once in an examination the students were asked to write an essay on the miracle of Christ turning water into wine. The hall was filled with students and they were writing. One poor fellow (Byron) was whistling, singing, looking at this corner and at that. He did not write a single syllable looking at this corner and at that. He did not write a single word. He went on making fun even in the Examination Hall, he went on enjoying himself. Oh, his was an independent spirit. When the time was up and the Superintendent was collecting the answers, he made a joke with Byron, and told him that the Superintendent was very sorry that Byron was fatigued by writing so long an essay. Byron. at that time took up his pen and wrote one sentence on the answer book and handed it to the Superintendent. When the result of the examination was out, he got the first prize. Byron got the first prize, the man who had written nothing, who simply took up his pen and with one stroke scribbled out a single sentence, got the first prize. The Superintendent of the Examination, who thought Byron to be an idler, was amazed, and all the other competitors asked the examiner to be kind enough to read before the whole classy before the whole congregation of students, the essay by which Byron got the first prize. The essay was: "The water saw her master and blushed." This was on the miracle of Christ by which he turned water into wine, that was the whole essay. Is it not really wonderful? In blushing the face becomes red; the water saw her master and blushed That is all. Splendid, is it not? Realise the true Self within you; like Christ, realise that the Father and Son are one. "In the beginning was the word; the word was with God" Realise it, realise it. The Heaven of heavens is within you. Realise that and wherever you go, the dirtiest water will blush into sparkling wine for you; every dungeon will be converted into the Heaven of heavens for you. There will not be a single difficulty or trouble for you; the master of all ye become.

MORAL: Self-realization makes you Master of all, and converts even Hell into Heaven.

The Way to Realization (The Parrot and the Sage)

At a certain meeting in India wise men were there, very wise men were present, and sacred texts from the Hindu Scriptures were being recited, and when explained by the savants, one of the audience, at the time when the meeting was about to dissolve, spoke about a certain sage who had come to the town, and was living on the bank of the river, and he praised this saint very highly. The people then became naturally anxious to know more about this saint. There was a parrot who was listening to the talk, or you might say a slave, hearing this conversation about the sage that had come to the town. This Parrot that was confined in the cage or this slave asked the gentleman who was talking about the sage, to go to the age on behalf of this imprisoned parrot or enslaved person and ask him to tell certain means of escape for this confined bird or enslaved person. Well, the gentleman, who had first interview d the great saint, went to him at the time when he was bathing in the river, and put to him this question, "How could that bird, parrot, or say, that particular person, confined in a cage, be released?

How could he be released?" Just when the question was put, the sage was seen to be carried off by the torrent; he was observed by the people of the town as dead. The people who were witnessing this state of the sage were astonished,' and they rebuked the person who put this message or who conveyed this message from the parrot or from the slave. The people thought that the saint was fainting or was swooning through pity for the imprisoned parrot, or through sympathy for the bound slave. The saint did not recover that day, so it appeared. Well, next day, when the meeting was held again at the place where the encaged bird was, or where the confined slave was, the parrot, or you might say, the slave asked the gentleman who had interviewed the saint, whether the parrot's message had been conveyed to him. The gentleman said that the message had been conveyed, and added that he was sorry to convey the message from such a wretched fellow as the encaged bird, or from such a sorry person as the bound slave. The parrot or the slave inquired why he was sorry. Then the gentleman said that just when the message was conveyed, the sage fainted away. And all the people were wondering, were astonished, what all this meant. But the parrot or the slave explained the whole secret. The parrot or you might say, the slave was not intelligent, but immediately after hearing that, the parrot fainted. He fainted and was dead to all intents and purposes. There the bystanders were surprised, lo, this must be a strange message, which had caused the death of two. When the message was conveyed to the saint, the saint died, and when the message was repeated to the parrot or the slave, the slave died. Do you know what happened next? When the bystanders saw that the parrot was dead, they thought it no longer worthwhile to keep the parrot imprisoned. They opened the cage, and immediately the parrot flew out and said, "O people, O audience, who gather here every day to hear the sacred Scriptures, you do not know how realization, salvation, inspiration is to be achieved.

I have learnt it to-day from the answer to my message that I received from that saint. The saint did not faint, the saint as it were answered my message; the saint by fainting, by falling in swoon, told me the way to realization. The path to salvation, the way to realization is apparent death, that and nothing else, crucifixion and nothing less, there is no other way to inspiration. The way to realization is getting above the body, rising to that state spiritually, rising to the state of inner salvation, where the body is as it were dead, where the small personality is conscious-less, is altogether lost, is entirely left behind, that is the way to Life.

MORAL: The way to realization is to rise above the body into the real Self, or to lose the consciousness of the little self.

The Vedantic Lullaby (Queen Madaalsa and her Sons)

Madaalsa, an Indian queen took a vow of seeing that all her children were perfect. She took the vow of making all her children free from transmigration. She also took the vow of making all her territories filled with men of realization, with God-men.

She also wanted to make all her subjects God-men. This was one vow by one mother, and she succeeded. Her sons were God-men, they were Krishnas, Buddhas, Philosophical men, men of renunciation, and they ruled the whole community; all her subjects were made free. One woman did that; and what was her process? She used to sing to her children while very young, she used to sing to her children while she nursed them at her bosom, she used to instill into them with her milk, the milk of Divine wisdom. The milk of Vedanta she drilled into them while she rocked the cradle, while she sang her lullaby to them as follows:

Sleep, baby, Sleep!

No sobs, no cries, ne'er weep,

Rest undisturbed, all fears fling, To praise Thee all the angels sing. Arbiter of riches, beauty, and gifts,

Thy innocent At man governs and lifts. Sleep, baby, Sleep.

Soft roses, silvery dew-drops sweet, Honey, fragrance, zephyrs, genial heat, Melodious, warbling notes, so dear, And all that pleases eye or ear,

Comes from Thy heavenly, blissful home: Pure, pure Thou art, untainted Om

Sleep, baby; Sleep, etc.

No foes, no fear, no danger, none, Can touch Thee, O Eternal One! Sweet, lovely, tender, gentle, calm, Of sleep Thy Atman doth embalm. Thyself doth raise the spangled dome Of starry heavens, O darling Om!

Sleep, baby, sleep, etc.

The sun and moon, The playing balls,

The rainbow arch bedecks Thy Halls, The milky ways for Thee to walk,

The clouds, when meet, of Thee they talk; The spheres, Thy dolls, sing, dance and roam, They praise Thee Om, Om Tat Sat Om!

Sleep, baby, sleep, etc.

In lilies and violets, lakes and brooks, How sweet Thy sleeping beauty looks. Let time and space, the: blankets warm Roll off Thy face by sleeping arm, Look half askance as baby lies,

Dear naughty boy with laughing eyes! Sleep, baby, sleep, etc.

The shrill, sharp echoes of cuckoos

Are whistles, rattles, Thou doth choose. The sparrows, winds and all the stars Are beautiful toys and baby's cars.

The world is but Thy playful dream, It is in Thee, tho' outside seem,

Sleep, baby, sleep, etc.

O wakeful home of rest and sleep! O active source of wisdom deep!

O peaceful spring of life and action! O lovely cause of strife and function! To limiting darkness bid adieu Adieu! adieu! adieu! adieu!

Sleep, baby, sleep, etc.

The beauteous objects, charming things, Are flattering sound of beating wings, Of Thee, O Eagle blessed King,

Or fleeting shadows of Thy wing, Bewitching beauty half reveals, And as a veil it half conceals,

The wearer of this veil, Sweet Om, The real Self, Om, Tat Sat Om.
Sleep, baby, sleep, etc.

This gives a kind of idea of the lullaby which the queen sang to seven of her sons. When the sons left home, they went abroad, filled with Divinity. Through them was Vedanta spread. The eighth child was not trained exactly that way, because the father did not wish this child to leave the throne; he was not wanted to become a perfectly free man. So to this child the mother did not sing this lullaby, but she had to carry out her vow in some way, that the child should not suffer sorrow or be pained in this life. As the eighth child was not to leave the royal throne, it was not brought up the same way as the other seven. The eighth son was placed in the care of a nurse, but when the mother was about to die, this son was brought before her, and she gave him this lullaby, which was written on the paper and wrapped in some rich, costly material and covered with jewels; she encircled it around his arm, and asked him to keep the amulet most sacred, she asked him to read the paper contained within, she asked him to think it, feel it, and it would make him free, it would take away all sorrow; she told him the amulet was not to be opened except in case of emergency. The mother died and the father died and their boy became king and ruled for many years. One day the elder brothers of the boy came to the capital of their father, and sent a message to the boy Alerk by name, and menaced him to leave the throne, because they were the elder brothers and they were the rightful heirs to the throne, and he ought to leave throne in favour of the eldest brother. When this Alerk was threatened by the authority of the elder brothers, when he was threatened by the precedence of his eldest brother, he trembled with fear, he was terrified and knew not what to do; he wept at the fear of losing all his grandeur and glory. On returning to his bed at night he noticed this amulet around his arm, and the last words of his mother flashed through his mind, and he opened it and read the paper, with tears in his eyes he read, "Thou art pure, thou art immutable; thou art all knowledge, all power; thou art the arbiter of all power; thou art the giver and restorer of all beauty, all joy in the world. Think not yourself to be the body, depend not on worldly things, rise above it, meditate upon it, think it over, friend and enemy ye are!" The son realized it through and through, his anxiety and fear were gone; cheerfulness and joy were brought to him. He sang it over and over again. What with the meaning and virtue of the song and the good wishes of the mother, he was resuscitated and became himself; all fears and anxiety had fled, all sorrow was gone; he bade adieu to all worldly expectations, all worldly asking, all petty desires. He realized it so much; so filled was he with purity and power that it was gushing out of him; he forgot to go to bed, and he dressed and went to the spot where his brothers were, and cried, "Come, come, come and release me of this burden—this head aching crown—here is the burden, take it, release me from it, I know I am all these bodies, desirous of sitting on the throne, and ruling the kingdom; and I am you, and you and I are one, there is no difference." When the brothers marked this sacredness on his face, it filled them with joy, and they said that they came not to take the throne, for they were the rulers of the whole world; they simply wanted to give him his true birthright contained within that body. They said, "O brother, this is not you who are the dupe of senses; you, brother, you are not the king of the earth only, but the king and ruler of the sun, the stars, the worlds and all the lokas that be. O brother, come, realize that you are the Infinite, the Immutable Self, the Sun of suns, the Light of lights." The prince realized this truth, and he (Alerk) went on ruling, but he looked upon the office of king as an actor's role in the theatre, imagining himself to be playing that part. Well, this prince was sane, and nothing could make him sorrowful. He ruled as a mighty monarch and was a most successful king of the world. Successful sought him.

Joy Eternal, Unbroken Peace is yours, nay, you are that. Realize your Centre and be there for ever and ever.

MORAL: The Vedantic Lullaby or Vedant, if drilled into the mind from the very infancy, is sure to lead to Eternal joy or Self-realization.

Realizing Everything as God (Prahlad and his Trials)

It is said in the Hindu Puranas that king Harankasyap wanted to turn his son Prahlad away from religious life. He desired him to remain a worldling like himself, but the remonstrances and admonitions of the parent did not prevail upon the child - they were all lost on him. In order to prevent the child from, his intention, the father cast him into fire but it burnt him not. The king then threw his child into running water but it bore the child up. To him the fire, the water, and other elements had ceased to be harmful - they were realized in their true state. The boy had dehypnotized himself into this real state.

Everything unto him was God, all Love. The threats, frowns, and brow beating, sword and flame were nothing else than sweet Heaven. How could he be injured?

MORAL: Nothing can harm him who realizes everything as God, as all Love.

Realizing God as Omnipresent (A Searching Test of Two Disciples)

Two boys came to a master and wanted him to instruct them in religion. He said that he would not teach them unless he had examined them. Well, he gave them two pigeons, one to each, and asked them to go out and kill the pigeon at some retired place where nobody might see them. One of them went straight into the crowded thoroughfare. Turning his back to the people who were passing through the streets and putting a piece of cloth over his head, he took up the pigeon, wrenched its neck and came back straightway to the teacher and said, "Master, master (Swami, Swami) here is your order carried out." The Swami enquired, "Did you strangle the pigeon when no one was seeing you?" He said, "Yes." "All right; lot us see now what your companion has done."

The other boy went out into a deep, dense forest, and was about to twist the neck of the pigeon, and lo! There were the gentle, soft and glittering eyes of the pigeon looking him straight in the face. He met those eyes and in this attempt to break the neck of the pigeon, he was frightened, the idea struck him that the condition laid upon him by the master was a very trying, hard one. Here the Witness, the Observer, is present even in this pigeon. "Oh, I am not alone! I am not in the place where no one will see me I am being observed. Well, what shall I do? Where shall I go?" He went on and on, and retired into some other forest. There also when he was about to commit the act, he met the eyes of the pigeon, and pigeon saw him, the Observer was in the pigeon itself.

Again and again he tried to kill the pigeon: over and over again he tried, but did not succeed in fulfilling the conditions imposed upon him by the master. Broken hearted, he came back reluctantly to the master and laid the pigeon alive at the feet of the Swami and wept and wept and cried: "Master, master (Swami, Swami), I cannot fulfill this condition. Be kind enough to impart the knowledge of God to me. This examination is too trying for me. I cannot bear this examination. Please be merciful, have mercy on me and impart to me divine knowledge. I want that, I surely need it." The master (Swami) took up the child, raised him in his arms, caressed and patted him, and lovingly spoke to him; "O, dear one, even as you have seen the Observer in the eyes of the bird that you were going to slay, even so, wherever you may happen to go, and where you are moved by temptation to perpetrate a crime, realize the presence of God, realize the Observer, the Witness in the flesh and in the eyes of the woman for whom you crave. Believe or realize that your Master sees you even in her eyes. My Master sees me.

Act as if you were always in the presence of the Great Master, ever face to face with the Divinity, all the time in the sight of the Beloved.

MORAL: Sin is committed only when God's presence is not realized; hence to cease from perpetrating crime, one should realize the Divine presence everywhere and at all times.

The Self is AH in All (Dr. Johnson's Dream)

Dr. Johnson, the Prince of talkers, with whom it is said there was no reasoning, because "If his pistol misses fire he knocks you down with the butt end of it." Johnson who would always have the last word to himself in an argument, in a dream found himself beaten by Burke. To a man of Johnson's character this dream was as bad as a nightmare. He started up and lost his ease of mind; he could not fall asleep; but mind cannot by its own nature - Divine nature - live long in unrest. He had to control himself, he had to console himself somehow or other. He reflected and came to the understanding that the arguments advanced by Burke were also furnished by his own mind* the real Burke knew nothing about them; thus it was he himself who appeared unto himself as Burke and got the better of himself. So it is yourself that appears to yourself as ghosts, spirits, enemies, friends, neighbours, lakes, rivers, mountains. The swelling rivers and giant mountains are all within you. You split yourself into the outside phenomena, the object on the one hand, and into the little thinking agent, the subject on the other hand. In reality you are the object as well as the subject. You are the Self, as well as the so-called not-self. You are the lovely rose and the lover nightingale. You are the flower as well as the bee. Everything you are. The ghosts and spirits, and angels, the sinners, and saints, all ye are. Know that, feel that, realise that and ye are free. Do not place your centre outside yourself; this will make you fall. Place all your confidence in yourself, remain in your centre, and nothing will shake you.

MORAL: Outside things trouble you only so long as you do not feel them to be your own Self; the moment you realize your Self in them, as the Self is all in all, they begin to give peace and happiness.

Godhead, Our Birth Right (Moses and the Hissing Snake)

Moses when walking on Mt. Sinai saw a bush flame.

He asked, "Who are you? Who is there?" He may have not spoken aloud, but he was very curious as to the marvelous blaze which lighted up but did not burn the bush. The answer came out from the bush "I am what I am." This pure "I am" is your Self.

When Moses heard the voice in the bush, he found a hissing snake beside him. Moses was frightened out of his wits; he trembled, his breast was throbbing, all the blood almost curdled in veins, he was undone. A voice cried unto him, "Fear not, O Moses, catch this snake, hold it fast; dare to catch hold of it." Moses trembled still and again the voice cried unto him, "Moses, come forth catch hold of the snake." Moses caught hold of it, and lo, it was not a snake but a most beautiful and splendid staff.

Now, what is meant by this story. The Snake (Sanp) stands for truth (Sanch). You know, according to the Hindus and Orientals the Truth or final Reality is represented by the snake (Shesh).

The snake coils round in a spiral form, making circles within circles and puts its tail back into its mouth. And so we see in this world we have circles within circles; everything repeating itself by going round and round, and extremes meeting. This is a universal law or principle which runs through the whole universe.

To catch hold of the snake means to put yourself boldly in the position of the wielder of the Divine Law, or Ruler of the Universe. Put yourself boldly in that Position; realize your oneness with Divinity.

Moses was at first afraid to do that. To him it was a novelty, unfamiliar. Moses belonged to a tribe living in slavery. Ordinary people are in the same state of mind in which Moses was when he heard the voice. Moses was in a state of slavery, and when he saw the serpent he trembled, so it is with the people. When they hear this sound "I am," this pure knowledge, the pure truth Om, when they hear this, they tremble and hesitate, they dare not catch hold of it Words, like the following sound like a hissing serpent to the people: "Yes are Divinity itself, the Holy of holies; the world is no world; you are the All in all, the Supreme Power, the Power which no worlds can describe. No body or mind, ye are, the pure "I am," that you are. Throw aside this little yellow, red or black scrap of paper from beside the crystal, and wake up in your reality, and realise <I am He.' "I am the All in all."

People want to shun it. They fear the serpent. O! Do catch hold of the snake, and then to your wonder of wonders this snake will become the staff of Royalty in your hands. The hissing serpent will feed you when you are hungry, will quench your thirst when you are thirsty, will sweep off all the difficulties and sorrows from your way. When in the woods Moses touched a rock with this staff, and bubbling, sparkling water came out from the rock. When the Israelites were fleeing for safety, they had to cross the Red Sea. There this terrible Sea stood before them as a gaping grave to devour them. Moses touched the Red Sea with this staff and the waters split in twain, dry land appeared and the Israelites passed over it.

Why depress your brains through fears and why use up your energies in supplications? Repress not your inner nature; crush not the Truth; come out boldly; cry fearlessly at the top of your voice "I am God, I am God";- that is your birthright.

This apparent hissing snake, this truth appears to be awful but have only to dare to pick it up and hold it fast.

To your wonder you will find yourself the Monarch of the Universe, the Master of the elements, the Ruler of the stars, the Governor of the skies. You will find yourself to be the All.]

MORAL: Truth should not be crushed, and as our inner nature is nothing else but God-head, so it is our birthright to assert our God-head.

The Price of Realization (Selling Nam - God)

There was man in India, famous, full of truth, mad with Divinity. He walked through the streets crying at the top of his voice, "O customers of Divinity, come." He used to go about selling Divinity. "O, customers of Divinity, O all desirous of God-consciousness, come; O ye that are heavy laden, come." He cried in the language of his country, and in that language Nam is the name given for God. He cried in his own language, "Nam le lo" which literally means, "I have an article to sell. Purchase it, O people, and that article is God", and he used the word Mam. Now Mam has two meaning; one meaning is God, and the other meaning of Mam is beautiful, bedecked, jeweled necklace; but that saint used the word Mam to mean god and not jewellery. One day while passing the streets selling Mam, God, a gentleman, who wanted to purchase a fine necklace, heard him crying through the streets, and he thought that this fellow must be an agent for some banker and wants to sell that necklace. When people in India are going to be married, very often they want very precious jewels for adorning themselves or their brides. The man asked where this hawker or sage lived and he went to his house and was amazed. The house of the hawker was very poor and he wondered how the house of a Nam-seller could be so poor. He entered the house and did' not find the hawker, he knocked at the door and there came out a dear little child and he asked for master of the house, and the child replied, "My father is away, he will be here in the evening; but sir, would you mind telling me what business you have with him?" He was very much impressed with the talk of the child and wanted to talk with her, so in order to exchange some words with her, he said that he wanted to purchase Mam. The child smiled and said, "I can give you Mam, it is so easy." He said, "All right, I will wait." He waited at the door and she went in. He waited and waited but the child did not make her appearance and he was about to lose his patience, as he had waited twenty minutes and he thought that time was long enough to dig out the treasure from under the ground. Losing patience he peeped into the house and there he found the child was whetting her large knife, and he said, "What does that mean?" and he spoke to the child and said, "Child, why are you playing childish pranks? This is no time to trifle with a gentleman of my rank; do not fool with me, please; this is no time to try your idle experiments; come out and say that you do know where your parents have buried the jewellery: but the child exclaimed, "Please excuse me; have patience and wait a minute. I am coming" and he said, "Come right away, why sharpen that knife?" She said, "Do you not want to receive Nam?" He said, "I want Nam; but please show it to me that I may take it to some banker or to those who can set the right value on the article," and then she said, "Our Nam is not an article which requires a valuation to be set upon it by the banker or jeweller of the streets. Our precious Nam has already got its value fixed; there is no going up or coming down. The value is already fixed and the price already determined." He said "Is it so? Then please come, show it to me, throw aside your knife." She said. "O, but you must pay the price first and then you get Nam afterwards." He said, "Do you intend to stab me, why do you sharpen your knife?" She said in the most trustful, pure way, "If you did not know the price of Nam why did you come here? Do you not know in order to get Nam, you must lose your life? Life is the price you must pay for Nam. He who will save his life must lose Nam". The girl said, "Sir, did you not know that the price is already fixed? In order to get Nam (Nam meant God to the girl, and it meant the necklace to the man) this head of yours must be cut off with knife; then and then alone you can get Nam" Boldly, cheerfully, and unflinchingly the girl made this statement. The poor customer was stricken aghast; he cried aloud and made such a noise that all the neighbours collected. He began to complain. "Look here" he said, "this poor hut contains butchers and homicides. I presume that the parents of this girl are the worst homicides. The matter ought to be placed before the court; let us call the police." But the people said, "Don't talk that way, the parents of the girl are noted for their great piety, etc.", and he said, "I come to see that all those very pious people are usually very bad; they are not religious; under the cloak of religion they perpetrate religious crimes." There was a great noise and confusion in their talk and all of a sudden the father of the girl appeared on the scene and this man was about to strangle the father of the girl. The pious father was tranquil and serene when the queer customer addressed him in very harsh language and said, "Why do you teach even your child to perpetrate such heinous crimes, why do you do such deeds every day as to make your children homicides in their very infancy?" The sage replied, "How is it, sir, what do you mean?" The whole matter was explained and when the sage heard the story, his heart was filled with emotion; his whole being was saturated with Divinity; tears like great beads appeared on his cheeks and he said, "O prophets and saints, O angels, God! Have matters come to this! Have matters come to such a low pass; is the name of God to be brought down to the power of a child like that; was this to be changed to a small thing like that? Pointing to his daughter he said that it is because the Divinity, God, has been taken up by an innocent, ignorant, child, that the name of God, the Divinity has become so ridiculously cheap that the name of God, Heaven, and Immortality is sold at such an awfully low price as the head or heart. O Divinity, O sweet Immortality! Is it dear if it were sold for one life? Let millions upon millions of lives be created and destroyed for the sake of one glimpse of that Reality. Let infinite lives and heads' be chopped off and cut to pieces for a moment of that Holy God-consciousness.

When these words were uttered by the saint, the heart of the queer customer melted and all the by-standers stood aghast. It was then that they came to know that the same word Nam meant something exquisitely sweet for the little girl and for the parents of the girl, and that their own minds were so grovelling in materiality as not to grasp the true meaning.

This story tells you the price you must pay in order to taste the sweet nectar of Heaven. It tells you the inevitable value set on Realization.

You cannot enjoy the world, you cannot enter into sordid, petty, low, worldly, carnal, sensuous desires and at the same time lay claim to Divine Realization.

MORAL: If one wants Realization, he must be prepared to pay its price, which is the total effacement of the ego or little self.

Self, the Master Musician (A stranger and the Church Organ)

There was a beautiful organ in a Church; in fact the organ was so fine that the custodian would not allow an amateur to touch it. One day while they were having a service in the Church, a stranger dressed poorly came in and wanted to play upon the organ but he was not allowed to near it. He was unknown to the minister and since this was such a choice thing, of course they would not let him play upon it. After the service was over and the musician had left the organ, this man stealthily crept up to the organ. The minute he laid his hands upon it, the organ recognised its master, and such music as it poured forth, though the congregation were on their feet and ready to go, still when such peals of grandeur came forth, they were spellbound, enraptured, and could not leave the Church. This wielder of wonderful harmony was the master musician, the inventor of the organ himself.

We do not give the Self, God, Love, a chance to manifest for us, we must care for this body, we must care for this mind, and it is plain to be seen that in that case only common place notes come forth of us. Let the Master play upon the organ, minute Love's hands touch the chords, music will pour forth - music that you never dreamed of before, wonderful light and harmony will begin to flow, divine melodies will begin to burst out, celestial rhapsodies will emanate.

MORAL: We suffer from disharmony, miseries and troubles, because we care only for the body or little self and do not give a chance to the higher Self, God or Love to manifest its wonderful powers of harmony, peace and bliss.

The Whole World Within (A Drop of Water)

A drop of water in the shape of a tear fell from the clouds. The tear fell, and when asked, 'Why this weeping?' It replied "O, I am such a tiny, puny, insignificant thing. I am so small, Oh, too small, and the ocean is so big. I weep at my smallness." It was told, "Weep not, do not confine yourself to name and form only, but look within you; see what you are. Are you not water; and what is the ocean? Is it not water too? Things which are equal to the same thing are equal to one another. Don't look yourself as being confined in space and time. Look beyond this Space and Time, and see your Reality." You become miserable when you confine yourself within time. Lift yourself above all. Not only matter and spirit are the same, but all are the same. True Self is beyond all time. The whole world is within you. Just as in your dreams, you think yourself to be in the woods or forests, on the mountains, by the rivers, they seem to be outside, but all are within you. If they were outside, then the room would be weighed down, and the bed would be wet with the water you saw.

Similarly, Vedanta says, "All the world is within you; the astral, the psychic worlds, are within you; and you think that you are in them. Just as a lady carrying a mirror on her thumb looks into the mirror and thinks she is in the glass, but it is just the reverse, so as a matter of fact, the world is in you, and you are not the world.

MORAL: The time and space, comprising the whole world, though seem to be outside, are really within you. Hence, confine not yourself to name and form only hut rise above them and realise your Reality.

Ways Differ (The Buddha's reply)

To Lord Buddha came a man who asked him to go to his father's cabin. You know, the same Lord Buddha, who was a prince and emperor, was a mendicant at one time, he gave up everything and became a mendicant. As a mendicant he went from place to place-, not asking anything, not begging anything. If anybody threw anything into the bowl, which he carried in his hand, well and good, otherwise he did not care a straw for the body, for this worldly life. He went into his father's kingdom and there he walking through the streets in the beggar's dress, in the mendicant's garb. It is a misnomer to call him a mendicant, it is no mendicancy, no beggary, it is kinghood, it is majesty. He does not seek anything, he does not ask for anything. What if he perishes? Let him perish; it matters not. He does not come to you to ask for food or clothing, not at all.

He was walking through the streets in that garb, and the father heard about it, came up to him, shed bitter tears and said, "Son, dear prince, I never did this, I never took this dress that you wear; my father, that is to say, your grandfather never had this mendicant's dress, your great-grandfather never walked as a mendicant through the streets. We have been kings, you belong to a royal family, and why is it that you are this day going to bring disgrace and shame to the whole family by adopting the mendicants' garb? Do not do that, please, do not do that, please. Keep my honour."

Smiling the Buddha replied, smilingly did he say, "Sir, sir, the family to which I belong, I look behind. I look behind to my previous births, I look behind to the previous birth before that, and I see that the family to which I belong has been all along a family of mendicants, and it is illustrated in this way:

Here is one street and there comes another street. Buddha says, "Sir, you have been coming from your births in that line, I have been coming in this line, and in this birth we have met on the crossing. Now I have to go my way and you have to go your way."

MORAL: Ways differ not in accordance with the outer circumstances but with the inner development of the persons.

Reality Concealed (Birbal and the King)

Birbal asked the king if the blind or men with sight were in majority. There was argument, and it was decided to put it to the proof. The king thought" the minority to be blind. So he came as a proof with a piece of cloth, winding it round his head, he asked, "What is this? "A turban," was the answer. He put it on his shoulder and asked people, "What is this? "Shawl," was the reply. The third time he wore it as loin cloth, and they called it as such. "Blind, blind, all! It is none of these, but cloth,—by names and forms is cloth concealed."

Realize what Atman is. To see gold you need not break it. When you think of man, woman, eddies, breakers, cloth and gold, you do not think of the reality behind.

MORAL: Reality or Atman is concealed behind names and forms. Hence realize It, think out the basis of every name and form.

The dilemma of an intoxicated man

One man sold away his house under the intoxication of alcohol. When he came to his senses, he submitted an application to the concerned court to the effect that, since he had sold away his house under the influence of alcoholic liquor, (when he was not in his proper senses), he disowned his previous deed. In the same way the man says, "O God! my all is dedicated to Thee. I am thine, my property is Thine, and my very life is Thine. Everything is Thine". But, he goes home and his wife says in an angry mood "my hair pin has been worn out, the daughter has to be married and soon and so forth". At that time he has to swallow such bitter pills from his wife that all his God intoxication is gone. Consequently, he takes back the previously surrendered body, mind and wealth from God. He is again imprisoned in the dungeon of egoism. However, in a way, it is also very good to dedicate his all to God, though only for a short time, under the temporary intoxication of wine of love for Him. But the permanent and real renunciation conies through gyan, the thorough understanding or the realisation of Self. While in perfect senses, if a man desires, he can do away with the curtain of duality forever. The method is to continue to reduce thickness of the layers of the curtain. Thus the curtain will become thinner, till it becomes so thin that there is no curtain at all.

To allow the curtain to slip down for a while is like a temporary meditation and to remove the curtain for good, by gradually, thinning it down, is "Realisation of Self".

The Story of Lord Shiva & Bhasmasura

Lord Shiva (the light of the Seed-body) once gave a boon to the demon Bhasmasura that anything on which he would place his hand will be burnt to ashes. On getting this power, he wanted to try it on Lord Shiva Himself. Realizing this, Shiva ran away from the demon. But the demon would not let Shiva go. He continued to chase Him (Shiva). It appeared that the demon was sure to catch hold of Shiva and destroy Him. But will he really destroy Him?

While the Devil Bhasmasura was running after Shiva, there appeared on the scene an extremely beautiful and charming young girl, smiling and dancing in various poses. It was Lord Vishnu, the light of Satva guna, who adopted the form of this charming young girl to save Shiva). The demon fell in love with and was attracted towards her.

She was dancing rapturously. Her dance was so rhythmical and infectious that the demon also could not help dancing with her. He was, as if, one with her in the dancing poses. While dancing, the girl raised her hands and made semi circles. The demon also did the same. Gradually, while dancing, she put one of her raised hands on her head and the demon also copied her in his infatuation and state of self-forgetfulness. And lo! No sooner did he put his hand on his head, than he was burnt to ashes.

The lesson from this allegorical story is as follows: As the sun shines on the snow, a river is created. So, too, when the sun of Atman (Shiva) shines on seed body steeped in inertness, Bhasmasura (the Vagrant mind) is born. As a matter of fact, there is nothing but Atman (Shiva) but due to the power bestowed by Atman, the vagrant mind (Bhasmasura) can destroy anything. There is Atman (Shiva) in front of you when Bhasmasura (vagrant mind) cast its shadow, it looked a tree. The Atma so to say, disappeared from there or ran away from there. What is to your right? It is Atman (Shiva). When Bhasmasura (vagrant mind) cast his shadow, it looked a wall. The Atman, as it were, vanished. But Atman cannot be killed on any account. Even in the names and forms of the tree, the wall, Atman is being expressed by its nature, Existence, Knowledge and Bliss. (Sat, Chid, Anand). What is towards your head? It is Atman. When Bhasmasura cast its shadow, it looked a moon. Atman, as if, disappeared. Atman is all pervading. There is nothing but Atman, everywhere. But wherever the demon Bhasmasura puts his hand (the mind exercises its influence) it all becomes dead carcass, matter of name and form. The reality, Atman, is not seen then.

From childhood till your old age, whatever you heard or did in sleep or waking state was all Atman, but the mind (Bhasmasura) could not see Atman anywhere.

According to Sanskrit Astrology, the same sun in different houses is named differently. Similarly, the same Atman is called differently in different states. In deep sleep state, it is called Shiva, because it enlightens the seed-body. In the waking state it is called Vishnu, because it enlightens the waking state. In order to subdue Bhasmasura (vagrant mind) this Atman (Vishnu) in the waking state, with excess of Satva guna or virtuous conduct, adopts the form of a charming girl to sing Divine songs. This means that the Divine songs of Upanishads make the vagrant mind enter into a state of self-forgetfulness. The teaching of the Upanishads makes you dance at her tune. And, when you are completely won over, she places her hand on her own head i. e. assures you with a vow that you are nothing but God. At this moment, Bhasmasura also puts his hand on his head to indicate his conviction that he is also God. This means that mind's vagrancy is destroyed. It becomes peaceful and it merges into Atman. This is the realization of the Self. At this stage all ego is gone and nothing remains except God and God alone.

The popular game of Gulli-danda as an aid to concentration

You might have played the game of Gulli-danda, during your boyhood. In this game the gulli is first quietly placed, with the help of a rod, in suitable and convenient position. Afterwards, it is made to spring-up, by beating it at one of its pointed ends with the rod. While it is still in the air, it is again struck by the rod with all the strength to throw it far away into the space. So, too, by reading the scriptures, you can throw your mind into the peaceful state of absorption or even beyond it to be lost in Self-Realisation. All this depends on the intensity of your feeling.

You should pay all attention to the study of your holy scripture so that you may continue to feel its peaceful and exuberant intoxication long afterwards. It is no tell tale. Rama tells you ail this from his own experience.

CHAPTER SEVENTEEN

Self-Reliance

Self-Reliance (Go, go and Come, come)

Two brothers involved in litigation appeared before a Magistrate. One of them was a millionaire, the other a pauper. The Magistrate asked the millionaire how it was that he became so rich and his brother so poor. He said: "Five years ago we inherited equal property from our parents. Fifty thousand dollars fell to his share and fifty thousand dollars to me. This man, regarding himself as wealthy, became lazy, and whatever work was to be done he entrusted to his servants. If he received a letter, he would give it to his servants and say, 'Go, attend to this business.' Anything that was to be accomplished he told his servants to do. He lolled away his time in ease and comfort. 'Eat, drink, and be merry.' He would always bid his servants, '.'Go, go; attend to this business or that." Speaking of himself the rich man said: "When I got my fifty thousand dollars, I never committed my work to anybody; when anything was to be none, I would always run to do it myself and I always told the servants, 'Come, come, follow me.'

The words on my lips were always 'Come, come,' and the words on the lips of my brother were 'Go, go.' Everything he possessed obeyed his motto; his servants, friends, property or wealth went away, entirely left him. My maxim was ' Come'; friends come to me, property increased, everything multiplied.

When we depend upon others, we say, "Go. go". Everything will go away, and when we rely upon Self and trust nothing but the Atman, all things flock to us. If you think yourself a poor, sneaking vermin, that you become, and if you honour yourself and rely on yourself, grandeur you win. What you think, the same you must become.

MORAL: Dependence on others makes us lose, while reliance on Self gains for us everything.

The Result of Dependence on Others (The Horse and a Stag)

A horse came to a man to be saved. You know, there was a time once when man too lived in the jungles. The horse also lived in the jungles; the deer and the stags too lived in the jungles, as they do in these days.. A horse was once worsted in a fight with a stag. The stag stabbed him with his antlers. The horse came to the man to seek help. The man said, "All right, I will help you. I have arrows in my hands. You take me on your back and I will go and kill your enemies." The man rode on the back of the horse, went into the forest and killed the stag. They came home victorious. The horse was very happy. Now the horse wanted to go. The horse thanked the man, and said, "Dear sir, I thank you. Now I want to leave you." The man came up and said, "O horse, O horse, where do you want to go? Now that I have come to know how useful you are, I will not let you go. You have to be my servant; you have to become my slave." The horse was saved from the stags, the deer, the other beasts of the forest, but he had lost his freedom; and the slavery which was the result of his outward success, did not counterbalance his loss of freedom.

So it is with man. After his marriage he is saved from many temptations, but the one temptation, the slavery or dependence to which he is reduced in relation to his wife, is just like the treatment that the horse received at the hands of man.

MORAL: Dependence on the strength of others may give you temporary comfort and pleasure but results in permanent loss of freedom and independence.

CHAPTER EIGHTEEN

Self-Respect

Value, Respect and Honour (A Gentleman Ill-treated by his Superior Officer)

A gentleman came to Rama and said that his superior officer ill-treated him all the time. Rama told him that the superior officer looked down upon him because he looked down upon himself. If we respect our own selves, everybody must respect us. If a value of one anna is put upon any book, nobody will pay two annas for it; but if a value of two rupees is placed upon the same book, everybody will be willing to pay that amount for it. Similarly, set upon yourself a small value, and nobody will take you at a high value. Set upon yourself the highest value, respect yourself, feel your Divinity, your Godhead, and everybody must take you in the same way.

MORAL: Your value, respect and honour are in your own hand. Have living faith in your Divinity, value and respect yourself, and everybody will value and honour you.

Belief in Self (A Criminal and the king)

A man was taken to be a criminal by a certain king of Asia, because he would not bow before the king. This old king got offended when people did not bow before him. The king said to the criminal, "Do you not know what a powerful and strict monarch I am? Do you not know that I will kill you, you are so audacious? The man spat in the king's face and looked so fiercely at him that he was exasperated. The man said, "O foolish dolly that you are, you have not the power or the authority to put me to death. I am my own master. It is in my power to spit in your face, it is in my power to insult you and it is in my power to see this body put on the cross or scaffold. I am the master of my body. Your authority is second-hand, my authority comes first." Similarly, feel and realize that you are always your own master. Look at things from the standpoint of your Atman, and not through the eyes of others. Feel your independence, feel that you are the God of gods, the Lord of lords, for that you are. So long as man does not realize his own Divinity there will be suffering always.

MORAL: Belief in the lower self makes you bold, but belief in the higher Self (Atman) makes you Divine.

False Idea of Respect (A Preceptor and His Disciple)

There was once a preceptor who being very tired, lay down on a sofa and asked his disciple to come and massage him by treading on his legs. (That is a practice, most frequently followed in India.) But the boy said, "No, no, master, never will I do that; your body is too sacred, your personality too holy. I dare not put my feet on your body, that would be sacrilege; I will not commit such a sacrilege; I will do anything for you. I will give my life for you, but I will not tread on your body" The preceptor said, "O son, come I am very tired, come, come and massage my body." The boy began to weep but could not be persuaded to commit such a sacrilege. The preceptor said, "O foolish boy, you do not want to tread upon my body limbs, you do not want to insult my body, but you trample upon my sacred lips, you trample upon my sacred face; which is more religious* Is it more sacrilegious to trample upon the word of the master or to massage his body?"

People will very readily trample upon the sacred Scriptures of Jesus or Mohammad or of the Vedas, but will regard this flesh and blood as sacred and holy.

MORAL: Paying respect to the personality alone but not minding its orders and sayings is a false idea of respect.

Sound Sense of Self-respect (Imam Ghizali and Khwaja Khizar)

It is said of Imam Ghizali, a Mohammeden saint, that in his student life, one night, after his usual strenuous work, he fell asleep in the study. In a vision appeared to him Khawaja Khizar, the God of Learning, offering to convey all the knowledge of the world to him by the simple act of breathing into his ears and mouth. Imam Ghizali's sound sense of self-respect refused, and he asked instead the boon of being provided with oil for his midnight reading. He preferred the longer road to the short cut not caring to steal Into the back-door of heaven.

MORAL: Sound sense of self respect does not allow one to accept an object of gift, when the same can be achieved by one's own labour however hard it may be.

CHAPTER NINETEEN

Selfishness

The Result of Greed (The dreams of the Master and his Servant)

There was a very cruel and funny master in India. He used to torture his servant 'in a most funny way. Once, the servant cooked a most delicious dish for the master. The master did not like that the servant should partake of it. It was cooked at night and the master said, "We won't eat it just now; we may eat it in the morning. Go to bed just now, and, we will eat it in the morning". The real intention of the master was to eat in the morning, because by that time he would have a very strong appetite. Having abstained from taking any food at night, he would be in a position to eat the whole in the morning, and not let the servant eat anything. That was the real intention of the master. He wanted that the servant should feed on crusts and crumbs, but this intention he could not lay plainly before the servant. He said to the servant, "Well, go to rest, and in the morning, that one of us will eat it who dreams the sweetest dreams, the finest dreams. If by the morning you have dreamed the finest dreams, the whole will be your share; otherwise, the whole will come to me and I will eat it up and you will have to satisfy yourself with crumbs and crusts." The morning came and now the servant and master sat before each other. The master wanted the servant to relate his dreams, and the servant said, "Sir, you are master, and ought to have the precedence; you had better relate your dreams first and then I will state mine." The master thought within himself that this poor servant, this ignorant, illiterate fellow, could not invent very fine dreams. He began to say, "In my dream I was the Emperor of India. In my dream I saw that all the European powers, all the American powers were brought under the sway of the king of India, and so I, as Emperor of India, ruled over the whole world."

You know this was the dream of the cruel master. True Indians do not wish to continue that childish custom of putting up before themselves lumps of flesh called kings and worshipping them. Well, that was the dream of that man. He regarded himself as sitting on the throne of India and governing the whole world, and there he found all the kings of all the countries standing before him and offering him homage. Besides, in his dream he saw all the gods and all the saints brought into his court and sitting on his left hand side, or right hand side. Now having related his own dream, he wanted the servant to tell his story, to tell his dream.

The servant, poor fellow trembling from head to foot, said, "Sir, Sir, I have not had any such dream as you had." The master was elated and very happy, and thought that all the delicious food would come to his lot. The servant began to say that in the dream he saw a big monster, a most ugly, heinous demon coming up to him, with a blazing sword in his hand. Well, the master began to ask, "What next, what next?" Then he said,. "Sir, he ran after me, he was about to kill me," The master smiled that that was a hopeful sign. "He began to kill me, he was trying to slay me". The master said, "And what did you do? What was his object in slaying you?" The servant said, ' Sir, he wanted me to eat that delicious food or to die." The master said, "And then what did you do?" He said, "I simply went up to the kitchen and ate up everything." The master said, "Why did you not wake me up?" The servant replied, "Sir, you were the Emperor of the whole world. In your court there was a grand, magnificent gathering and there were men with drawn swords and cannon. Had I tried to approach your majesty, they would have killed me. I could not come to you and inform you what a terrible plight I was in, so I was forced to eat that delicious food, to enjoy it by myself."

MORAL: Greed very often results in the loss of what one has in possession already.

The Cause of False Interpretation (Join At Once)

There was a man employed in the army. He was in love with a lady, and his superior officer was also in love with the same lady. This lady had given her heart to an officer of the lower rank, the subordinate officer took leave from the army and went home, and the lady embraced the opportunity to be present at his home also. The marriage was arranged and he though it necessary to get his leave of absence extended, so he wired to his superior officer to extend his leave of absence. The superior officer came to know about the whole affair and he knew that the leave of absence was wanted so that this officer might marry the lady. Now the superior officer was jealous and did not wish to grant the leave, and in answer, telegraphed this hasty message, in laconic language, "Join at once." He meant this subordinate officer should join the army at once. This man was reading the message which said, "Join at once," and he wanted very much to stay away, but the message said, "Join at once." He felt very much disappointed and worried over the matter. While he was in this state of mind, the lady came in and seeing him so despondent wanted to know the cause. He showed her the telegram. The quick wit of the lady helped her to interpret the message to her own advantage, and she put a most gladsome interpretation upon the message, and she was rejoicing and dancing. She asked him why he was so miserable; she thought he ought to rejoice. She was preparing to leave the room when he asked her why she was leaving so quickly, and she replied, "To make all preparations for a hasty marriage."

That is the way people read their own meaning into the sacred Scriptures. Such interpretation might have done well for the lady who wanted to get married, but it won't do for the interpretation of the Scriptures.

MORAL: Self-interest is generally the cause of false interpretation. To interpret truly one must rise above self-interest.

The Result of Egoism (Dodging Death)

Once there was a man so clever as to reproduce himself to such perfection that you could not tell the reproduction from the original. He knew that the angel of death was coming for him, and as he did not know just what to do to avoid the angel, finally settled upon what might be termed an able device. He reproduced himself a dozen times. Now when the angel of death came, he could not know which was the real person and therefore did not take any. The angel returned to God and asked Him what to do, and after a consultation, returned to the earth to try again to take this man and remarked, "My! But you are wonderfully clever, why, that is just the way you have made these figures, but there is one thing wherein you have erred, there is just one fault." The original man immediately jumped up and asked suddenly, "In what, in what, have I erred?" And the angel said, "In just this," singling out the clever man from the mute statues.

The only wrong is to ask, "Am I right?" Dear one, what else could you be? The little imp of doer-self is claimed by death.

MORAL: The assertion of egoism in punished by death.

The Result of Selfishness (This is my Carrot)

In famine days a poor woman died. The Judge of Death in his post-mortem investigation into her case, while assorting her good and bad deeds, could discover no act of charity except that she had once given a carrot to a starving beggar. By order of the Judge the carrot was reproduced. This carrot was to take her to Heaven. She caught hold of the carrot and it began to rise lifting her with it.

There appeared the old beggar on the scene. He clutched at the hem of her tattered garment, began to be elevated along with her, a third candidate for mercy began similarly to be uplifted being suspended from the foot of the beggar, nay, a long series of persons, one below the other, began to be drawn up by that single carrot elevator. And strange to say, the woman felt no weight of all these souls hanging from her!

These saved persons rose up higher and still higher till they reached the Gate of Heaven. Here the woman looked below, and don't know what moved her, she said to the train of souls behind her, "Off, you fellows! This is my carrot!"

And unconsciously waved her hand to keep them away. The carrot was lost and down fell the poor woman with the entire train.

MORAL: One selfless act of piety is enough to lift up to the Heaven not only the doer of the deed but many other souls connected with him. On the contrary a single selfish act brings all down.

Fall of Indians due to short-sightedness

This room is well lighted by the sun, and the light looks pleasant. If we say, "This light of ours should not be polluted by going out of this room," and in order to prevent the light from going out, we draw the curtains, close the windows and the doors, our light will vanish altogether and we will be left in pitch darkness. It is, however, a pity that the Indians adopted this wrong policy. Alas! Why did we do so to our great distress and disadvantage?

Distortion of Truth

Ramanuja, Madhavacharya and others have interpreted the Vedas in their own way and tried to prove their point of view on the authority of the Vedas. It is like the story of a drunkard Muslim who supported alcohol drinking on the authority of Koran. It is said to be mentioned in Koran, "you drink wine and you are sure to go to hell". The drunkard took only the first portion of this sentence, "you drink wine", and supported his point on the authority of Koran. That is how they have tried to prove their point of view on the authority of the Vedas. But the Truth is the Upanishads have preached the ultimate aim of the Vedas as later on supported by Shri Sankaracharya.

Result of selfish and deceitful action

A foreigner was studying in Japan. One day he brought a book from library. The book contained a map which he desperately needed. But the boy didn't care to take the trouble of copying it down. Instead, he just tore off that page and returned the book. Sometime later, a Japanese student happened to see the torn page with that boy. He reported the matter to the principal of the college. It was announced soon after that no student of that country would be allowed to take books home from the library. Alas! For his own selfishness and for just saving himself a bit of trouble this student caused irreparable loss to his own country. You le may also commit the same mistake. It is a matter of grave concern that we don't at all hesitate in causing irretrievable damage to our country, if our personal gain is at stake. Ultimately, we ourselves have to suffer, too.

In Hong Kong the British had employed a Muslim force i.e. soldiers were paid Rs. 45 or so per month. Two soldiers some other community, who were getting Rs. 9 or Rs. 10 per month, made an application to the government to the effect that they would be willing to go to Hong Kong provided they were paid Rs. 15 per month there. The government was obviously gaining in the deal. So, their requests were granted and the Muslim soldiers were told either to work for Rs. 15 a month or quit. No Muslim soldier agreed to stay on for Rs. 15 a month. So they were made to quit. They later represented their case to the British throne but nothing was done. Why should the government have paid more when the work could be got done for a much less amount? Better and braver soldiers were recruited for a much smaller sum. As a result, the new soldiers went to Hong Kong and the Muslims were dismissed. Frustrated and infuriated, the Muslim soldiers went to Africa td enlisted themselves for Mulla's force. They successfully instigated Mulla against the British. In the ensuing battle, the British Government sent the new regiment from Hong Kong. When the Muslim soldiers learnt that the new force which was responsible for their dismissal at Hong Kong had come from there, they fought with utmost valour and venom to settle their old account. Many British soldiers were killed and many wounded. Many others failed to stand the heat of the desert. Many fell ill. All of them were ruined. One reaps as one sows. These new British soldiers had deprived the Muslim soldiers of their Rs. 45 a month just to get an increase of Rs. five only a month. They had to suffer the consequences in the shape of deaths, wounds, diseases and other ravages. Selfishness is a double-edged evil. It first harms others and then mars those who fall a prey to it.

Dear ones! As all the different limbs and organs of the body are essential for a smooth and normal life, similarly all the different races, sects and peoples are needed for an active, healthy and lively society. Who can we harm, then? Who should we look down upon? If the eyes refuse to help all the other limbs by showing them things or if the hands refuse to co-operate with the other limbs in the interest of the body or if the legs refuse to carry the burden of the whole body, what will happen? Can the body function even for a minute in the midst of this confusion? If he eyes were to say, "I have the power to see. Why should other parts of the body take advantage of my faculty," will it be in the interest of the body? If the hand which toils decides to keep itself whatever it earns, that is not possible. It will only harm the hands. The same is the case of all the limbs taken in isolation. When it is proved beyond doubt that selfishness ultimately harms the person who tried to harm others, there is no fun in becoming selfish. The foreign student, who tore the page out of the book, smote not only his country but himself also. The new soldiers of the British regiment stabbed themselves by wanting to wrong the Muslims. Innumerable instances can be quoted to show how these egotists have mauled themselves and their country. The battle between the Kauravas and Pandavas, Muslim rule in India, constant quarrel among Shahjehan's sons, the expiration of the Muslim reign, establishment of the British Empire in India, the doom of Marathas and Sikhs, are some of the examples. All this was caused by our selfishness. We would never have been enslaved but for this egoism. It is this selfishness which has made you an animal, pushed you out of the heaven into the hell and converted you into cowards from the lion-hearted peoples. Shall you not give it up even now?

The story of a selfish and greedy man

A saint gave one of his disciples a magic item which could fulfill all his desires. The only snag was that his neighbour would automatically get double the amount. That man got all that he wanted-money, elephants, horses, cows, buffaloes etc. but his neighbours got all that too, doubled. He was jealous of his neighbours on that account. He was always thinking of desiring something that would harm his neighbours. At long last, an idea struck him and he wished that he might lose one of his eyes. Then he got one arm and leg broken, and the neighbours lost both their arms and legs. He at this stage happened to have an attack of paralysis which completely immobilized him. Even his normal eye, the leg and the hand were rendered unless. He requested the magic article to restore his normalcy but this was rejected, because the neighbours had to get the double the amount and they couldn't possibly get four eyes, legs, arms etc. In desperation he asked for just one eye, leg and arm and this time his request was granted. And lo! The neighbours were also as hale and hearty as ever. He remained deformed for the whole of his life, while his neighbours enjoyed normal health. This is what happens if you wish others ill.

Note: Selfishness must be purged in practical life in order to obtain peace and bliss.

CHAPTER TWENTY

Sin

The Cause of Sin (A Man who misused Medicine)

A man was suffering from two diseases. He had a disease of the eyes and a disease of the stomach. He came to a doctor and asked him to treat him. The doctor gave to this patient two kinds of medicines, two kinds of powders. One of the powders was to be applied to the eyes. It contained Antimony or lead Sulphide, and if taken internally, it is a poison. It can be applied to the eyes and the people in India use this powder for the eyes. So the doctor gave him the powder for the eyes containing antimony or lead sulphide. Another powder he gave him to be taken. This powder contained pepper and chillies; chillies which have a very cold name, but which are very hot. He gave him one powder containing chillies to be taken. This man being in a state of confusion just interchanged the powders. The powder which was to be taken he applied to the eyes, and the antimony and the other things which were poisons he took in. Here were the eyes blinded and the stomach worsted.

That is what is being done by the people, and that is the cause of all the so-called sins in this world. Here is the Atman, the Light of lights within you, and here is the body, the stomach, so to say. What is to be done to the body is being done to the Atman and the respect and honour and glory of the Atman are being paid unto the body.

MORAL: Misapplication of the qualities of the body to the Atman and of the nature of Atman to the body is the cause of sin.

The Phenomenon of Sin (A Man who did not believe in God)

A man who did not believe in God wrote everywhere on the walls of his house, "God is nowhere." He was an atheist. He was a lawyer, and at one time a client came to him and offered him Rs.

500. He said, "No I will take Rs. 1,000." The client said, "All right. I will pay you Rs. 1,000 if you win the case, but I will pay afterwards: if you want to take Rs. 500, then you may have it first." The lawyer felt sure of success and took up the case. He went to the court, feeling sure that he had done everything right. He had studied the case carefully, but when it came up for hearing, the lawyer of the opposite party brought out such a strong point that he lost the case as well as Rs. 1,000 which he had expected to receive for his services. He came to his house dejected, crest-fallen and in a sad plight. He was leaning over his table in a state of dejection when there came to him his darling child who was just learning to spell. He began to spell out "G-o-d, i-s," further was a long word of so many letters: that word the poor child could not spell. He divided it into two parts, "n-o-w h-e-r-e," and the child jumped up with joy; he was amazed as his own success in spelling out the whole sentence, "God is now here," "God is now here." The same "God is nowhere" was read "God is now here." That is all. Vedanta wants you to spell things in the right way. Do not misread them; do not misspell them. Read this "God is nowhere," (that is to say, the phenomenon of sin, crime) as "God is now here." Even in your sins is proved your Divinity; the Divinity of your nature. Realize that and the whole world blooms for you a Paradise, is converted into a garden or Heaven.

MORAL: Misreading of things causes the phenomenon of sin or crime.

The Wrong Way of Instruction (The Monkey Grip)

A customer of mystic power once went to a trader in religion, asking the venerable Siddha (or Pir) to teach him some *'divine" formula by repeating which he might gain the worldly end nearest to his heart. The Fakir told the Mantram, but imposed a rather queer condition for its fruition. "Let not the thought of a monkey cross your mind while repeating the formula for a prescribed length of time." The poor fellow returned to the Guru next day complaining: "Sir, the idea of monkey could never occur to me, had you not warned me against it. But now the monkey-thought clings to me with monkey-grip, I cannot shake it off."

Thus impurity and other sins would long have left the world, had not our blessed teachers kept them up by continual dwelling on them in condemning them. Adams poor Adam, in the magnificent grand Garden of Eden would never have thought of eating the fruit of particular tree in a neglected quarter, had not the Biblical God distinguished it as "forbidden".

MORAL:—Forbidding such evils, as are unknown to people, is to implant the very evils in them, and hence it is a wrong way of instruction.

Commandments without Reason (Don't must be my Name)

A child being once asked his name replied: "Mamma always calls me Don't! That must be my name."

So have people lost their real Self under the weight of rules and orders, and they fancy themselves to be merest name and form.

All our "Do's" and "Don'ts" appeal only to the animal nature in man. When we tell even a boy or girl "Thou shalt do this or that," the rational in him or her resents or rebels because of being ignored and slighted. Our imperative commandments are like trying to drive away the horse (the animality) from its rider (rationality). We teach children the spirit of rebellion in trying to rule them or exercise on them any authority other than their own reason. Where forced rule does not create rebellion, it creates decay and death. According to a law of Psychology, the more indirect hint in the normal state of the man, the stronger is its effect. In our forced moral teachings the ordinary person naturally takes a suggestion to the contrary. Desire for anything is increased by prohibition or condemnation.

MORAL: Commandments and prohibitions without giving reasons generally aggravate evil or produce contrary effects.

CHAPTER TWENTY-ONE

Spiritual Powers

Thought-Reading (A Spiritualist)

A certain gentleman in India was a spiritualist. He was taken to a place, his eyes were blindfolded and a book on mathematics was placed before him. This book he had never seen. In that state he could go on reading. Mathematics has signs of its own and this work contained names which he was not supposed to know. He asked for blank sheet of paper and went on copying all that was in the pages of the mathematical book. He could not call the symbols by their proper names, but he copied them all: he possessed that power. He could read your thoughts and could copy instantly all that you could write with your own hand, apart from him.

Here was a spiritualist but he was far from being a holy man, no, not in the least; worldly, worldly he was, and not a holy or happy man. Spiritualism is often designated as a science, and as a science we may respect it, but it must not be confounded with that which brings the real Joy, the perfect Bliss, that which places you above all temptations.

MORAL: Thought-reading or the possession of any spiritual power does not indicate that the man is surely holy or happy.

Suspending Life-Functions (Khechari Mudra)

There was a man in India who was apparently dead for six months. This process of suspending life-functions is called Khechari Mudra and is given in full detail in the works on Hatha Yoga. He put himself in that state. There was no sign of life; no blood flowed through his veins. After six months he came to life again. Here was a man who might be considered a wonder of wonders, another Christ. He came to life after having been apparently dead for six months, not three days only. This man was far from being happy or free. Rama need not mention the crimes he committed. The prince in whose court he practised these things drove him out of the State.

MORAL: Suspension of life-functions, or possession of similar wonderful powers is no sure sign of happiness or freedom, or of holiness or purity.

Levitation (Becoming Light) (A man who walked on the Waters)

There was a man who walked on the waters. A real saint laughed and asked him how long it took him to acquire this power. He replied that it took him seventeen years. The saint replied, "In seventeen years you have acquired a power worth two annas, we give two annas to a boatman and he ferries us across the river."

All personal power is limited, it binds you just as much as any possession or property binds you. Chains are chains whether of iron or gold; they enslave you all the same.

If these powers make a man so very holy, then dogs must be holy. Dogs smell out where the stag is. The dogs have the power of smell that man has not; hence they must be holy.

MORAL: Levitation or any other personal power does not make a man happy, holy or free; on the other hand, it limits and binds him, just as any other possession does.

Possession of Powers (A King Maker Fakir)

There was a Fakir who could make a king of any person. How had he acquired this power? He answered that he fasted and after that ate the droppings of cows. He lived in a certain way and thus acquired this particular power. A brother said to him, "You give this power of a king to be enjoyed by everybody, but to you fall only the cow's droppings." Thus Indians respect and honour persons having these powers, that is all, they know that that which puts us beyond all want is simply the knowledge of Self.

MORAL: Possession of any kind of power does not put us beyond all wants, nor does it lead to Self-knowledge.

Hatha Yoga Samadhi (A Hatha Yogi)

A Hatha Yogi came before an Indian Prince and threw himself into a long trance. There was no sign of life. The people built a cottage over him to protect him from rain and storm. One night there was a very severe storm and the bricks fell on the head of the Yogi. He came to life again and the first words he uttered were "A horse as my reward, O king! a horse, a horse, O king!"

So long as persons of this kind are in a state of concentration, they are in a good state, they are happy: but when on the material plane, they are just as miserable as anybody else.

MORAL: A Hatha yogi may be happy as long as he is in a state of concentration (Samadhi) but no sooner than he is out of it, he may feel just as anybody else. Hence, Hatha Yoga Samadhi does not give lasting happiness.

Success

Practice without Understanding (Superstitious Theory)

A doctor used to heal wounds by keeping the diseased part under linen bandages for a full week and touching it daily with a sword. The -wounds were healed, being kept from exposure by the bandage. But he ascribed the wonderful healing property to the touch of the sword. So thought his patients too. This superstitious theory gave birth to failures upon failures in many cases that required some other treatment than mere bandaging.

MORAL: Practice without understanding leads to superstitious theories, and hence to failures. Success depends on right theory and right practice.

The Secret of Success (Akbar and Two Rajputs)

Once two Indian Rajputs went to the court of Akbar, the great Moghal Emperor of India, and sought employment.

Akbar inquired about their qualifications. They said they were heroes. Akbar asked them a proof of their heroism. Both drew out their daggers from the scabbards. There the two lightning flashes shone in Akbar's court. The flash of the dagger was symbolic of their inner heroism. Immediately the two lightning flashes joined the two bodies. Each kept the point of his dagger on the other's breast, and both gave proofs of their heroism by running through the daggers with stoic calmness. Their bodies met on earth and fell bleeding to the ground, but their souls united in Heaven. A very queer proof of their heroism was given to the emperor. This is an illustration of the fact that true work is accomplished only when the self-asserting worker is sacrificed.

MORAL: Sacrifice your little self, forget it in the performance of your work, and success must be yours. It cannot he otherwise. The desire for success must die in your work before achieving success. This is the secret of success. When shall I be free? When I shall cease to be!

The Secret of Invincibility (The Three Asuras)

In the Hindu Scriptures there is a magnificent story told about three persons called Asuras. These three persons had wonderful powers. They were warriors, nobody could get the better of them, they were wonderful people. People who came' and fought with them, were defeated immediately, hosts of enemies came, and were defeated. The men, who fought with them, came in thousands but were defeated by these three persons. The enemies being defeated so frequently, went to a great saint and asked how they could beat these three fellows; and the saint told them they must enquire into the cause of their invincibility, how were these three Asuras invincible? With great effort and trouble it was found out that the secret of their invincibility lay in the fact that these persons never entertained the thought that they were workers or enjoyers. When the victory was gained, they thought nothing of it. They did not stoop down to enjoy the victory. When they were fighting, the idea that "I, as this body, am fighting" was entirely lost, and the idea that "I am fighting" was entirely absent. Such are the heroes in this world. You know every hero in war, while engaged in action, as people say, "I am all ears," so the hero is all action. There is no room left for the idea "I am doing." There his body gets mechanical, so to say. - He is all action. His head and feet are saturated with Divinity. So, such people whenever they fought, became all action, they never for a moment allowed the idea, "I am acting." Just as a machine worked, their bodies worked; machines of God, machines of Divinity, their bodies worked. This was the secret of their success, nobody could win them. Now the secret of their invincibility being found out, the great sage told the enemies of these three warriors the means of conquering them. He told those enemies to engage in action with them and then run away from them; go to them and call them out into action, and just when they begin to attack them, to leave those warriors as conquerors. Thus to draw them out and flee away from them. The enemies of those warriors drew them out and fled from them. Thus a few times more were the enemies of those warriors defeated. By and by those three invincible warriors were drawn out of their true position, were drawn out of their real invincibility, and were brought down into their bodies, they were made to believe that they were conquerors. They were made to believe that they were great, that they were victorious. Those continued victories engendered in them the idea that they were victorious, they were conquerors. Here were the three men brought down into the cage of the body; here were the three men put into the prison house of the body. The idea of "I am doing," or the thought of "I am great" got hold of them, and held them in prison. There the God in them was replaced by the small ego and then it was no hard task to win them and catch them and imprison them. It was not a hard task they were defeated immediately, immediately were they caught.

So long as you are doing a work, as it were, your body being a machine in the hands of God, your personality being merged in Divinity, so long as you are in that position, you are invincible, you are like those three Asuras above the idea of "I am enjoying, or I am doing." You are invincible; but when people come to you and begin to praise you, to puff you up, flatter you, favourably review you from all sides, you are made to, believe that you are a conqueror, a hero, you are victorious, others are defeated, your rivals are against you. They are like those three Asuras. The idea of "I am doing it" and."I must enjoy the deed," "I am the enjoyer," that very thought imprisons you, brings you down into the cage of the body. You are undone, the power is lost. Go out of the cage and you are inspired, go into the cage again and you are no more.

MORAL: Merging of personality into Divinity leads to invincibility and power; getting out of Divinity into personality leads to defeat and ruin.

The story of a retired soldier

A soldier returned to his village home, as a pensioner, after thirty years of service in the army. One day he purchased some milk in the market and took it in an earthen pot holding it with both the hands. Someone cracked a joke with him, and with a commanding voice, he cried out, 'Attention'. The man had worked in the army for full thirty years and it was a mechanical action for him to implicitly obey this Military Command. It had, so to say, become his nature to act mechanically, without meaning it. Accordingly, on hearing the command, 'Attention', the man, ex-soldier as he was, immediately stood at attention. The earthen pot fell from his hands and the milk was poured out and spilt on the ground. They all enjoyed this joke and laughed heartily.

Now Rama asks, 'Will you call it a work?' No. It is not a work. Why? Because it was all mechanical. It was not done with any higher intention. If, however, you call it a work, then, breathing can also be called a work. Even the circulation of blood in your arteries and veins can be called a work. But, no! It is no work. It goes on automatically, mechanically and involuntarily i.e., even without your knowing or willing it or without making you exercise your intention or attention. You cannot be held responsible for the work which has no intention on your part to help you evolve according to our scriptures, unless you definitely mean to do it. If, while doing any work, your mind is thinking of something else, that work will surely be spoiled. Even the so called big persons are likely to be absent minded at times. They do not, then, achieve the success in their work. Please note that all these persons who put-in all their heart and head in doing the real and useful work, are readily wise men. It is only such persons who could do wonderful jobs in life.

The importance of honest and truthful work in life.

You might have noticed that the proprietor of a business firm has no liking for the servant who always gives respectful salutes to him but does not discharge his duties properly. On the other hand, there is another servant who discharges his duty properly and with all sincerity, but does not indulge in unnecessary sycophancy. It is quite natural that the proprietor, the Master, will love and like only the servant who is a sincere worker. So, too, God loves only that man who discharges his duties properly and not the one who indulges m mere sycophancy and lip flattery. Only repeating the name of God on a rosary, bowing or kneeling down again and again or reading Ramayana, Koran or Bible, without caring to implement its teachings in actual life, will not help you. One may succeed in deceiving the world, but not God. God knows you through and through. You cannot throw dust into the eyes of God. Remember that He loves and patronises only those persons, who love Truth more than any-thing else, who sincerely and lovingly discharge their duties in an unattached way, in right earnest, with faith in God or Self, without caring for the result and who act according to the Laws of Nature. This is the essence of the philosophy of work or action, commonly known as Niskam Karm Yoga. This will give you peace of mind, howsoever, bothering responsibility it may involve*

CHAPTER TWENTY-THREE

Suffering

No Gain without Pain (A Wrestler Unable to bear Pinpricks)

There was in India a great wrestler and athlete. He wanted a barber to tattoo him, to engrave on his arm the picture of a lion. He told the barber to paint great, magnificent lion on both his arms. He said he was born when the sign of Zodiac, the Lion or Leo, was in Sinha Rashi. So he was born under the right influence of the sign Zodiac—Lion, Leo, and he was supposed to be a very brave man. The barber took up the needle to paint or tattoo him, and just when he was pricking a little, the athlete could not bear it. He began to pant for breath, and addressed the barber, "Wait, wait, what you are going to do?" The barber said that he was going to draw the tail of the lion. This fellow, in reality, could not stand the pricking sensation, but made a very queer pretence, and said, "Don't you know that fashionable people cut off the tails of their dogs and horses, and so that lion which has no tail is considered a very strong lion. Why are you drawing the tail of the lion? The tail is not needed," "All right", said the barber, "I won't draw the tail. I will draw the other parts of the lion". The barber took up the needle again, and just pricked it through his skin. This too the fellow could not bear. He remonstrated and said, "What are you going to do next?" The barber said, "I am going to draw the ears of the lion". The man said again, "O barber, you are very foolish. Don't you know the people cut off the ears of their dogs? They don't keep dogs with long ears. Don't you know that the lion which is without ears is the best?" The barber desisted. After a while the barber took up his needle and was again pricking him. The man could not bear it and remonstrated, saying, "What are you going to do now, O barber?" The barber said, "I am going to paint now the waist of the lion." There the man said, "Haven't you read our poetry, haven"t you read the accounts given by Indian poets? Lions are always painted as having a very small, thin, nominal waist? You need not draw the waist of the lion." The barber now threw aside his colours and his painting needle and asked the fellow to go away from his presence.

Here is a man who asserts that he is born under the influence of the sign of the Zodiac called the Sinha Rashi or Leo. Here is a man who pretends to be a great wrestler, a great athlete; here is a man who calls himself a lion. He wants to have lions tattooed all over his body, but he cannot bear the sting of a needle.

Such are the majority of people who want to see God, who want to realise Vedanta, who want to know the whole truth this moment, this second, who want to accomplish everything, to become Christ in half a minute. When the time comes, to get that lion (Truth) painted in their souls, to get that lion of Righteousness painted or tattooed in their being, they cannot bear the sting, the stinging sensation, there they hesitate. The price I will not pay, but the thing I want.

MORAL: Sufferings are necessary for the achievement of the Goal, as there is no gain without pain.

The Nature of All Pains (The Tramp and the Lady)

A poor tramp begs b.ead from the lady of a ranch. She, poor soul, envies the freedom of the homeless wanderer. When the tramp is gone, she feigns before her husband to have received a letter announcing the death of her mother. Thinking that the mother may have left some property for them, the husband allows her that evening to leave home for the departed mother's. The lady purchases a ticket and gets off at the nearest station. Away she flies into the woods like a bird let loose from the cage after along wearisome imprisonment, relieving long wearisome burden by laughing a hearty laughter in the woods. Freely she roamed, bought her meals from the country peasants, and slept under a haystack when the sunset over her head. Next morning she resumes her happy wandering, and lo! To her utter horror, what voice does she hear? It is her own husband's wandering with the tramp of yesterday. He had been suffering from the distressing burden of ennui just as much as she, and wanted a life of liberty and vacation for some time, but neither would disclose the anguish of the heart to the other for fear of seeming faithlessness. Of this nature are all our pains to please others. To your own Self be true, and just as night follows the day, to none could you be false.

MORAL: All our pains are mostly due to pleasing others without being true to our own Self. In being true to one's own Self alone can one be truly happy and a light to the world.

The Snares of Flattery (Benjamin Franklin's Experience)

Benjamin Franklin in his Autobiography relates an experience of his boyhood. When he was a boy, he was going to school in Philadelphia, and one day on his way to school, he happened to see a blacksmith at work. In those days, the machinery was not in such a high state of development as it is to-day. The blacksmith was working in his shop. Just like a curious boy, Benjamin stopped at the shop and was looking at the man at work. Children lose themselves in any thought that comes up before them. He had a satchel in his hand and he was just going to school, but he forgot all about his school to enjoy the sight of the working blacksmith. The blacksmith noticed the interest of the boy. He was sharpening his tools and knives. The assistant of the blacksmith having gone on an errand was absent. On seeing the little boy taking so much interest in the work, he asked him to come up to him. Benjamin moved up and the blacksmith said, "What a nice boy, what a fine boy, how intelligent you are!" Benjamin was puffed up and felt flattered, and when he noticed the beaming smiles on the face of Benjamin, he asked him if be would take the trouble to help him in turning the grindstone. Benjamin immediately began to do that work. (Children are naturally very active and they want to do something which will keep their muscles employed. You can send them to the other end of the world if you can tackle their humour). While Benjamin was working at the grindstone, the blacksmith went on humouring and flattering him. The boy went on doing the work. In the meantime, he whetted a number of knives and axes. By that time the little boy felt fatigued and he remembered his school time and recitation hours, and wanted to leave the shop. But there was that man upon him with his flattery and humouring spirit saying, "Oh good boy, I know you are never punished in school, you are so fine, so smart. What the other boys take three hours to accomplish; you can do in one hour. The school master never gets angry with you, you are so good. One by one the swords were whetted and when one was half done. Benjamin wanted to leave, but he could not. The recitation hours commenced at 10 and he was released at 12. He went to school and was flogged for being late. He was tired and his arms were sore. For a week he had to suffer the consequences. He could not prepare his lessons.

Ever afterwards when any one flattered him, the thought came to his mind. "He has an axe to grind." After this event never was Benjamin Franklin entrapped in the snares of flattery.

MORAL: Beware of the snares of flattery; else you are bound to experience suffering.

Rest and Unrest (A Dog in the Mirror-House)

In India some houses have many mirrors; in fact the walls and ceiling are covered with mirrors. Once a dog entered such a house, and on all sides of himself he saw hundreds of dogs. When he looked up, he saw them on the top of him, and thus being very much frightened he began to jump, and immediately all the hundreds of dogs began to jump also; then he barked and scampered about, and they too scampered and opened their mouths. He behaved in this way until he became so tired that he lay down and gave up the chase, gave up the body and the owner of the house came in and removed the remains of the dog. Now a handsome young prince entered this room and admired himself very much in all the mirrors, first he admired his hair, then his mouth and other features, then his dress, and so on. He was very happy with all these pictures and knew that these many hundred people were himself.

It is only when we know that there is only one Self and that all the shapes and forms we see under the various names are really our Self, then there is rest; otherwise it is like the case of the dog. We are afraid: this one is going to deceive us; that one is going to harm us; the other one is going to take something from us, and there is a continual struggle against the forms which we imagine to be different; but once we realise the Truth and sit quietly as did the prince, we know that nothing can deceive the Self, for It is Immutable and Free. While we jump about as the dog did, we merely live on the surface; but when we realize the Self, we dive below the surface into the realms of Absolute Truth.

MORAL: Seeing and realizing the Self under all names and forms brings rest and peace, otherwise there is continual struggle and unrest.

Sensual Pleasure (The Rose with a Sting of Bee)

A young man in the presence of Rama plucked a beautiful rose with a view to enjoy its smell. No sooner did he bring it in contact with his nose than a bee stung him just on the tip of the nose. The man cried with pain, the rose fell from his hand.

Do the petals of every rose enfold a bee? Certainly, there is not a rose of sensual pleasure which has not got the bee of injury concealed in it.

MORAL: The enjoyment of sensual pleasure ends inevitably in pain and suffering.

Human Suffering - boon in disguise

You might have marked that an elephant is controlled and directed with a small iron prick-hook (Ankush). The troubles and miseries of the human being are also a sort of prick-hook to guide him and to keep him on the proper path of progress and evolution.

CHAPTER TWENTY-FOUR

Thought Power

Unbecoming Modesty (The Bashful Boy)

An inspector came to a school in India. One of the school-masters, pointing to a student, said that he was so bright as to have learned by heart such and such a piece of literature, say, Milton's Paradise Lost; be could recite any part of it. The student was presented to the inspector, but he had no Vedanta in him. He assumed bashfulness and modesty, and when asked, "Do you know that piece by heart?", he said, "No sir; I am nothing, I know nothing." Those words he thought to be an indication of modesty, a sign of bashfulness. No sir, I know nothing; I did not learn it." The inspector asked again, but the boy still said, "No sir j no, sir; I do not know it." The master was put out of countenance. There was another boy who did not know the whole book by heart, but he said, "I know it; I think I shall be able to recite any passage you may desire." The inspector put to him a few questions. All the questions were readily answered by the boy; this second boy declaimed passage after passage and secured the prize. No one can even estimate you at a higher value than you set upon yourselves. Do not please make yourselves cringing, sneaking, miserable creatures. As you think, so will you become. Think yourselves to be God and God you are. Think yourself to be free and free you are this moment.

MORAL: Modesty carried to the extreme is unbecoming and will launch you into misery and slavery for as you think, so will you become.

Right imagination (The Imaginary Curry)

There was a man who was hungry, and in order that he might appease his hunger, he sat down at a certain place, closed his eyes and began to eat imaginary curry. After a while he was seen with his mouth open, endeavouring to cool his burnt tongue. Somebody asked him what the matter was. He said that in his food there was a very hot chilli. The name is cool, but the thing itself is very hot. Thereupon a by-stander remarked, "Oh, poor fellow, if you had to live on imaginary food, then why not select something far sweeter than hot chilli, pepper? As it was your own creation, your own doing, your own imagination, why did you not make a better choice? According to Vedanta, all your world being but your own creation, your own idea, why think yourself a low, miserable sinner? Why not think yourself into a fearless, self-reliant incarnation of Divinity?

MORAL: Right imagination is to think yourself not a low, miserable sinner but a fearless, self-reliant incarnation of Divinity.

The Effect of Prohibition (The Monkey Thought)

There was a man in India who was practicing Mantram in order to win his lady love, but the sage who told him the Mantram that he was to repeat to himself, asked the man to beware of one thing. Now what was that? The sage told the man never to allow the idea or though t of a monkey to enter his mind when he was practicing this Mantram. Well, the man began to practice the Mantram and he was trying hard not to think of the monkey, but every time he practised the thought of the monkey, the monkey kept all the time before him. He could not for a single second repeat the Mantram without the thought of the monkey coming before him. He went to the sage and said. "Sir, sir, if you had not cautioned me not to think of the monkey, I would have been able to chant the Mantram, and would never have thought of the monkey, but when you want me to keep out the thought, then it haunts me, over-shadows me. Similarly, by the very attempt to shut out ignorance and weakness, you post weakness and ignorance there.

MORAL: The effect of prohibition is aggravation, as an attempt to shut out a thought does not remove it but aggravates it.

Thought the index of Man's Nature (A Thief Turned into a Saint.)

A thief related the way he once managed to break into the house of a rich man and steal away the jewellery of the house. He said that he came to know about the jewellery that this rich man had got recently into his house by some means. He went to break into the house, but could not devise any method or means of doing it. By thinking and thinking again he made a plan; he saw that near the house there was a gigantic tree growing, and he saw that this tree was opposite the window of the third storey of the house. Then he devised the plan to put a swing at night, when it was dark to put a rope at the top of the tree, and he made a kind of trapeze, and he began to swing upon the trapeze, went on swinging and swinging in that hot country. It was summer, and he had come to know that people of the house slept on the fifth storey, they were not on the third storey. When the trapeze reached the window, he gave it a kick, and he kicked it a second time, and at the third kick window-sash flew back. Now in the seventh or eighth attempt, by making the window-sash or door fall down he entered the house, and there he had some ropes with him, he let down the ropes and drew up two or three of his companions. Then he began to think within himself of the place where the jewellery was expected to be found. He concentrated his mind; his mind was all merged in concentration. There he said that the people did not keep their jewellery at such places where the thieves might expect to find it; the people keep their jewellery where it is least expected to be found. Then he began to dig at a place where the jewellery was least expected to be found. 11 was buried in the ground, (That is the way people did in those days, and some do today in India, but now they are beginning to put their money in banks. The people used to keep their money buried under-ground) He got the money and then he heard a sound upstairs. He said that he and his companions, after they had got the money, heard that sound, and that sound sent a thrill throughout their body. Their whole being was throbbing, shaking, quivering, shivering; they were trembling from head to foot. Then he said that that was a time of death. They found themselves almost dead, and there they said that even a small rat might come and kill them. The sound, in fact, was the sound of rats only. There he said that he repented, he prayed to God, he gave up his body and resigned himself entirely to God. There he resigned himself, repented and asked God to forgive him, and there was he in a state of Samadhi in which the mind was no mind, all selfish interests were gone. Here he was in a very queer, wonderful state of mind, he and all his companions. There he prayed, "O God! save me and I shall become a hermit, I shall become a Sannyasi, I shall become a monk, I shall devote my life entirely to your service, O Lord! Save me, save me." Here was offered a most fervent, heartfelt prayer, a most sincere prayer that came from the bottom of his heart and soul. Here was prayer that sounded through the depth of his whole being; merged in God he was at that time. What was the result? All sound subsided, and he and his companions came out of the house safe.

Do not draw any inferences from the external actions of people. If a man commits murder or theft, you ought not to look down upon him. Judge not things from the external actions; man is not what his actions are, man is what his thoughts are. A man who lives in a house of ill-fame may be a saint.

MORAL: The true index of man's real nature is his thought and not his external actions and behaviour.

The Way to uplift the Dead or the Living (A Lady who wanted to save her husband)

A lady came to a saint and put the question, "My husband died a few months ago; what shall I do to save him?" Another, a gentleman came and said he was going to commit suicide because he had lost his only child; he could not bear the separation. Another man said he had lost his wife and he did not think it worth his while to live any longer. Now what answer did the saint make?

The lady was very despondent and very anxious to save her husband. The saint said, "You can save your husband; you need not be despondent; you should abide by my advice. Every day whenever you feel despondent, or when the thought of your husband comes to you, sit down at once, close your eyes, and place, before your mind the body of your husband, and you know that the object of your affection can immediately appear before our mind. When you get this picture before your mind, or when you get the body of your husband before the mind, do not grieve or be sorry, do not sob or cry; by sobbing and crying, by shedding tears you simply make your husband cling to the earth, you fasten him to the world, and your work is perverted and degrading. You should not try to bring him down, you should not try to lower him or retard his progress. You can think of the different world of your husband, you can think of him not as dead (because with your eyes closed, the picture of the husband comes most vividly before you) but as living. When you have it before you, then feel, feel, realise that he is God; tell him, preach to him, say continually, pour forth this idea before him, "You are God, Divinity, you are the Lord; in your picture, in your body, in your form, it is the Divinity that is appearing to me."

When we approach a telephone apparatus and apply it to your ears, we hear something; we know that the sound does not come from that steel apparatus but from the friend behind the scenes or at the other end. Similarly, when you see the picture of your departed husband before you, realize that this picture has the Divinity behind it; tell it, (You are Divinity, you are God). This way you can save your departed husband.

If we can save and raise and help our departed friends, we can no doubt save, raise and help our living friends by the same method.

MORAL: The way to help and uplift the dead or the living is to bring their picture before the mind and infuse it with the thought of Divinity.

Like cures like (Diarrhea versus Purgative)

A man suffered from diarrhea, and the Doctor gave him a purgative, and he was cured. The diarrhea made his go to the bath-room over and over again. Now a purgative taken willingly acts the same way, but there is a world of difference between the two. A purgative is a remedy while diarrhea is a disease; and while both work in the same way, there is a world of difference between them.

Worldly thought enslaves you, it is a disease, it binds you and keeps you at the mercy of all sorts of circumstances; every wind and storm can upset you. The diarrhea of thought is human idea. Take up the purgative which Vedanta furnishes. This is also thought to be a kind of imagination. So is all thought of the world; but worldly thoughts and human ideas are a diarrhea, and the kind of imagination or thought advocated by Vedanta is a purgative. Take up this purgative and you will be cured of your malady, your disease; you will be relieved of all suffering, anxiety, and trouble.

In India, people do not wash their hands with soap but with ashes. Ashes are one kind of dirt, one kind of earth, and the soil which is polluting your hands is also dirt or earth. When the ashes are applied to the hands and the hands are washed in water, they not only remove the dirt from the hands but are also removed themselves.

Similarly, the kind of thought which you will have to dwell upon, the kind of imagination, according to the teachings of Vedanta, is like ashes; it will wash you clean of every impurity and every weakness, it will raise you above the kind of imagination which is inoculated in this.

It is imagination and the current of ideas in the wrong direction which binds you and it is imagination directed in the right channel which liberates you. *Similia similibus curantur* - like cures like.

MORAL: Imagination or thought, directed wrongly, binds, a man; while, directed rightly, liberates him.

Contrary cures contrary (The Dream Lion)

A man dreamt, and in his dreams all sorts of things appeared. Those things in the dreams were mere ideas, mere thought, mere imagination. He saw a lion, tiger, or serpent in the dream. No sooner he saw the lion, the tiger, or the serpent, he was startled at once and was awakened.

The tiger was a kind of nightmare and woke him up; but this tiger or lion in the dream although a creation of his own thought, this object of his dream was a wonderful thought, a wonderful imagination. It took away all other ideas in the dream, it took away all other objects. The fairy scenes, the beautiful landscapes, the flowing rivers, the majestic mountains, of which he was dreaming, were all gone after the tiger or the lion was seen in the dream. Now the tiger or lion never eats grass or stones, but the tiger of his dream was a wonderful creation, for the tiger ate up all the landscapes, the woods, the forest; all were gone, it had disturbed the dreaming self, and at the same time had eaten itself up, it was seen no more when he woke up.

Similarly, the kind of ideas or imagination, inculcated in Vedanta, is like the tiger in the dream. The whole world is a dream. This tiger will rid you of all false imagination and ignorance, and will at the same time rid you of its own self. It will take you where all imagination stops, where all language stops, it lands you into that indescribable Reality.

The ladder, from which you feel, so to speak, is the ladder which will lead you up. You will have to retrace your steps by the same road down by which you fell to anxiety and misery. The kind of imagination which Vedanta recommends to you for liberation is just opposite to the form of imagination which brought you low. Thus you are sure to be cured by the process *contrara contraribus curanta*; the contrary cures the contrary. Vedanta proves that all this world is nothing else but your own ideas, nothing else but your own imagination and your own thought. Now, purify this thought, elevate this thought, direct it-aright, and you become the Light of lights, the All throughout the universe.

MORAL: The imagination, which leads one to bondage, also leads to liberation if applied contrariwise.

Ludicrous Fright (A Penniless Lad)

They say it was a penniless lad. And nothing, nothing to lose he had. He heard that thieves were at him still. They must pursue, go where he will. Thus haunted, worried, he for escape Ran uphill, down ditch, into the cape. He hurried and flurried in fear and fright, Wore out his body and mind in fight. Yet nothing, nothing to lose he had, They say it was a penniless lad!

O worldly man! Such is thy plight, Thy arrant, ignorance and fright, O scared fellow, just know thyself. Away with dread of thieves and theft, Up, up awake, see what you are. There is nothing to lose or fear for, No harm to thee can ever accrue, Thy thought alone doth thee pursue. "Afraid of what? Of God? Nonsense! Of man? Cowardice! Of the Elements? Dare them. Of yourself? Know thyself. Say, I am God."

MORAL: It is your own thought that makes you fear, no harm can come to you, if you know and realize your true self.

Heaven or Hell our Own Creation (When Rama was a Student)

When Rama was a student preparing for the Bachelor of Arts Examination, a fellow-student used to live in the same room with him. This fellow-student was a very playful young man. He used to while away his time in singing, dancing and playing. One day a gentleman asked this friend how many hours he used to devote to his studies. He smilingly said, "Full 18 hours." The friend said, what does that mean? You waste four or five hours in my presence, before my eyes, I know that you sleep about 8 or 9 hours out of the 24, and that leaves you only 10 or 12 hours, and yet you say that you read for full 18 hours. The young man said, "You have not studied Mathematics." I can prove that I read for full 18 hours. The gentleman said, "Well, how is that?" The young man said, "I and this Rama live in the same room; as a matter of fact I read for 12 hours and he reads for 24 hours, that makes up to 36; strike the average, 18 falls to his share and 18 to mine". The gentleman said, "Well, admitting that you read for 12 hours, but this I cannot admit that Rama reads for full 24 hours.

How is that possible? I know that Rama is a very hard working student, I know he is preparing so many subjects, and he is not only doing the University work, he is doing four times as much work extra and preparing many other subjects, and doing all sorts of works, but still the laws of nature will not allow him to work for 24 hours*" This fellow student began to explain. He said, "I can show you that when he is taking his dinner, he never allows his mind to idle away a single second; I can show you that he always has with him a paper on which there is some scientific problem to reflect upon, some mathematical or philosophical subject, or some book or some poem which he may commit to memory; he may be writing a poem or doing some sort of work or other, he never wastes a moment when he is taking his meals. When he is in the toilet room, he is drawing with a piece of chalk figures on the wall; when he goes to sleep, he is working at some problem or other, he is always dreaming of the same subjects which occupy his mind during the day. Thus his 24 hours are devoted to study."

Well, there was some truth in his statement. The man who devotes full 18 hours of his time to study, in his dreams he can do nothing else but the same kind of work which he has been doing in the day time.

This being the case, in your long, long sleep of death, what should you expect; the period between the death and the next birth, that period of long sleep, how is that to pass? Vedanta says this will pass in your hells or heavens; this will pass in your paradises, or your purgatories. What are these paradises, these hells and heavens? These are the dreamlands which pass between one death and the next birth. Here is a man, a true Christian, who has been living a most pious, religious and devout life, who has been attending the Church every Sunday, who has been offering his prayers every morning and1 every evening, he has been invoking the grace of God at every meal that he has taken, and has been keeping the Cross of Christ on his breast all his life, he has meditating upon Christ all the while that he was awake, from his birth until his death; he was all the while living, moving, and having his being in the holy presence of Jesus the Christ. This man is a man who has devoted his wakeful state to the love of Christ, the wakeful state of 80 or 90 years, he has devoted all his thought to Christ, he has been expecting after death to find himself seated on the right hand side of Jesus the Christ, and he has been dreaming and thinking all his life, about the angels, seraphims, and cherubims that will greet him after death. According to Vedanta, a devout Christian of this kind will find himself after death on the right hand side of Jesus the Christ. Verily, verily after death, during that long, long sleep, between this death and the next birth, he will find himself surrounded by the cherubims, the seraphims, and the angels who are singing hallelujahs all the while. He will find himself in their midst. There is no reason why he should not find himself in their midst. Vedanta says, "O Christians, if you are devout, if you are really in earnest and faithful, you will get the promises in your books fulfilled, but find no fault with the Mohammedans and the Hindus. If a Mohammedan is a true Mohammedan, if he has been devoting all his wakeful state of 70 or 80 years of his life in the same way, as prescribed by Mohammed, and has been thinking of and looking up to Mohammed, and he has been offering up his prayers four or five times a day (Mohammedans offer prayers four or five times in every 24 hours, and they are very strict, very devotional), if he has been all the time living in the name of Mohammed, and if he has been always ready to lay down his life in the name of Mohammed, (These Mohammedans are very earnest, most zealous, and you might even say sometime bigoted fanatics), then what will become of a Mohammedan of this kind, the dream of whose life has been to serve the cause of Mohammedanism, to make the name of Mohammed resound from one end of the world to the other? A Mohammadan of this kind, when he dies, what will become of him? To him will befall nothing which is contrary to the laws of nature. The law of nature is what we are dreaming in our wakeful state, the same we shall dream when we go to sleep. He has been dreaming of Mohammed, of the Paradise, of the beautiful gardens, and of the beautiful damsels; the rivers of wine that are promised by their Prophet after death; he has been dreaming about magnificent palaces and objects of luxury in heaven after death. Vedanta says there is not a law or force in nature, which can prevent him from enjoying the kind of heaven about which he was dreaming. He must see a heaven of the same sort, he must find himself, after death, in a paradise of the sort promised by his Prophet.

But Vedanta says, "O Mohammedans, you have no right to place all the people in this world, after death, at the disposal of your own Prophet, at the mercy of one Mohammed only. Let Christians enjoy their thoughts: make them free, do not want to subject all these, whether they die in Europe, America, India, Japan, or China, to the mercy of Mohammed. 'If they believe in Mohammed, all right; otherwise they are damned.' You have no right to speak that way, to be so cruel. If you are a follower of Mohammed, you will have a heaven of the kind which you desire, and so with all religions. If you are true to your ideas, if you are true to your dogmas or creed, or your religion after death, you will have a heaven of the same sort as you are expecting. In reality, hell or heaven after death is dependent upon yourselves. You make the heaven after death, and you make the hell after death. In reality the heavens and hells are simply your dreams, nothing more, dreams which appear to you to be real at that time. You know dreams appear to be real when we are dreaming. So these hells or heavens will appear to you to be real after death, but as a matter of fact, in reality, they are nothing more than dreams.

MORAL: Whatever we are always thinking about in our wakeful state, the same we dream when we go to sleep. Similarly, whatever ideas about hell or heaven we cherish constantly in daily life, the same will appear real to us in our life after death.

1. The Companion's Effect on Transmigration (A Sage Questioned by a Cat and a Bog)

There came two men to a sage in India, one of them with the temper of a dog and other with the temper of a cat, or it might be said, a cat and a dog came to the sage. The dog put this question to the sage, "Sir, sir, here is this cat or this catlike man. He is very wicked and sly, he is very bad. What will become of him in the next birth?'* Afterwards that cat-like man came to the sage and put the same question, "Sir, sir, here is the dog, or doggish fellow. He is very bad; he is snarling, barking. What will become of him after death in the next birth?" The sage kept quiet but after the questions had been repeated very often, he said, "Brothers it would have been better if you had not put these questions." But they insisted upon a reply.

The sage said, "Well, here is this cat; the cat keeps company with you, O dog, and he or she is imbibing your habits, is living with you, and is all the time partaking of your character. Well, in his or her next birth, this cat will become a dog. What else can it become?' And as to the dog, "Well, it is keeping company with you, O cat, and is all the time imbibing your characteristics and is sharing your habits; well, in his next birth, he must become a cat."

MORAL: Just as you imbibe the qualities of your companion in this life, so you are bound to become in the next.

CHAPTER TWENTY-FIVE

Truth

Everything Indispensable (The Mountain and the Squirrel)

The mountain and the squirrel Had a quarrel;
And the former called the latter 'Little Prig'. Bun replied:
"You are doubtless very big;
But all sorts of things and weather Must be taken in together,
To make up a year And a sphere
And I think it no disgrace To occupy my place.
If I'm not as large as you, You are not so small as I, And not half so spry,
I"ll not deny you make
A very pretty squirrel track.
Talents differ; all's well and wisely put. If I cannot carry forests on my back, Neither can you crack a nut."

Your body may be like that of a little squirrel and another body beside you may be as big as a mountain, but don't think you are small; be as wise as the small squirrel. Remember that even if your body is very little, you have a function to discharge in this world, which the big body cannot perform. Then why look down upon yourself? Be cheerful and happy.

MORAL: Everything looking however insignificant, is important and useful in its own place, and hence indispensable.

The True Companion (Yudhishthira and the Dog)

There was a king in India named Yudhishthira; He trod the path of Truth. It is said that he was going up the Himalayas to let his body melt down in the snows. For some reason, for a great reason he was going with his parents, with his wife and wife's brothers, and his four brothers, on the summits of the Himalayas. It is said that he was treading the path of Righteousness, he was going to seek Truth. He was going ahead, marching on. His younger brother was following him and after his younger brother came his other brother, and so on in the right orders and after the brothers was the wife of this king. He goes ahead his face towards the goal, and eyes set upon the Truth. He found that his wife was bewailing behind him, tottering down she could not follow him; she was fatigued and about to die. Here the king did not turn his face back. He asked his wife to run to him a few feet and. then he would carry her with him. "Come up to me, come up to me." But she could not go up to him for those three feet. She was lagging behind, she could not manage to go up to him, and he did not turn back: to turn back one step from the Truth is not allowable. Never will king Yudhishthira turn back one step. The wife totters down but for her sake the king is not to turn back from the Truth.

Thousands of wives, you have had in your previous births, and if you have any future births, you don't know how many times you will be married again; how many relatives you have had, and how many relatives you will have in the future. For the sake of these ties and relations you have not to turn back from the Truth. Go ahead, go ahead. Let nothing draw you back. Have more respect for Truth than for your wife. Have more respect for Divinity. The Truth concerns the whole human race, Divinity or Truth concerns all time, is eternal, and your worldly ties are not so. They are momentary. Bear in mind the law that what is really good for you, must be really good for your wife or your companions. If you see that for you it is really beneficial to live apart from your wife, remember that for her also it is really good to live apart from you. This is the rule. The same Divinity or Truth that underlies your personality underlies the personality or being of your wife also.

The wife of king Yudhishthira fell down. But the king went straight on and asked his brothers to follow him. They ran on with him for some time, but the youngest brother could not keep pace any longer. He was tottering down, overtaken with fatigue and was about to fall down when he cried: "Brother, brother Yudhishthira, I am going to die, save me, save me." King Yudhishthira did not turn his eyes away from the goal, from the truth: on he went, went ahead. He simply calls out to his younger brother to gather courage enough to run up to him those two or three feet, and he would take him along on that condition, but for nothing, nothing would he go one step behind to give him even a pull. On he goes. The youngest brother dies.

After a while the second brother who was at the end of the rope, cried and was about to totter down. He called for help, "Brother Yudhishthira, help me, help me. I am going to fall down." But brother Yudhishthira does not turn back. On he goes. This way all the brothers died, but king Yudhishthira did not swerve or turn back a single step. Away he goes, on he goes to the path of Righteousness. The story runs that when king Yudhishthira reached the pinnacle of Truth, when he reached the goal, God Himself, Truth personified appeared to him. Just as we read in the Bible that God appeared in the shape of a dove, so in the Hindu Scriptures we read about God appearing to certain persons in the body of an angel or in the shape of the King of Heaven. So the story goes that when king Yudhishthira reached the pinnacle of Truth, Truth personified approached and asked him to go in person to Heaven, to ascend to Heaven. As we read in the Bible about certain people being raised alive to Heaven, so here is the story of king Yudhishthira being asked to ascend to Heaven alive. When he looked at his right hand side he found a dog with him. King Yudhishthira said, "O God, O Truth, if you want to raise me to the highest Heaven, you will have to take this dog also with me. Let this dog also ascend to the highest Heaven with me."

But the story says that God or Truth personified said, "King Yudhishthira, that cannot be. The dog is not worthy of being taken to the highest Heaven, the dog has yet to pass through many transmigrations, the dog has yet to come into the body of man and live the right life, and live as a pure, immaculate person, how then can it be raised to the highest Heaven. You are worthy of being taken to the highest Heaven in body, but not the dog." There King Yudhishthira says, "O Truth, O God, I come here for your sake and not for the sake of Heaven or Paradise. If you want to raise me to the highest Paradise and to enthrone me there, you will have to take this dog also with me, my wife did not keep pace with me, she staggered on the path of Righteousness. My youngest brother did not keep pace with me, he staggered on the path of Truth; my other brothers did not keep company with me, they forsook me, yielded themselves to weakness, they allowed temptations to get the better of them, they did not keep pace with me, but here is this dog, he alone comes up with me. Here is the dog. He shares my pains, he shares my struggles, he shares my fights, he partakes of my anguish, he labours with me. Here is this dog. If this dog divides with me my difficulties, my hard fights and struggles, why should not he enjoy my Paradise or Heaven? I will never go to your Paradise or Heaven if you do not make this dog share equally with me that Paradise or Heaven. I have no use for your Paradise if you do not let in this dog with me." There the story says that Truth personified or God said once more to King Yudhishthira, "Please do not ask this favour of me, do not ask me to take this dog with" But King Yudhishthira said "Away, ye Brahma, you are no Truth or God personified. You may be some devil, you cannot be God or Truth, because if you be Truth, then why should you allow any injustice in your presence? Don't you mark that if you give me the exclusive enjoyment of Heaven, and don't allow the dog to share it, my happiness, then you are unjust to the dog which shared my troubles? This is not worthy of God or Truth personified." The story says that on this, Truth personified or God appeared in His true colours, and that very dog was immediately found to be no longer the dog but to be in full glory the Lord Almighty Himself. That king was being examined and tried, and in the final examination, in the final trial, he came out successful.

This is the way you have to tread the path of Truth. Even if your dearest and nearest companions, those who are next of kin to you, do not keep with you on the path of righteousness, do not look upon them as your friends, and if a dog accompanies you on the path of righteousness, that dog should be the nearest and dearest being to you. Thus make your friends on the principle of favouring your righteousness, select no friend on the principle of favouring your evil nature. If you select your companions on the principle that they enjoy the same kind of evil propensities that you do, suffering, anguish and excruciating pain will be your lot.

MORAL: The true companion is one who accompanies you on the path of Truth right up to the goal, and not he who may be dearest and nearest of kith and kin but does not do so.

Standing by Truth (Rama and Truth)

It is said in one of the Hindu scriptures that Sri Rama Chandra, the greatest hero of the world, or at least of India, when he went to search out Truth, to discover or regain Truth, all nature offered him her services. It is said that monkeys formed his army, and squirrels helped him building a bridge over the gulf. It is said that even geese came up on his side to assist him in overcoming his foes. It is said that the stones offered him their services. The stones forgot their nature; the stones, when thrown into water, instead of sinking, said, "We shall float in order that the cause of Truth be advanced."

It is said that air, the atmosphere, was on his side, fire helped him, winds and storms were on his side. There is a saying in the English language that the wind and wave are always for the brave.

All Nature stands up on your side when you persist, when you overcome the primitive seeming difficulties. If you overcome the struggles or temptations in the beginning, the whole of Nature must serve you. Persist in standing by the Truth, and you will find that you live in no ordinary world. The world will be a world of miracles for you. You will be the master of the Universe, the husband of the whole world, if you persist by the Truth.

MORAL: The whole Nature is bound to co-operate with and serve one -who stands by Truth.

Majority no Proof of Truth (A Man in Parliament)

A man in the house of Parliament in London, who was a great orator, was hooted. Do you know what words lie spoke afterwards? He said, "What, if you have the majority on your side." He spoke to the opposite party, "Opinions ought to be weighed, they ought not to be counted." Majority is no proof of truth.

MORAL: Majority does not always consist of wise men; hence it is no proof of Truth.

Connection with the Eternal (Newly Married Bride)

There was a newly married girl in India. She was sitting with her sister-in-law and with her mother-in-law. They were having a very pleasant chat. The husband of this new bride was away from the scene. He was absent.

Then the sisters-in-law of this new bride passed some remarks against the husband of this girl. They made some statements which depreciated the husband of the new bride. Sweetly she said, "For your sake, for your sake, you who have to live with him for a few days only, you that have to pass with him a week or so, for your sake I will not play the child's part to break with the bridegroom with whom I have to spend my whole life."

Similarly, all these worldly ties, worldly relations, worldly connections will not last for ever. You have to spend your whole life with the true Self, that is Eternal, you cannot break with it. For the sake of this fleeting present, you should not break with the true Self.

MORAL: Our connection with the Eternal or the true Self should not be broken for the sake of the fleeting or the worldly things.

CHAPTER TWENTY-SIX

Vedanta

Vedanta in Everyday Life (When Ram was a Boy)

When Rama was a boy, he was one day walking along the roadside reading a book. A gentleman came along and cracked a joke with Rama. He said, "What are you doing here? This is not a school, young sir, throw aside your book." Rama replied: "The whole world is my school." Now does Rama realize what your school should be.

If Vedanta is not practised in everyday life, what is the use of it? Vedanta, printed in books and placed on shelves to be eaten up by worms, won't do. You must live it.

MORAL: Vedanta in theory alone is no good. It must be lived in everyday life.

The Way to Learn (Yudhishthira)

There was a man, Yudhishthira. He was the heir-apparent to the throne of India. There is a story related of his boyhood.

He was reading in school with his younger brothers. There were many brothers. One day the Head master, the Examiner came to examine those boys. This Head master came and asked them how far they had advanced, and the younger boys laid before the master all they had read. When the time came for this boy, the master put the usual question to him, and the boy opened the Primer and said in a cheerful happy tone, not the least ashamed, "I have learned the alphabets, and I have learned the first sentence." The master said, "Is that all?" and pointed to the first sentence. The master said, "Have you learnt anything more?" The boy said hesitatingly, "The second sentence." The prince, the dear little boy, said this cheerfully and happily; but the master was exasperated, because he expected him to apply himself to possess, high knowledge and great wisdom, and not to be snail-slow. The master asked him to stand before him. He was very cruel and thought "To spare the rod was to spoil the child." You know professors think that to break rods upon children moulds them, and the more rods they break the better moulded are the children. That condition of mind made the master very cruel, and he began to beat and thrash the boy, but the latter kept his calm: he was cheerful as before, he was as happy as ever. The master beat him a few minutes, but found no signs of anger or anxiety, fear or sorrow on the beautiful face of the prince, and his heart relented, even as stones might have melted, so to say, looking at the boy's face. The master reflected and said to himself, "What is the master? How is it that this boy who by one word can get me dismissed, who is one day to rule me and the whole of India, is so calm? I am so severe on him and he does not resent it in the least. 1 was harsh to the other brothers and they resented it, and one of them took hold of the rod and beat me; but this boy preserves his temper. He is cheerful, calm and quiet." Then the eyes of the master fell upon the first sentence which the boy had learned.

You know, in India, the Primers do not begin with dogs and cats.. In India Primers, begin with beautiful advice. Now, the first sentence after the Alphabets in the book in Sanskrit was "Never lose your temper, never get annoyed, have no anger." The second sentence was "Speak the truth, ever speak the truth." The boy had said he had learned the first sentence, but he hesitatingly said he had learned the second sentence. Now, the master's eyes fell upon the first sentence, "Lose not your temper, have no anger," and then he looked at the face of the boy. One eye of the master was on the boy and the other eye on the sentence in the book; then of the meaning of the sentence flashed through his mind. Then the face of the boy told the meaning of the sentence. The face of the boy was the incarnation of the sentence written in the book, "Never get angry." The calm, placid, bright, happy, cheerful and beautiful face of the boy brought home to the heart of the teacher the meaning of the sentence, "Never get angry."

Heretofore the master had transgressed; he had learned the substance of the sentence originally through the lips. Now did the master know that this sentence was not to be talked out like parrots, but could be lived, could be carried into effect, and then he realized how little was his own knowledge. He felt ashamed within himself that he had not learned the first sentence when a boy had really learned it. You know the boy, by learning a thing, did not mean learning it by rote; but by learning he meant practicing into effect, realizing, feeling, and becoming one with it. This was the meaning of learning to this boy.

No sooner did the master understand the meaning of learning than the stick fell from his hand; his heart relented. He took up the boy and clasped him in his arms and kissed his forehead; and then he felt his own ignorance and his lack of practical knowledge to such an extent that he felt ashamed of himself, and he patted the boy on the back and said, "Son, dear Prince, I congratulate you on having truly learned at least one sentence. I congratulate you that you have properly learnt at least one sentence of the Scriptures. Ah! I do not know even one sentence, I have not learnt even one sentence; for I get angry and I lose my temper: anything will put me in temper. O my son, pity me, you know more, you are more learned then I." When the master spoke thus, when he cheered the boy, the boy said, "Father, father, I have not yet learnt this sentence thoroughly because I felt some signs of anger and resentment in my heart. When I received a five minutes thrashing,

I felt signs of anger in my heart." Thus was he speaking the meaning of the second sentence; thus was he speaking out the truth, when there was every temptation to conceal his inner weakness, on an occasion when he was being flattered. To reveal by his own acts the weakness, lurking in his soul, the child proved that he had learned the second sentence also, "Speak the truth." By his acts, through his life, he lived the second sentence.

This is the way to read things; this is the way to learn Vedanta, live Vedanta, practice Vedanta.

MORAL: The way to learn a thing is not to commit to memory only but to put it into practice in daily life.

Model of a Vedantic Life (The Royal Resignation)

In a certain country there was a very noble, scholarly and majestic prince who had just inherited a throne. Years and years passed on, yet he did not marry. The people were very anxious that he should marry, as they wished for an heir to the throne. They persistently urged him to choose a wife, and he finally consented to do so, provided they would allow him to make his own selection. You know in that country, no freedom was allowed to any one even in the matter of love and marriage. They were bound by custom. He wanted to marry according to his own wishes. His subjects, thinking if they did not consent to his will, he would remain a bachelor all his days, thought it advisable to let him make his choice. He ordered his courtiers and officers to make preparations for a great wedding festival. Everything was prepared in a most royal, and magnificent style.

With great éclat on the appointed day the army was ready. Everyone was arrayed in his most gorgeous clothes, and drove in the best carriages and victorias.

This king rode in the middle, one half of the army on one side and the other half on the other. They went on according to the king's orders, not following any particular road. They went through very deep, dense forests. They said among themselves, "What is the king going to do, is he going to marry a lake, or stock and stones?" They were astonished. They went on and finally came to a place in the forests where there was a small hut, and near that hut was a beautiful, clear crystal lake. On the banks of the lake they found beautiful, magnificent, natural orchards, and from the branches of one of the trees there hung a hammock or trapeze, on which an old man was lying. They said, "Is he going to marry that old man?" One half of the army passed on and when the king's elephant reached that place, the king ordered halt. Immediately there appeared on the scene a beautiful, fair; lovely maiden who was gently swinging the hammock on which her father was lying.

The king, before he came to the throne, had been to that forest many times. He had watched the girl and always found her most dutiful; she cared for her father most faithfully, brought water and bathed

him, and fed him She did all sorts of rubbing and scrubbing work. But while doing this work she was always happy, bright, merry and cheerful as a caroling robin. This happy disposition of the girl impressed itself on the king and he vowed to marry her if he ever married. The girl gazed in amazement at all this grand array, little thinking that the man who rode on horseback by their door many times before was this king. She asked her father what this magnificent spectacle meant. Her father told her that it was a bridegroom going to a distant country for a princess-to be his wife. Now the king alighted from his elephant, went up to the old man and fell at his feet as in the oriental custom. The old man said to him, "My son, what do you want?" The face of the king brightened. He said, "I want you to make me your son-in-law." The old man's heart leaped with joy. His ecstasy knew no bounds. He said, "You are mistaken, king, you are mistaken. How could you wish to marry the daughter of a poor mendicant? We are poor, very poor."

The king said he loved no one as much as that lovely girl. The father said if such was the case then she was his. This parent was a Vedantic monk and he had imparted his knowledge to his daughter. He now told the king that he had no dowry to give his child, the only thing he could give was his blessing. The king then presented his bride with all sorts of beautiful clothes which he requested her to put on. She accordingly did so. But the girl did not go to the king empty handed. She had a dowry. What was it? Into one of the caskets, the king gave her, in which was to be kept jewels, she put in her dress of rags which she wore while living with her father. Now the old man was left alone, one servant was left at his disposal. He wanted nothing else from the king.

The king took his bride to the palace. At first his courtiers did not like her as she was low born. These noblemen and aristocrats wished the king to marry their daughters or nieces, and here they were all superseded by this low girl. They were very jealous of her. How could they pay homage to this low born girl. But the new queen by her sweet temper, gentle ways, and lovely manners charmed them all. By and by they all began to love her very dearly. She was always calm and tranquil, never disturbed or ruffled about anything, no matter what the circumstances might be. After a year or so a daughter was born to the queen. A beautiful baby girl. How happy were the king and queen! When the child was three or four years old, the king came to the queen and told her that there was going to be a revolt in the kingdom, a mutiny which was most undesirable. The queen inquired the reason of such a condition of affairs. Her husband replied that the officers and ministers were jealous when he married her, and now they could not bear the idea of this girl inheriting the throne, being low born on her mother's side. They wanted their king to adopt the child of one of the prime ministers. But the king said that if they did so, when the girl grew up in all probability there would be an antipathy between them. So in order to obviate that result he had been meditating and meditating, and had finally arrived at the conclusion that the best thing to be done was to have the girl killed. Then Griselda, which was the name of the queen, made this most characteristic answer to the king. This answer typifies her conduct and duty towards the king. She said, "You know from the day I came, I had no desire of my own to enjoy this throne with you. I have made my will and desire entirely yours. My individuality and personality is merged in yours and it is kept up only so far as it may be of service to you and not to obstruct your purpose. If it is your will that the daughter be taken away, let her be taken away. I have never called the daughter mine in my heart of hearts." The daughter was taken away at the dead of night and after a few hours the king returned and said the child had been given away to the executicners to be slaughtered. The queen was collected, calm, quiet, and cheerful as if nothing had happened. This is Vedanta. Never be disturbed by any outward circumstances.

The king now said that everyone would be pleased. After a year or so, there was a little boy born. This child was loved by everyone. The boy grew up to the age of five or six years, then, again there was uproar. The king said, "As circumstances are at present, it is advisable to kill this child also. If the child remains, there will be a great civil war; so to preserve the national peace the child ought to be killed." The queen was again smiling and cheerful, and said, "my real Self is the whole nation, I have nothing personal, I am like the Sun, I give away. Like the Sun we do not receive, we would give away. When we have no clingings and are not attached to anything, what can happen that will mar our happiness? The Sun- goes on giving away all the time, but still constantly shining. That boy was also taken away. After a few years the third child was born, and when about three or four years of age, was taken away in the same way.

Now, how did the queen keep up her spirits? Since the day she came to the palace she would retire into a solitary chamber wherein she had preserved her old rags- That was her solitary chamber, and there stripping herself of all her beautiful clothes she used to put on those old rags, and in this simple dress she would realize. 'That I am.' And in the mendicant's dress she would feel and realise her Divinity. Shakespeare says, "Uneasy lies the head that wears the crown," She knew in her heart of hearts that she was the woman caroling and singing on the banks of the lake. Here she was confined in the palace of the king and. bereaved of her freedom and liberty, but she did not make herself miserable, she did not allow herself to get entangled in affairs. She was not attached to this or that; her real Self was continually held aloof from the surrounding circumstances. She was continually merged in Divinity. In this way she purified herself by casting aside all attachments and clingings, no responsibilities she had, she was bound to nobody, no duties. Thus it is, whenever you are in dumps or in blues, strip yourself of all attachments, connections, desires, wants and needs. Free you are.

In this way the queen always kept herself up during her stay in the king's palace.

One night the king approached her and said that it would not do for them to go on killing their sons and daughters all the time, and he did not like the idea of adopting a child. So after thinking the matter over he had come to the conclusion that it was best for him to marry again, and thus peace would be restored. The queen consented willingly because she never derived her happiness from the king, her happiness came from her own Self, and not from others. She got all the pleasure from the God within, not from husband, father and children. The king was amazed at her happiness and asked her what she would like to do. She told him his will was her will. He told her that if she remained, the harmony might be broken, and it was best for her to go away. Immediately, the beautiful clothes were taken off and the old rags, the mendicant's dress, was put on again, and she left the palace. She was cheerful and happy and went to her. father, who was also as happy as ever. The servant of the king, who was left with the old man, was immediately sent back to the king.

One day the king passed the hut with the intention of sympathizing with her, but when he saw her cheerful, smiling countenance, he saw that there was no occasion to do so. He then asked her if she would come and receive the new bride. She willingly consented. She planned and arranged everything in such a lovely way that the magistrates and their wives were astonished at the beauty of the arrangements. According to the arrangements made, the bride had to come to the king with a great army and a magnificent dowry of gold and jewels. She came with great pomp and glory and was received most loyally by Griselda and the other ladies of the king's court at his request. When Griselda saw the new bride, she loved, kissed, and embraced her as if she had been her mother. The ladies with Griselda were astonished at the beauty of the new bride, but were more astonished at the moral beauty of the old queen. The new bride brought with her two little brothers. According to the custom of that country, the noble ladies and aristocratic chiefs had to enter the palace and enjoy a great feast. Griselda presided over the ceremonies. When the people saw the calm, peaceful, placid manners of their former queen, their hearts relented and tears came into their eyes. She was to leave and retire to the hut of her father after the ceremonies. But as they went on eating, all their feelings of sorrow for the queen soon vanished and they forgot all about her. But when she was bidding them good-bye and telling the king if he ever needed her again not to hesitate to call on her, the hearts of the gentle ladies relented and they burst into tears. They repented of their hard heartedness. They said, "You are not the daughter of a mendicant, you are the daughter of God." Then they told how this queen had permitted her children to be murdered in order to preserve the peace of the country, and the new queen also began to weep. She said, "Your daughter and your sons were murdered and I have come here wading through a stream of blood.' Then they began to rebuke the king. All were present, the new bride and the queen who was about to depart. The king then rose up and said, "O officers, magistrates, and noble ladies, you are all weeping and crying with the exception of Griselda alone. I am also weeping with feelings of mingled pleasure and pain. I do not blame you, O people, ye are my children; my eyes are filled with tears, but they are not tears of sorrow but tears of joy and gladness. Let your tears be also tears of joy." Then turning to Griselda he said, "Be of good cheer and happy, happy you are alone in the whole king-dom." Now it seems that the new bride was the daughter, of the king of the adjoining country, but she was his daughter by adoption only,, and also her little brothers. These children as orphans fell in the way of that king, and he on account of their beauty loved them and reared them as his own. These three children were the children of the king and Griselda, as the executioners to whom they were given to be killed did not have the heart to do the deed and took them to this country. Now all these things were explained to the people. And when the king of this adjoining country saw these beautiful children in the hands of those dark coloured executioners, he thought they must be children of some king and he reared them as his own. Of course the king could not marry his own daughter, so to the happiness of all, Griselda remained the queen and her children inherited the throne. So you see, God is always very grateful. He pays His debts with interest.

Let such be the royal resignation of things in Love by every married woman. In India, such are called Pativrata and Patnivrata which means that woman is to live in her husband and her husband is to live in his wife. The woman is to see God in her husband. She is to give away her body and mind to her husband, and her husband is to give himself to God in her. There is nothing personal, nothing selfish.

MORAL: A life without clingings or attachments to anything and full of happiness and joy under all circumstances is Vedantic life.

True Vedanta (Arjuna and Krishna)

A great warrior, Arjuna, who was the hero of the battle of Kurukshetra, was about to give up his worldly action; his duty required him to fight, and he was going to give that up, he was going to retire, he was going to become an ascetic, he was about to do that, and there came Krishna. Krishna preached Vedanta to .Arjuna, and it is this Vedanta properly understood, which braced up the courage of Arjuna, which infused energy and power into him, which breathed a spirit of life and activity into him, and he rose up like a mighty lion, and there he was the mighty hero.

Vedanta fills you with energy and strength, and not weakness. In the Vedas there is a passage which says that this Atma, this Truth can never, never be achieved by a man who is weak. It is not for the weak; the weak hearted, the weak of body, the weak in spirit can never acquire it.

MORAL: True Vedanta fills one with energy and power, and not weakness.

CHAPTER TWENTY-SEVEN

Work

Hell turned into Heaven (Scientists in the Lowest Hell)

There was a priest, a Christian priest in England. He read about the death of some great men, great scientists, Darwin and Huxley. He began to think in his mind whether they had gone to hell or heaven. He was thinking and thinking and thinking. He said to himself: "These people did not commit any crimes, and yet they did not believe in the Bible, in Christ, they were no Christians in the proper sense of the word. They must have gone to hell." But he could not make up his own mind to think that way. He thought: "They were good men, they had done some good work in the world, they did not deserve hell. Where did they go." He fell and dreamt a most wonderful dream. He saw that he himself had died and was taken to the highest Heaven. He found there all the people whom he had expected to find; he found all his Christian brothers who used to come to his Church. He found them all there. Then he asked about these scientists, Huxley and Darwin. The door keeper of Heaven or some other steward told him that these people were in the lowest hell.

Now, this priest asked if he could be allowed to go to the lowest hell on a flying visit simply to see them, and there to go and preach to them the Holy Bible and show them that they had perpetrated a most heinous crime in not believing in the letter of Bible. After some fuss and trouble the steward yielded, and consented to get for him a ticket to the lowest hell. You will be astonished that even in hell and heaven, you come and go in your railway-cars, but so it was. The man had been bred in the midst of surroundings overflowing with railway traffic and telegraphs. So in his thoughts, in his dreams, it is no wonder if the railway got mixed up with hell and heaven.

Well, this priest got a first-class. The railway train went on and on and on. There were some intermediate stations because he came from the highest Heaven to the lowest hell. He stopped at the intermediate stations, and found that there was a change for the worse as he went on down and down. When he came to the lowest hell but one, he could not keep himself in senses. Such a stench was coming out that he had to put all his napkins and handkerchiefs before his nose and yet he could not but be senseless, he had to fall into a swoon. There were so many crying voices, weeping and crying and gnashing of teeth down there; he could not bear it. He could not keep his eyes open because of those sights. He repented of his persistence to come to see the lowest hell.

In a few minutes the people on the railway platform were crying, "The lowest hell, the lowest hell", for the convenience of the passengers. There was engraved on the station, "The lowest hell." But the priest was astonished. He asked everybody, "This cannot be the lowest hell? It must be about the highest Heaven. No, no, it cannot be. This is not the lowest hell; this is not the lowest hell; it must be heaven." The railway guard or conductor told him that this was the place and there came a man who said, "Just get down, sir; this is your destination."

He got down, poor fellow, but was surprised. He expected the lowest hell to be worse than the lowest hell but one. But this well nigh rivaled his highest Heaven. He got out of the railway station and found there magnificent gardens, sweet scented flowers, and fragrant breezes blowing into his face. He met one tall gentleman. He asked his name, and he thought he saw in him something or somebody whom he had been before. The man was walking before him, and he followed after him, and when the man called out, the priest was delighted, they shook hands, and the priest recognized him. Who was he? That was Huxley. He asked, "What is it, is it the lowest hell?" Huxley said, "Yes, no doubt it is." And he said, "I came to preach to you, but first of oil answer how it is that 1 find such a strange phenomenon before me?" Huxley said, "you were not wrong in your expectations for the worst. Indeed, when I came here, it was the worst possible hell in the universe. It was the most undesirable that could be conceived." And here he pointed out certain places: "There were dirty ditches." and he pointed out another spot: "There was burning iron." And he pointed out another spot; "There was hot sand"; and "There was steaming dung."

He said, "We were first of all placed in the most dirty ditches, but while there, with our hands we were throwing water to the next adjoining hot burning iron; and we went on with that work, throwing that dirty water out of the ditches on the hot burning iron that was on the banks. Then the stewards of the lowest hell had to take us to those places where there was a burning liquid iron, but by the time they took us to that place, most of the iron had become wholly cooled, most of the iron could be handled, and still a great deal of iron was in its liquid burning condition, fiery condition. Then, with the aid of the iron which had cooled down and holding it before the fire, we succeeded in making some machines and some other instruments."

"After that we were to be taken to the third place where was the dung. We were taken to that place, and with the help of our instruments, iron spades and machines, we began the digging work. After that we were taken to the other kind of soil, and there by means of machines and other instruments that we had got then ready, we threw some of these things into the soil to which we were taken; that served as manure, and thus we succeeded, by and by, in turning this [hell into a veritable heaven."

Now the thing is that in that lowest hell, there were present all the materials which, being simply placed in their right positions might make the highest Heaven. So it is, Vedanta says, in you is present the Divine God, and in you is present the worthless body; but you have misplaced the things. You have done things upside down; in a topsy-turvy way you have put them. You have put the cart before the horse; and that is how you make this world a hell for you. You have simply not to destroy anything, not to dig up anything. This ambitious spirit of yours, or this selfishness of yours or this angry nature of yours or any other sin of yours, which is just like a hell or heaven, you cannot destroy, but you can re-arrange. No energy can be destroyed, but you can re-arrange this hell and convert it into the highest Heaven.

MORAL:—Even Hell can be turned into Heaven by the right application of energy and proper arrangement of materials.

Work for Work's Sake (A Pond and a River)

There was a quarrel between a pond and a river. The pond addressed the river thus: "O river, you are very foolish to give all your water and all your wealth to the ocean; do not squander your water and wealth on the ocean.

The ocean is ungrateful, the ocean needs is not. If you go on pouring into the ocean all your accumulated treasures, the ocean will remain as salty as it is today, the ocean will remain as bitter as it is today, the brine of the sea will not be altered. "Do not throw pearls before swine. Keep all your treasures with you." This was worldly wisdom. Here was the river told to consider the end, to care for the result, and regard the consequences. But the river was a Vedantin. After hearing this worldly wisdom, the river replied, "No, the consequence and the result are nothing to me, failure and success, are nothing to me; I must work because I love work; I must work for its own sake. To work is my aim, to keep in activity is my life. My Soul, my real Atman is energy itself. I must work." The river went on working, the river went on pouring into the ocean millions upon millions of gallons of water. The miserly economic pond became dry in three or four months; it became putrid, stagnant, full of festering filth; but the river remained fresh and pure, its perennial springs did not dry up. Silently and slowly was water taken from the surface of the ocean to replenish the fountain heads of the river; monsoons and trade winds invisibly, silently and slowly carried water from the ocean and kept the river source fresh forever.

Just so Vedanta requires you not to follow the sophistic policy of the pond. It is the small, selfish pond that cares for the result. "What will become of me and my work." Let your work be for work's sake; you must work. In your work should your goal be, and thus Vedanta frees you from fretting and worrying desires. This is the meaning of freedom from desires which Vedanta preaches. Worry not about the consequences, expect nothing from the people, bother not about favourable reviews of your work or severe criticism thereon. Care not whether what you are doing will tell or not; think nothing of that. Do the work for its own sake.

This way you have to free yourself from desire; you have not to free yourself from work, you have to free yourself from yearning restlessness. This way how splendid does your work become! The most effective and best cure for all sorts of distracting passions and temptations is work. But that would be only a negative recommendation. The positive joy that accompanies faithful work is a spark of Salvation, unconscious Self-realization. It keeps you pure, untainted and one with Divinity. This happiness is the highest and surest reward of work. Corrupt not this health-bringing, heavenly treasure by setting your heart on selfish motives for work.

Sordid ambitions, and petty hankerings retard rather than accelerate our progress; outward and concrete allurements are detrimental rather than beneficial to our efficiency of labour. No prize or appreciation can be more benign or salubrious than the immediate joy which accompanies earnest action. Follow then action to realize the renunciation, religion or worship it involves and be not led by the childish frivolities it promises. Feel no responsibility, ask for no reward. Mow here should your goal be.

MORAL: Work is its own reward, for work done for work's sake brings positive joy.

Reflex Action (A Retired Veteran)

There was a man, a retired veteran, who had been accustomed to military discipline and drill to such a degree that the performance of those feats of drill were automatic for him. This man was walking through the street with a heavy pitcher of milk, or some other eatable in his hands. He carried a heavy pitcher on his hands or shoulders. There appeared a practical joker in the streets; he wanted that all this milk or other delicious food should be spilled into the gutter. This man stood aside and just ejaculated, "Attention!" You know when we say, "Attention", the hands ought to be dropped down. As soon as this veteran soldier heard that word "Attention," his hands dropped down and all the milk and other things that he had, fell into the gutter. All the by-standers and shopkeepers in the street had a very pleasant time of it.

You will see that when he heard the word "Attention," he dropped down his hands, but Psychology says, "He did no work; that is what is called a reflex action. Reflex action is no work; because the mind is not engaged."

MORAL: Reflex or involuntary action is in reality no work, as it is not done by the mind, and, therefore, produces no reaction (Karma).

Half-hearted Action (Two Boys of different Tastes)

Two boys met each other in the street. They were friends. One of them urged his fellow to go with him to a church, and there hear a sermon, or say some music, or something. The other pleaded play. Now, what was the use of wasting time in going to church and hearing a monotonous sermon? They had better play. They did not come to an agreement, so one went to the church and the other went out seeking play. But when the boy who went to church found himself face to face with the preacher, he could not understand, or enjoy the sermon at all, he repented of his having gone to the church. Then he began to think of the play-ground. He began to think of the boy who was being joined by his friends at play. Two long hours he spent in the church, but all the time his mind was in the play-ground. Now, the boy who went to the play-ground did not find congenial company, did not find any other boy who might come and play with him. He found himself alone, and he felt very lonely. He thought of the church, and then he thought within himself that it was too late to go to the church. He remained in the play ground, but his mind was all the time in the church, he was all the while in the church. After two hours, those two boys met each other again in the streets. One said he was sorry for not going to church, and the other said he was sorry for not going to the play-ground.

This is what is happening everywhere with men. If your mind or attention is not occupied with what you have got in your hands, then you are not working; there you are idling away your time. In some work our mind is thoroughly occupied, while doing some other work, our mind is half occupied. In work where your mind is half occupied, you are doing half work; the other half of your attention you might utilize; and when your attention is entirely idle, you might utilize your full attention. Your minds are not where your bodies are. By utilizing your mind's attention you may increase your lives. You can do more work in one day than you could do by not utilizing the unengaged attention.

MORAL: Half hearted action is incomplete work. It produces unsatisfactory results and wastes time.

CHAPTER TWENTY-EIGHT

Faith in God

Fight between gods & demons

Once there was a fight between the gods and the demons. The gods were lesser in strength than the demons.

Vrihashpati, the Lord of gods, preached to the demons the philosophy of 'charvak', the principles of which are to eat, drink and be merry and not to care for anything that is metaphysical. As the story goes, gods won the war. Why? Because gods had faith in their good cause and in God.

The nation, which has no faith in God, Truth or goodness, can never be victorious.

Spear with which Jesus was touched

Rama now tells you something about the Christian crusade in which Richard I, King of England had also participated. When the Christians were being defeated in Jerusalem, an old warrior spoke out, "I have seen Gabriel. He told me that just here, where we are fighting, there lies buried the spade with which Lord Jesus was touched. If we could find it out, we are sure to win the battle". On hearing this, all of them began digging the ground, and, after exhaustion of considerable time and energy, they succeeded in digging out an old and rusted spear. Taking that spear to be the one connected with Lord Jesus, they resumed the fight, heart and soul, and won the victory in the end. The old man confessed at the time of his death to the priest that he had concocted the story, concerning the spear, in order to achieve victory in the holy war of Jerusalem. Whatever the case may be, the fact remains that the story worked wonders due to faith alone.

That portion of the story which infused the hearts of men with conviction was „faith" and the story itself is 'creed'. The strength of conviction is life.

Lord Krishna's grace over Kubja

It was of vital importance for Lord Krishna to kill the King Kansa, in order to acquire His inherent right. But Kansa could be killed only when Kubja was straightened. Madam Kubja was going to Kansa to serve him cosmetics, lavender, scent etc., and she met Lord Krishna on her way to Kansa. She was not only physically crooked, but her talk with Lord Krishna was also unpleasant. She needed to be tackled properly. Faith (Kubja) must be set right. She was, therefore, set right with only one bang of blow. On losing her hunch, she fell on the feet of the Lord to express her feelings of gratitude. She abandoned her path to Kansa and surrendered herself to Lord Krishna. It is only after winning over Kubja that Lord Krishna could gain victory over Kansa and recapture His birth right of Real Freedom. This is only an allegory, a symbolic narration. Let it be explained further. In order to capture the Real Kingdom, you have first to come out of the thick and deceptive forest of senses. It is only then that you can gain victory over the ego, the King Kansa; otherwise this ego will never let you have rest or peace even for a moment. But, mind you, this ego (Kansa) will be killed, only when Kubja, after being set right, has been won over to your side.

Now, what is Kubja? Kubja is Faith. Generally the common man, due to his ignorance, resorts to perverted Faith to serve his ego, day and night. 'This is my house, this is my wealth, this is my wife or son, this is my body or mind etc., etc.' In this way the perverted Faith (Kubja) goes on nourishing the ego (Kansa), all the time. Unless this evil eyed and misguided Kubja is straightened and put on the right path, so as to be able to associate with Krishna (Atman), neither Kansa (ego) can be vanquished nor can you gain the Real Kingdom of Heaven. Kick this Kubja with dispassion and hammer a blow of awareness to this perverted faith (Kubja) and straighten the hunch in her back to turn her towards Krishna (Atman).

The astounding work of Shri Sankaracharya

Adi-guru Shri Sankaracharya lived for only thirty years, yet in this short period he wrote six hundred fifty books and made several rounds of India, even though there was no railway, motor, bus or any other fast means of conveyance. He travelled all through on foot. How could he accomplish all this stupendous task within a short life of only thirty three years? What was at the back of his Unbelievable power to work?

It was because of his purity of heart, disciplined mind, sincerity of purpose, strong will-force based on his unshakable faith in God. All these factors combined to make his life fu)l of peace, tranquility and serenity which helped him to devote himself with one-pointed concentration to accomplish these unbelievable tasks in such a short span of life.

The examples of Prophet Mohammad and others in achieving great tasks through unflinching faith

Look at Prophet Mohammad. He began his real work only after the age of forty years, yet he created a flaming sensation in the whole world. The black particles of sand of Arabia, turned, as if, into the particles of gunpowder which exploded the myth of the old religions of the then known world which was later infused by the prophet with a new strength to develop a living faith in one God.

In America, too, there were several remarkable poets who wrote a number of valuable books within thirty two or three years of their age. When even one man can do a thing why not you? You can also achieve the same success, if you could only know how to do it. The secret of their success was their Peace of mind and resolute will to find time to do it. But alas, you say that you have no time. Are you really short of time? No. You have ample time at your disposal, but you have no will to utilise it. Where there is a wall, there is a way. But you do not want to assert your will due to your laziness and indolence. What a shame!

Story of Hercules

There is a story in Greek mythology about the fight of Hercules with someone. Hercules defeated his opponent and pinned him to the ground. But it was surprising to note that no sooner he fell to the ground than he picked up his original strength to renew his fight, because the earth was his mother. It so happened a number of times. As soon as he was made to fall on the ground, he gained strength and stood up to fight again. He derived the renewed strength from his mother earth. The lesson of this story is that the main source of strength in this world is God. The Divine nature, God or Rama, is the basic substratum of everything in this universe. He is energy personified. He is also, so to say, the mother of every one of us. Accordingly, they, who remain in mental touch with Him, never suffer from want of energy, power-or strength.

You will feel strength and vigour and be fresh and energetic, like the opponent of Hercules, provided you keep contact with God, Almighty, the Source of Power and Energy.

If you want to be triumphant in your daily activities, if you want to be victorious against the struggles in life and if you want to come out as strong and invincible in the world, have a living, practical and unflinching faith in Almighty God in order to draw inspiration and strength from Him.

The Example of Duldul

At Lahore and even at Lucknow the Shia community of the Muslims take out in a procession a decorated horse, called „Duldul". The Shia devotees respect this horse and offer flowers on it (taking it to be the horse of Imam, the grandson of Prophet Mohammad). No worldly man rides on it. So, too, this ego of yours may be taken as your Duldul. Let only God ride on it to control it. They, who do so, are. worshipped in the world. If you really keep within you the true faith in God, with strong determination and firm resolve, you will move not only the world but will inspire thousands of worlds like this in an effortless way.

An English boy with strong faith in his love

A boy in England was taking his examination and while writing the answers of the question paper, he would occasionally take out a paper from his pocket and look at it. The invigilator suspected something foul. He went to the boy and asked him to show the paper in his pocket. The boy explained to him that there was nothing wrong. But on insistence of the invigilator, he showed to him that paper. It was only a photo of a girl. The boy said, 'This photo is that of my girl friend. I have come to take this examination only on account of her. She had promised to marry me, only if I could pass this examination. When I am tired of writing the answers or when I feel discomfort or uneasiness, I look at the photo of my sweet beloved. All my fatigue, then, disappears and I feel refreshed. Not only this, all the forgotten answers become vivid to my memory."

Similarly, in the examination of this world, if you keep the remembrance of God, your Beloved, who is already within you, you will ever foe successful with distinction, without losing your peace of mind.

CHAPTER TWENTY-NINE

Love for God

The Sweeper and the fallen pearls of the queen

There was a sweeper who used to sweep and dust the palace of a certain king. Often, she got pieces of gold or pearls, while sweeping. She would pick up those fallen pearls. She had a son who had been out of the country, since his child-hood. After about fifteen years, he returned home. He found that his mother had accumulated precious stones in her hut. He enquired of his mother the source of those precious articles. The sweeper replied, "I am in the employ of the local king. This accumulation consists of the pearls fallen from his queen."

The son pondered, "If the pearls of the queen are so beautiful, how much more beautiful the queen herself would be". He was lost in love for the queen and requested his mother to show him the queen.

These stars, the moon, the sun, the shining rivers and the worldly beauties are but the fallen pearls, the beauty of that Reality. If such is the attraction of the fallen pearls, the beauty of that Reality must simply be exquisite. It can better be realised than described.

It is He who distributed the beautiful flowering plants in this garden of the world, and decorated it with the sun, the moon and the stars.

When girls are married, their relations throw over the palanquin silver and gold coins in charity for the welfare of the bride sitting inside the palanquin.

O, Worldly Souls! You may pick up these coins. Others may pick up the pearls. Rama does not possess even a piece of cloth to keep them in, nor does he need them. He is in love with the Bride and only wants to become one with Her, that Beloved, God.

The Story of Guru Nanak

In the Punjab, there was a saint called Nanak. Like others, he was also of the higher stage. Once, when he was employed in a ware-house, a few cheats came to him in the guise of saints. He started giving them grains, after filling the measure repeatedly. He was orally counting the measures, but in his heart of hearts, he was absorbed in some other thoughts. A poet says,

"I have been admitted to the school of love just today. Although alphabet is uttered outwardly from the tongue, my heart is burning with love for Him," Absorption in spiritualism was permeating Nanak's thoughts, even through his worldly actions. Seemingly, he was counting the numbers, but this counting had no impression on his heart. By the time he counted thirteen (terah), he had forgotten everything. (In Hindustani the word „Terah" also means thine.) He entered into a state of spiritual forgetfulness or complete absorption in God. From the word (Terah) "thirteen" he was reminded of the idea that he was His. "I am Thine. I am Thine, Thine, I am Thine, Thine". Completely lost in his thoughts, he went on measuring the grains and repeating the word "Terah" (thirteen), (thine, thine) thereby meaning that "all is Thine" and; all are Thine". While repeating this he fell on the ground unconscious. Although his tongue stopped, yet it seemed, as if from every hair of his body the sound was coming out, Terah, Terah, "I am Thine. I am Thine". As a result, God changed the hearts of those cheats. They were themselves thieves but their hearts were stolen by God who is the Thief of all the thieves (because He steals away the hearts of His devotees). The cheats were so much affected that they also started saying, "Terah, Terah", "Thine, Thine". In this example of those thieves, the curtain was lifted, but only temporarily, through self-absorption.

The Story of a shepherd boy and Moses

Maulana, Room, has quoted the story of an illiterate but a sincere shepherd. He says that the shepherd was pray- . ing at the top of Mt. Tar us. "O Lord, be kind and have pity on me. Show me your face. I have brought for you milk of my goat of the best breed. I have myself prepared curd with which I will wash your hair. I will shampoo your feet. I have heard that you are One without a second; all alone, and All in all. I am afraid, when you might be walking, thorns and small pieces of stone might be pricking the sole of your feet. I wonder who must be taking them out. I will take them out one by one. O Lord, be kind unto me. I will fan you to cool your body. I will take the lice out of your hair and I will serve you with all sincerity. Only do me the favour of showing your beautiful face".

When the shepherd was thus praying and weeping, the prophet Moses reached there. On hearing his prayer, he was full of anger, struck him with the rod and said, "O thou infidel (Kafir)! What dost thou say? Thou insultest God and sayest unbecoming words against Him. Has God lice in his hair? Do the thorns and pieces of stone prick the sole of His feel?

O fool, thou canst meet God in this way".

The shepherd said in amazement, "Shall I not meet God"? Moses replied, ''No, Thy cursed soul shall not meet God". On hearing this, the shepherd was very much disappointed and he said, 'If it is so, I shall also not live". Hardly had the shepherd uttered these words, when a reverent old man appeared and, to console him, put his hands on his shoulders and said, "If God exists, as He really does exist, He must appear and protect you. If He does not extend His hand of protection even on such an occasion, He shall cut asunder His own hands". According to a Persian poet:

"Hundreds of lives should be sacrificed for him whose heart and tongue are one".

This sort of sincere love for God is religion. Religion is the back bone of the body, mind and intellect. It is the essence of the very existence of man. The merging of mind and intellect in Him is religion. Of whatever caste, creed or colour that shepherd might have been, and whatever might have been the condition of his body, mind and intellect, he did not consider God as something alien. He was all absorbed in God. This was his sincerity. Such was his firm faith in Him.

Moses said unto him, "O shepherd, thou art making fun of God". Rama says "It is they, who might possess greater knowledge of God, but little sincerity for Him, and whose hearts and words are not in unison, are really jeering at God, and not that shepherd."

To have some knowledge about God is one thing, but to have firm faith in Him and to feel His presence is quite a different thing. Truly speaking, that shepherd had faith in God and felt His presence.

CHAPTER THIRTY

Awareness

Lord Jesus' advice to Romans

Once, the Romans asked Lord Jesus, if they should pay tax to the King. This question was put to him with an ulterior motive. If Christ was to reply in negative, they would immediately inform the King that Jesus was preaching sedition. And, if he replied in affirmative, it would mean that he was not the "KING OF KINGS", as he called himself to be. They would, then, get an excuse to call him a liar. In reply to their question, Lord Jesus put a coin in his plam and put a counter question to them to let him know the name of the king whose seal was on it. They all said that it bore the seal of Caesar. Then Jesus said, "Render unto Caesar that belongs to Caesar, and render unto God that belongs to God". Similary, put all your efforts to achieve God-realisation which has the seal of God, and leave your body enjoyments to Destiny which controls them. When a man works for a higher position, all the lower jobs are automatically achieved. Similarly, as a man makes efforts to advance towards his goal of God-realisation all his worldly necessities connected with his body are automatically fulfilled. This is the Law of Nature.

Spiritual Power

Alexander the great and the Indian Saint

When Alexander came to India, he discovered that, of all the countries he had conquered, the most truthful, wise and beautiful persons were found here. He desired to see the heads of India, i. e. the philosophers and the saints. He was then taken to the banks of river Indus, where he found a saintly personality. Alexander was known as the Emperor of the world, while the saint did not have even the loin-cloth round his waist. Alexander had a great personality. The eyes of the saint were also sparkling with spiritual lustre, saying, as it were, "I bestow grandeur on the kings and beauty on the beautiful ones, whenever I look at them".

Alexander the great was overwhelmed by the spiritual personality of this saint. He said, "O great soul! Be kind unto me. People here in India keep even the jewels like you hidden in obscurity. But in Greece great importance is attached even to small things. I request you to be gracious enough to accompany me to my country. I shall offer you kingdom, wealth and precious stones. I shall offer you anything you might require but pray, do accompany me".

The saint only smiled and said, "I am everywhere. I am omnipresent. I am beyond space."

Alexander could not understand the saint and repeated his request and the temptations. The saint replied, "I do not stand in need for anything. I am not a man to like my own discarded sputum."

Alexander got annoyed and felt insulted; for nobody till then had ever refused to comply with his orders. He drew his sword to kill him. There-upon the saint burst into laughter and said, "You could never have told such a big lie in your life before".

"I have yet to see a sword which could cut me". Children sit on stand, play with it, construct small houses and then demolish them themselves. The sand does not lose anything in the process. It remains the same as before. Similar was the case with the saint.

This body is like a house of sand which is built according to the innate tendencies of man. I am the sand, the base, the all-pervading. I was never' a house. If anyone wants to .demolish it, he is in reality damaging his own house The sand does not run any risk of losing anything. It remains the sand all the same.

"The stars are never separated from the light. So you are myself and I am yourself."

On this retort from the saint, the sword fell down automatically from the hands of Alexander, the great and he apologised for his arrogance.

Expansion of the limited self

Regarding achieving unlimited powers, Rama may further explain it with an example. If you put a piece of salt in an empty tumbler, it occupies only a limited space. And, if you put it in a tumbler full of water, it is dissolved in water or, so to say, it becomes one with water, gives up its limitation, and spreads itself in the water, making it all saltish. Or, in other words you can say that, to the extent the piece of salt gives-up its limitation of name and form by being dissolved in water, it develops to the same extent the power to expand itself and make the water saltish. Similarly, though the mind is said to be limited, yet the more it gives up its limitation by identifying itself or being one with the unlimited ocean of its Real-Self, the more' it will develop unlimited powers. It means that the mind will then develop power to express itself in an unlimited way. Similarly, if you want to develop unlimited powers within you, you will have to identify yourself and try to be one with the Absolute, the unlimited source of Power and Energy.

The strong minded Lord Buddha

Lord Buddha was one of such strong minded persons of super-resolve. He was extremely popular for his sincerity and compassion. You know, one-third of the total population of this world consists of his followers.

The person, who can discipline his mind, who possesses pure and unblemished character, is above the worldly temptation and will ever be successful in any sphere of his life. He alone can enjoy the real peace; power and prosperity. There cannot be the least doubt about it.

CHAPTER THIRTY-TWO

Will-force

Maharaja Ranjit Singh-Lion of Punjab

Like Cromwell, amongst the Englishmen, or Babar, amongst the Muslims, there was only recently one Ranjit Singh amongst the Hindus. I am here relating the story of this Lion of Punjab. Once his enemy was on the other side of the river, and his own men were hesitating to cross the river. Seeing this, Maharaja Ranjit Singh boldly jumped with his horse into the river and crossed it saying, "God is everywhere. One should not have any doubts. Only those who are incapable of making advances are hesitant". Seeing this, his entire army immediately followed him and crossed the river in no time. Noticing their fearlessness, the enemy, who outnumbered them, got frightened, fled away from the battlefield and, lo! the Indian hero, Maharaja Ranjit Singh, wedded victory with utmost ease. He could accomplish this, because his heart was full of faith in God or reliance in Self which gave him real strength. He used to pass his nights in meditation of Almighty. Tears would roll down during his prayers. In other words, he had realised his Self. It is not merely a theoretical statement. Self-realisation is, the stage, where happiness percolates through every fibre of one's body.

It is said that the name of „Rama" was written on every particle of the body of Hanuman. Similarly, Ranjit Singh's heart was full of strength, emanating from faith. For men of realisation even the rivers and hills make way. The secret of worldly success is the strength of Self, emanating from the faith that "Lord within me is All-powerful".

The story of devotee child - Nam Deo

There are other examples too. I shall now relate to you story of a Hindu child. There was a child whose name was Nam Deo. His maternal grandfather used to worship God in the form of (Thakur Ji's) idol. Once the child said to his maternal grandfather, "what is this"? His grandfather replied, "This is Gopal Ji. It is God's representation in the form of baby! Krishna". The child observed the idol of Gopal Ji minutely. He saw the figure of Lord Krishna as a child in the, pose of walking on His knees, holding a ball of butter in his hand and looking behind to see if His mother was not watching Him. In one hand he had a ball of butter while the other was resting on the ground. Nam Deo did not know that it was only an idol made of stone or metal. He thought it was Lord Krishna Himself, as a child in the form of Gopal Ji. The child saw the child God in the form of Gopal Ji.

"Birds of the same feather flock together".

A small child cannot have love for an aged God. A child can love only a child God. Love does not evolve out of any recommendation. We develop love only for our desired objects. Love is natural and spontaneous. The young heart of Nam Deo could not conceive the idea of the formless omnipresent God. His heart could be impressed only by this butter eating child God. When Rama was young in age, his heart was also stolen by this very butter eating form of Lord Krishna. The child, Nam Deo, requested his grandfather to give him one day the turn to worship Gopal Ji. But the grandfather rejected his request and said, "You are not yet fit to worship Him. You are not clean enough to perform the worship, as you do not take your bath every day". One day, when the grandfather had gone out of the town, the child said to his grandmother, "I shall perform the worship of Gopal Ji today". The grandmother agreed and said, "You are allowed to worship Him, but not today, only tomorrow in the morning, after you have taken your bath".

The child could not sleep the whole night. He woke up from his sleep now and then. He woke up his mother and grandmother and requested them to bring Gopal Ji down for him to worship. But they said, "It is still night. Close your eyes and sleep". After all, the night was over. The child got up, ran to the nearby river and soon returned after a dip or two. But he did not know the rituals of worshipping an idol. He dipped the small idol in water which he had brought from the river, took it out and wiped it with a small dry towel. He then requested his mother to get some milk for the child God. The milk was brought and put before the idol, so that He might drink it. But, to his utter surprise, the idol did not drink the milk. The child did not know that his grand-father only put- up a show of feeding Gopal Ji, and that Gopal Ji did never drink milk. More often, persons have only lip sincerity which does not touch the heart at all. But the child was untainted and free from any showy rituals. His heart was full of sincere love for Gopal Ji. So the child insisted upon the idol of God to drink milk, and said, "How is it, you don't drink my offered milk? Is your heart stony?" But it was all in vain. The child said to himself "my mother is ever ready to do anything for me." But he wondered that God had no consideration for his request, not even as much as his parents had. In the words of a Persian poet:

"O, beloved! You are white like silver but your heart is hard like a stone. I had never seen before a stone hidden inside silver".

O, dear God! This innocent child is requesting you with folded hands to drink milk and you are not obliging him. What sort of God are you? The child then thought that God might drink milk if he closed his eyes. He, accordingly closed his eyes with his fingers but was occasionally peeping through them to see, if God was drinking milk or not. But God would not drink milk. He thought that God might drink it, after repeated requests. He did so again and again, but to no good. The child was already tired, due to sleepless night. He was hungry also.

One, two, three hours had passed but Gopal ji would not yield to his request. Good God! Rama also gets annoyed at such a Thakur Ji. The child then started weeping so much so that his voice became hoarse and he could hardly speak. His eyes became red. After all, the child lost his temper. Though he was quite young, he had a strong will behind. According to Hindu scriptures:

"The weak willed cannot realise the Self"

What was the child's strength? It was his perseverance, his faith and his strong belief in his success.

Such strength can perform wonders and can bring about even storm which could uproot the trees, dry the rivers and move the mountains. Unshakable faith of a man is his real strength. They say Farhad of Persia had also such a strong will force. The mountains were coming down with the heavy strokes of his spade. When persons of faith move about, they can create upheaval in the whole world. You have never tested the force of strength of "faith". The child Nam Deo had also such a faith in him. The faith of the child attracted, rather personified God Himself. An Urdu poet says:

"If there is any effect in my true love, you are sure to be attracted towards me, I, therefore, do not mind, if you remain aloof from me or are unmindful of me".

The child out of intense disappointment caught hold of a sword and, putting it on his neck said, "If you do not drink milk, 1 AM putting an end to my life. If I will live, I will live for you, otherwise I have no mind to live at all". A poet says:

"It is better to die, rather than live for one's own self. One, who dies for God, lives forever."

In America psychological experiments are being performed which make you see a table as a horse. As such, you should accept the story of your own country. This is also believable that, when the child was putting a sword on his neck, all of a sudden, nobody knows from where, God materialized and, taking the child in his lap, began to drink milk with His own hands. Seeing this, the child was very happy. But, when he saw that He was drinking away all the milk, he gave Him a slap and said, "Do keep some milk for me, as well". The child had a very thick curtain over his eyes, for he had no knowledge of God at all. Let the curtain be thick or thin, true love, sincerity and faith will surely remove the curtain. When a small child can develop such a faith in God, it is a pity, if a grown up man, fails to acquire it. An Urdu poet says: "If it is possible for a small insect to penetrate a stone, one does not deserve to be called a man, if one fails to win the heart of beloved."

"My Namaz is the informal bow out of respect for Him. The aching of my heart for Him is my Koran".

The story of Whittington, Lord Mayor of London

A boy was being brought-up in an orphanage of Scotland. Like any other boy, he loved to play and was also naughty. One day he ran away from the orphanage and reached London on foot. On the way, he somehow managed to satisfy his hunger by begging for bread, etc, At London he entered the garden of the richest man, Lord Mayor. While this boy was in the garden, he saw a cat and began to play with and talk to her. He was passing his hand over her back, and also pulling her tail in his boyish mood. Close by, a church bell was ringing. He asked the cat, "What is this mad bell saying?" He called the bell mad because generally the bell of the clock strikes four, eight or at the most twelve, but this bell was continuing to ring indiscriminately, as if it was mad. Poor cat could not say anything, but the boy himself was replying to his own question. This boy's name was Whittington.

He said, "Ton, Ton, Ton, Whittington, Lord Mayor of London".

Just reflect. This little boy, who has run away from an orphanage, is dreaming of becoming Lord Mayor of London. He hears in the "Ton, Ton, Ton" of the bell, the becoming of Whittington, Lard Mayor of London.

While the bell was still ringing, Lord Mayor also came walking in his garden. He saw the boy and said, "Who are you? What are you saying?". The boy in his care-free mood replied, "Lord Mayor of London, Lord Mayor of London". Lord Mayor was not annoyed at it. As a matter of fact, he was very much impressed by the boy. After all, who would not like to love care-free life? He enquired if the boy would like to be admitted to a school. The boy said, 'Why not? But only if the teacher does not beat". Accordingly, the boy was admitted to a school.

In the school, Whittington gradually passed all the classes and ultimately became a graduate with honours. By this time; Lord Mayor died. He had no issue. He had already assigned the great portion of his property to the boy who gradually added to the inherited estate and one day he, after all, rose to the status of Lord Mayor of London. You can find his name in the list of Lord Mayors.

There was a very poor student in China. He could not afford even oil for his lamp to study at night. He would collect fire-flies, keep them in little muslin bag and put it on his book to study at night with the help of their light. Somebody remarked "why do you work so hard? Do you want to become the Prime Minister of China"? He replied, "If God's laws concerning thought-force are correct. I must be the Prime Minister or China one day". If you see the history of China, you will find this boy as one of the Prime Ministers of China.

Note: from the above be visualise the importance of will force.

CHAPTER THIRTY-THREE

Thought Power

The curse of adverse suggestion

A man wanted himself to be initiated by a saint. The saint did so and gave him the sacred word to be repeated on a rosary. He said that after three repetitions on rosary, the sacred word shall produce the desired effect on him. But the saint warned him that, during the repetition of the sacred word the idea of monkey should not enter his mind. After a few repetitions, the man went to the saint again and said, "My Lord, I never thought of a monkey even in a dream. But now ever since your warning the monkey has been haunting me, and does not leave me." Do you know why it is so? It is because of the adverse suggestion. Such adverse suggestions are avoided in the American system of education.

Thinking of dog & cat

Lord Buddha used to say, "As a man thinks, so he will become" Two persons once paid a visit to him. One of them said, "This companion of mine thinks and acts like a dog. Will he not be a dog in his next life?" The second man said in respect of the first, "My companion acts in every way like a cat, Will he not be a cat in his next life"? Lord Buddha said, "Well, you must get the result according to your own thoughts. But unfortunately you are taking it in a wrong way. He is calling you a cat and you are calling him a dog. Now mark. The man who sees his companion as dog, he is all the time thinking of dog. He will be a dog in his next life. Similarly, the man who is regarding his companion as a cat, is having an idea of cat in his missed, all the time. He will therefore, be a cat in his next life."

A clever poet wrought in perversity

Professor Azad in his book, "Taazkirae Abehayat", has described a strange event. One day, at Lucknow, a poet was entertaining the Nawab and his courtiers with his poems and couplets. When the Nawab reached his harem late in the night his Begums enquired the reason of his being late. He replied that he was enjoying the poems and the witty humour of a poet. The Begums also expressed their desire to be entertained by him. The very next day the poet was called in and the Begums of harem, who heard him from behind the purdah (curtain), very much enjoyed his humour. They requested the Nawab to be pleased to allot him a room to stay in the palace. The Nawab was hesitating in allowing him to stay inside the palace, for fear of his seeing the ladies in the harem. The poet could see through the hesitation of the Nawab. He, accordingly, said, "I am quite all right. But, unfortunately, I am totally blind and cannot see". This excuse of the poet proved effective and produced the desired result. The apprehensions of the Nawab were falsified and he ordered a room to be allotted to the poet in harem. The evil intentioned hypocrite thus succeeded in deceiving the Nawab by saying that he was blind, in the hope of getting the opportunity of watching the ladies of the palace, without being suspected. But it is impossible to deceive anyone else, except one's own self. Success in depravity is like poisonous liquor.

One day the poet felt the urge to ease himself. He wanted the maid servant to give him the mug of water. The maid servant said, "There is no mug here in the room". She was fed-up with the too frequent orders of the poet and, therefore, she had told him a lie. But the poet was feeling a great urge and, since he could not control himself, he spoke out, "Don't you see? The mug is already there". Truth cannot be suppressed. It must come out one day. On hearing this, the maid servant ran to the Begums and said, "The devil has eyes. He can see. He is a liar and not blind". He was then immediately turned out of the palace. But, as it happened, he became blind the very next day. This event teaches us a very good lesson. As you think so you will have to be.

A poet says:

If you think of a flower, your mind takes the shape of a flower. And if you think of a restless nightingale you are a nightingale for the moment. If you think of sorrow, you are sure to become sorrowful. And if you think of goodness for all, you will be "All".

You might have observed that, while playing, the children often walk backward with closed eyes. Their mothers beat such children, saying» "You should entertain only good wishes. Yon should not copy blind persons or you might become blind yourself ".

Mira has said correctly, "By thinking and repeating the name of Krishna, I have become Krishna myself".

You have now marked out that, by acting as a blind man, the poet became blind, by contemplating on being a Minister, the poor student achieved Prime-Ministership, and, by thinking of becoming Lord Mayor, Whittington became Lord Mayor of London. So, too, in order to help yourself and to discharge your duty in your own interest, you must first develop purity of thought, high hopes, good conduct, holy mind, large heartedness, perseverance and firm faith in yourself, so that you may accomplish everything.

Lord Indra & his piggish thoughts

In an allegorical story, it is said that once Lord Indra, became a pig in his dream and he miserably suffered from itch and other troublesome diseases. Other gods were deeply concerned at this condition of their king. They entered his dreaming state and reminded him, "How is it Sir! Have you forgotten the nymphs of the heaven? Do not you remember the taste of nectar? Have you no idea of your own golden throne studded with precious stones?" But Indra in his piggish tone said, 'No, no, no. Your nymphs, nectar and golden throne are no match to my she-pig, excreta and cushion like mud in the ditch. I enjoy greater pleasure in rolling in this mud than in sleeping in the bed of roses.

You might be laughing at the foolish reply of Indra. But please reflect what are you at present? Are you any better than Indra in his dream? You, also in this worldy dream, are taking death as a physician and the disease as its remedy, i. e., you take everything in a perverted way. Is it the correct state of affairs? No, never. You will continue to suffer, unless you know your Self. You are the Lord Indra of Indras.

The intensity of Koonj bird's love For her offspring

In the plains there is a bird, called Koonj. It is said about it that, when the bird dies, its off-springs and young ones also die. And, if the Koonj lives, its young ones also continue to live. Why? What is the cause of this strange phenomenon? The reason being, that the life of the young ones of Koonj depends upon the thought-force of their mother. Even though they do not directly nurse or look after their young ones, being away from them, they always keep their welfare in their mind, with the result that their young ones remain hale and hearty and continue to live. And, if the mother bird dies, after giving birth to its off-springs, they (off-springs) also die, because there is none left to exercise its thought-force for their welfare. If it is true that the koonj birds can keep their young ones alive and healthy through their thought-force, even if they are far away in jungles or at the hills, is it not, then, strange, if a man, the highest evolved being, fails to keep his mind attached to his Rama or God who is his father, mother, well-wisher and everything?

The awareness of a pregnant woman

You know that a pregnant lady, does the entire domestic job, but never, never forgets the embryo in her womb. Is it not a pity, then, that the man forgets his Lord, Rama, who is always nearest to him and who is present in his very heart? Has the man degraded himself to such a depth that he is even worse than an ordinary woman?

CHAPTER THIRTY-FOUR

Self-Confidence

SELF-CONFIDENCE

Lions and Elephants

There is a vast difference between the physical body of a lion and that of an elephant. But the elephant, in spite of his huge bulk, is humbled down by the lion The elephants have no faith in their own strength. They, therefore, live and move in groups, because they are always afraid of being harmed, if they live separately. The lion is very small in stature as compared to an elephant but he is full of courage. The elephant, therefore, dares not stand before him. The lion has the will and courage emanating from his Inner-Self (Atman) or Cod. He is only expressing it in practical life.

The ocean & the Tateri

Have faith in 'Atma', i.e. your Inner Strength. Tateri, a small bird, developed faith or conviction within herself. She gathered courage, opposed the ocean and was ultimately victorious. There is a story that the ocean swept away the eggs of „Tateri". She argued that the ocean would sweep away the eggs of other birds also. It was, therefore, worthwhile to teach the ocean a lesson. With this determination the birds started taking water in their beaks and throwing it out of the ocean. They did not allow themselves to be dejected. In the meantime a 'Rishi' reached there and, seeing their absurdity, remarked, "You cannot empty the ocean in this way. Stop this nonsense". The tateries replied, "Respected Sir! We wonder, how you, a Rishi, can teach atheism? You see only our bodies and fail to realise our inner strength, our firm determination".

The same reply was given by Dattatreya to Kagbhusundi, "My friend! After all you are a crow, because your sight does not penetrate the skin of the body to see the Atman. Feel and realise that you are not this body and that you cannot be correctly estimated even by the holy Vedas. Real-Self is the One which is eternal and Everlasting.

On hearing the above reply of the tateries, the Rishi realised his mistake and asked the ocean in anger, "Why hast thou swept away the eggs of these birds?" The ocean thereupon returned the eggs and said, "It was only a joke, Sir".

In the above story the belief in the immortal Self is Faith, Religion or Islam. The rest is a story or creed. Rama aims only at the inspiration of Faith and has nothing to do with the rest.

Lion-hearted-Frederick the Great

Frederick the Great of Germany was fighting against France. His army was beaten and defeated. Many of his men were either killed or made prisoners by the French. This king was a learned and godly man. He had some experience of his inner strength. He asked a few of his remaining men to advance with war music from different directions towards the fort in occupation of the French. This lion-hearted king himself somehow managed to enter the fort all alone and unarmed. He challenged the enemy in a thunderous voice, ''Hands up. Leave the fort or my army which is advancing from all the directions, will cut you to pieces*'. Having heard the war music on all sides and been struck by the boldness of the king, the enemy got nervous and left the fort. Thus Frederick the Great conquered the fort all alone, even without the aid of any weapon* If you want to be victorious and successful in this world, you should also develop this strength of self-reliance. You need it and there is no substitute for it.

CHAPTER THIRTY-FIVE

Universal Unity

The Large-Hearted Abraham Lincoln

In spite of their being non-vegetarians, they love all the living beings. The American President Abraham Lincoln was once going to the Senate House. On his way he saw a pig in the marshes. The more the pig tried to extricate himself, the deeper he went. The President immediately ran to save the pig. In his soiled clothes he, thereafter, went to the Senate House. The senators were taken aback. The President narrated the entire incident to set their doubts at rest. They started praising the President for his kindness. He told them not to do so, because he had not, in fact, shown any mercy on the pig. He was pained to see the pig thus suffering. By helping the pig out of the marsh, he had only relieved himself of his affliction. He said that he was helping himself and not the pig. The real Vedanta is to consider the miseries of others, as your own. If you relieve others of their miseries, you will get the desired relief. If you are showing kindness to others you are doing kindness to your own self. This is practical Vedanta which you have to adopt in your actual life. Would a rich king or minister have done likewise? No, never. Please recall that your religion teaches you to be kind to all but you have drifted away from this tenet. All sorts of punishments have consequently been inflicted on you. Unless you follow the path of kindness and doing good to others, you cannot escape your miseries.

Lord Buddha and the hunter-King

Once Lord Buddha saw a king aiming at a deer. On seeing the frightened deer and the sharp pointed arrow, he prostrated and pleaded with the king. "You can surely shoot me with your arrow, if you so like but kindly spare this deer with beautiful eyes. I will gladly sacrifice myself to save the life of this innocent animal".

Dear readers, you can imagine the magical effect of Buddha's humble pleadings of the King. His request stopped the King from his cruel designs against the helpless deer. Thousands of years have passed, but even today Lord Buddha is reigning in the hearts of millions of people. Why? Because of his feeling of oneness with all.

Saint Kabir and one of his disciples

One day, a young man, named Ram Das, bowed before the saint Kabir and, with tears in his eyes, requested him, "You can perform miracles. Kindly help me to see God." The saint Kabir could not refuse the sincere request of Ram Das and, after some hesitation, he promised to show him God after two days. He also gave certain instructions to Ram Das for arranging the necessary preparations. The next day, Ram Das sold away all his property etc. and purchased rice, sugar, butter, flour, milk etc. Saints from far and near were also invited to participate in this feast on the fixed day. Delicious varieties of food were prepared. While the invitees were engaged in their usual prayers, Ram Das was deeply absorbed in meditation in the hope that he would soon have the blessed opportunity to see God. All the invitees were told that good food would be served to them only after God had appeared before Ram Das. They were, therefore, waiting accordingly. Noon passed away but God did not appear. Afternoon also passed away but God did not show His face. Some of the invitees, who felt very hungry, were very much disappointed. Some were blaming Saint Kabir; some considered Ram Das to be a fool to be hoping against hopes. Some were happy with the idea that, when God will appear before Ram Das, they would also be blessed to get a glimpse of Him. Everybody was however anxiously waiting for God to appear.

In the mean time, they all saw some commotion and heard hullabaloo in the kitchen. Every man was agitated. They could not know from where a buffalo had entered the kitchen and knocked down everything topsy-turvy. The big pots of pudding were turned upside down. He put his mouth in 'halva'. All the mal-puvas were either eaten or made dirty. He had damaged the oven and pulled down the fire places with his horns. The entire place was made dirty by his hoofs and dung. After destroying everything, he started making loud noises. The invitees were already feeling very hungry.

Seeing all this havoc in the kitchen, they lost their patience and were excited with anger. Ram Das was also very much enraged. He ran with a stout staff in his hand to beat the buffalo. The invitees had already surrounded the animal to prevent him from doing further damage. Ram Das then started beating him mercilessly with his staff and wounded him badly. They were all cursing the saint, Kabir, for fooling them in this way. They were badly agitated with anger, excitement and hunger.

The wounded buffalo, bleeding and crying with pain, ran limping for his life towards the corner of the garden where the saint Kabir was staying. Ram Das and other invitees were also running after him to punish him further and to express their anger against Kabir as well.

On reaching there, they were taken aback. They were surprised to see Kabir hugging the buffalo and weeping bitterly. 'O my Lord, you have received injuries which you did not have, even when you were fighting against the demon Ravana, or against Kansa. O my Lord, I am very much pained to see all this...' Seeing Kabir weeping in this way, the hearts of the invitees and the viewers were altogether changed. If any inflammable article is touched by fire, it also becomes fire. So, too, the hearts of all those who were present there were filled with godliness. Nothing remained except God. Dualism was gone. They were all experiencing God everywhere. All their sorrows, desires, expectations etc., vanished and instead of regarding their individual bodies as their own, they also realised all the other bodies also to be their own. Not only this, they also realized their own Self to be the all-pervading Universal Self. It was a strange sight to see that the viewers and the viewed were no more different. They were all one.

To realise God in everything in this way, is the real Darshan (sight) of God.

CHAPTER THIRTY-SIX

God-Realization

A patient and a doctor

A patient was suffering from two ailments, one concerning eyes and the other with regard to stomach. He went to the hospital and mentioned to the physician about his two ailments. The doctor gave him surma (Eye powder) for the eyes and a digestive powder for his stomach ache. But, unfortunately, the patient confused the packets of the two powders. He ate the eye-powder and put digestive powder into his eyes, with the result that both of his troubles were very much aggravated. Similarly, here too, there is a great confusion with regard to the conduct in our daily life. We should have left the body and the body connection to destiny, but, instead, we make efforts for it. In other words, we are eating the eye-powder. We should have made earnest efforts for realisation of the Self, but, instead, we have left it to destiny. It means, we are applying the digestive powder to our eyes. That is why we are going down instead of rising up. Under such circumstances, it is impossible for anyone to enjoy the true happiness without God realisation.

Dear friends, if you are really keen to enjoy the real happiness due to realisation of the Self or God, you have to work hard very sincerely to achieve that end. You have to give-up all desires, and leave the bodily enjoyments to destiny which will automatically look after them. Your real efforts should be to lose yourself in Atman and establish yourself in Godhood. In this way, you will be in position to enjoy the Eternal-Bliss in the „Kingdom of Heaven". This is the real Purushartha. If you only sit on the 'Royal Throne' of your Godhood, you will see that all your desires will be automatically fulfilled even without your wishing.

A judge in his court

When the judge sits in his chair in the court, his only work is to listen to the cases and deliver his judgment. The remaining jobs in the court are automatically done. So, too, when a saint is merged in Godhood, all his worldly jobs are automatically performed by nature, as if, due to his fear, even without his gesture. But, dear friends, you will reach this stage, only when you make the right use of your efforts, i.e. when you leave the body enjoyments to destiny and make earnest efforts to achieve spiritual development.

CHAPTER THIRTY-SEVEN

God-Consciousness

Rama Chandra's determination

Lord Rama Chandra is all alone. He has only a brother with him to get back Sita from across the ocean. Was it an easy job? There were no boats or ships. But he was the man of extraordinary courage and firm determination. As such, even the wild animals were ready to help him. Even the naughty animals like monkeys were ready to assist him. The birds also offered their help in his cause. The squirrels helped in constructing the bridge across the ocean by bringing sand in their little mouths. They were all serving the Maryada Purushottam Bhagwan Ram Chandra. If a man develops the same indomitable courage and determination, as Rama had, the whole universe will be his. If, however, you are not prepared to believe that "I am He", you can surely believe that "He is within me". If he is within you, you are the Lord of everything you like. This very thought should be entertained and hammered all the time, so that the inner strength begins to manifest itself.

Miraculous horn

An important condition for success in life is spiritual love. This will be illustrated by a legend of the king of Norway. He kept a horn in his room, the cavity of which was filled with water. He made an announcement that he would give the whole of his kingdom to the man who would drink all the water in the horn. Most of the persons came to drink water but none could empty the horn.

Although that horn was very small to look at, yet it was connected with the ocean and this was why it could not be emptied. In the same way, although your bodies are very tiny to look at, yet they have got their inner and latent connection with God-the Ocean of all the oceans. The man, who keeps his contact with God alive and maintains his adhesion to the ultimate source of unlimited power, is endowed with unlimited strength. When you are all absorbed in God, you are nothing else but God, and God's determinations are always fulfilled. Hence all your ideas, which have their root embedded in your Inner Self, are sure to be crowned with success.

A prince and his vulgar companions

You are not this limited body of any particular name or form. You are Divinity. When you are that Infinite Self, it does not become you to indulge in narrow and debased worldly thoughts. It is like a royal prince, who is given to some bad habits, enjoying pleasure in the company of his illiterate servants or of those who utter filthy and vulgar language. He is, however, ashamed and repentant of his folly, when he is made to realise his royal position. Similarly, you must also realise your Royal Universal Self. You must know that your Real Self is God who bestows eternal happiness and bliss on the universe and grants grandeur and light to the Sun and the Moon. So, like the repentant prince you, too, must realise your true Self, feel ashamed of your misdeeds and free yourself from the attachment for the worldly attractions.

The saint and the lion

The following is the story of a place near Rishikesh, near the river Ganges in India. On one side of the Ganges lived a number of saints, and on the other, was another saint who was all the time absorbed in the only thought "I am God" and uttering it, too. Day and night, this sound was heard "I am God. I am God. I am Shiva". One day, a lion came towards the saint. The saints, of the other side of the Ganges, were witnessing this. Even by seeing the lion, the saint was not terrified. He continued to repeat, "I am God. I am Shiva," as if this was ingrained in his mind that he was the lion or the lion was he and that he himself was roaring in the form of a lion. "I am Shiva, I am God." The lion caught hold of him. But the saint was, as if enjoying the taste of. human flesh in the form of the lion, still calmly repeating, "I am God, I am Shiva," as though nothing had happened. During Dewali (an Indian festival) sugar-toys are made. There is a deer made of sugar and there is also a lion made of sugar. Will the deer considering himself to be a deer on account of his name and form, fear that the lion made of the sugar will eat him? If he considers himself to be sugar, then he will just say that, by virtue of his being made of sugar, he is deer here and a lion there. Similarly, when you know yourself to be the universal God, like sugar in the toys, you can say in His capacity that you are a saint here and a lion there.

If you examine the realities of handkerchief or the coat, they are all, in fact, cotton yarn or only cotton. Likewise, when the armlet is melted, it can be reshaped into a bracelet or any other ornament. But in the eyes of Truth, it is all gold (God).

O dear Ones! This saint had the same sight of truth. When the Hon was eating him, he was enjoying, as if, he himself, was the Hon that day, tasting the human blood. When the lion was eating his legs, he was still saying, "I am God, I am Shiva". To him the roars of the lion seemed to be saying, "I am God. I am Shiva". The curtain was already thin and now it had been removed for good.

Two men and the pigeons

Two persons approached a saint and requested him to initiate them as his disciples. The saint said that he would first test their merit, before initiating them. After a few days, the saint gave each one of them one pigeon, and promised to initiate the man who comes first, after killing his pigeon. He also put a condition that nobody should ' see the pigeon being killed.

Both the young men left the place with their respective pigeons. One of them twisted the neck of his pigeon in a corner in the market itself, after turning his back towards the crowd of the passersby. He returned to the saint and asked him to initiate him as his disciple. The saint asked him to wait till the arrival of the other candidate. They waited for the other man's return for further two days, but he did not turn up. On the third day he returned and said, "Sir, I could not fulfill your condition. Please put some other condition." On being asked the reason, he said "When I went to the jungle to kill this pigeon in a lonely place, its beautiful and enchanting eyes were looking at me. Every time I tried to twist its neck, I noticed that its eyes were staring at me. I was then reminded of your condition and abstained from killing it. Some one sitting inside the pigeon was always looking at me. How could I have killed it? I am sorry, I could not do it." The saint was very much pleased at this man's version and remarked that it was God Himself who was looking at him through the eyes of the pigeon. God is everywhere* He is omnipresent. One who feels His presence everywhere and in everything is a real saint.

The designer of piano and his magnificent music

In one of the biggest churches in America, there was a very big piano. It was used only on Sundays. On one Sunday, when a huge gathering of the devotees was there, an unknown person wanted to use that piano, but the clergy man did not allow him to approach it. "You being unskilled, you will spoil the instrument and damage it". The man was, therefore, turned out. When the church service was over and the devotees had started going out of the prayer hall, the same man stealthily reached the piano and started playing on it with a melodious tune which was so enchanting and attractive that even the persons, who had gone out of the .church came back and listened to his musical notes with rapt attention. They were, as if hypnotised, like the snake at the music of Vina.

Who was this stranger? It was afterwards learnt that he was the same person who had designed this instrument and also tuned it. That is why the people enjoyed its wonderful music with entranced rapture. And, when the clergyman also came to know about it, the man was allowed to continue the music. He struck still more melodious notes on the instrument so much so that the audience was delightfully charmed and refreshingly fascinated.

Similarly, our body is like a musical instrument. Who is the clergyman? The clergyman is our limited ego which does not allow anybody else to interfere in our personal affairs. But, it is very necessary that we should surrender our body, mind and intellect to the designer for the pleasant music. But who is the master designer of our instrument? It is none else, but the designer of this universe, God, the Master of the masters and Emperor of the emperors. If you surrender your body, mind and intellect to Him, He will produce such beautiful notes out of you, that the world will be surprised at them. You will do such wonderful acts that the whole world will be moved to admiration at your excellence and perfection. The more you develop this divine faith within, the more you will enjoy peace and happiness.

The maid servant who sought nothing but king's grace

On his birthday, a King ordered his servants and others to ask for anything and they would be granted the same. Some wanted money, some desired emoluments, promotions etc and as promised, the King granted all their requests. But he noticed a maid-servant with dirty clothes, standing with a sorry face in one of the corners of his palace. The King was surprised to see her in such a condition. He drew her attention to the fact that his birthday rejoicings were being held everywhere and that all his employees were happy. He asked her the reason of her being indifferent to all those happy celebrations. He then asked her as well to be happy and to demand from him anything which she may like.

The maid-servant said, 'Yes, my lord, I will surely demand something from you. But, I am afraid, you may not be in a position to grant my request.'

The King assured her that her demand would be fulfilled without fail. Let her only speak out her desire.

The maid-servant, then, asked the King to extend his hand, she caught hold of it and said, 'Your Majesty, I only want your hand in my marriage. I do not want anything else. I hope, your Majesty will honour your word most willingly.'

The King was taken aback, but having already confirmed his promise, he had no option but to keep-up his words. He married her.

Similarly, we should ask from God nothing but God Himself. If God is ours, the entire pleasure of His Universe is ours. There remains nothing to be desired. We should, therefore, demand from God Himself. This is the way for fulfillment of all the desires, if any. They, whose all the desires are fulfilled, get the real peace in life. Seek God and be happy and peaceful.

The practice of allowing roots of godly ideas to penetrate deep into your heart and mind

You know that the height of an oak tree is even higher than that of a *sakhu* tree. But Rama has seen some of the oak trees in an exhibition in Japan not higher than a foot and a half, even though they were about three hundred years old. As a matter of fact, these trees go as high, as their roots go deep into the earth. Taking advantage of this principle, they, the growers cut away the roots as they penetrate deeper into the earth below, with the result that the height of the tree is automatically stunted. They continue this process of cutting away the roots, again and again, as they (roots) go deep, with the result that the trees are prevented from growing to their natural height. Similarly, if you do not allow the roots of Godly ideas to penetrate deep enough into your heart and mind, you will not be able to attain the natural height of spiritual evolution. Your progress will be retarded and you will remain spiritually stunted. This is the Law which holds true in every sphere. Drink deep the godliness, so that it may penetrate every fibre of your body, mind and heart and you may be free to grow higher and higher in the realm of spiritualism.

CHAPTER THIRTY-EIGHT

Truthfulness

Saint Tuladhar

The story of the famous businessman, Tuladhar, is well known. Honest trade made him a saint. He gained knowledge and insight denied to many saints. One saint once came to have a religious discourse with him. The moment he met the saint, he knew the purpose of the visit. The saint was surprised that the divine knowledge which he could not gain after so many years of devotion to God was imparted to that low-caste trader. On enquiry, the trader told him, "This is nothing surprising. I am honest in my dealings. I never try to cheat my customers. My rate of profit is very marginal. I don't tamper with the weights. I neither give nor take less. My prices are fair. I treat all equally and politely. Truthfulness is the best religion and I follow it. I don't resort to deception. This is why I have gained this knowledge which fortunately brings such great people, as you, to my place". This is the importance of truth. If all the Indian traders follow this example, they need not go to the woods to worship God or to look for teachers or saints.

The story of a simple boy

A simple boy was shy of going to school. One day he decided not to attend the classes at any cost. He put a bandage on his knees and under the pretext of serious injury, applied to the Headmaster for leave.- He wrote, 'Dear Sir, kindly excuse my absence for today, as I am unable to walk up to the school.'

The application was written but there was none to take it to the school. Accordingly, he went to the school and handed it over personally to the teacher and said, 'It is not possible to reach the school today.' Hearing this, the teacher and other students burst into laughter. O Simpleton! your bringing the application up to the school is a proof against your submission. When you are already in the school, the plea of your 'inability to go there,' is incredible.

O dear, your real nature is the embodiment of Supreme Consciousness, As per your daily assertions, you are knowledge incarnate. Or, if you do not agree by saying whatever 'Rama' has written is not correct and that you are right from your point of view, this, too, amounts to your being Consciousness personified.

The example of crooked and straight wood

Question: There is a saying that „they cut away only the straight wood from the tree". So, you want us to become plain, straight forward and simple. If, however, we act, as you wish us to do, they would not let us live peacefully in this world. How shall we, then, carry on in this crooked world? The worldly wise and the crafty persons will, then, surely wreck and ruin us.

Answer: It is true that they do not cut away the bent or the crooked pieces of wood. I want to know, if it is allowed to remain as it is in a tree? Is there no use of it?

No. It is all wrong. When the time comes, they are all cut sooner or later. So far as these are concerned, they are all cut. But there is of course some difference. The bent or the crooked wood is used as fuel. And, the straight wood, after it has been smoothly polished, is used as a walking stick by the rich, elderly and fashionable persons. If, however, it it thick and heavy, it is used as a beam in the construction of temples and the houses or is utilized as a supporting pillar. At any rate, its utility is muchbetter, as compared to the bent or the crooked wood which is used only as a fuel, and is ultimately burnt and destroyed. So, too, is the case of pure and simple hearted persons. If, however, they are harmed by some crooked man, the great Lord, the real Cause of all the causes, will elevate them, to much better status and higher position. The harming enemy will only watch him helplessly. The good and the pure hearted man even though he may be seemingly harmed, shall go higher up and achieve more exalted distinction.

O you worldly men! Please do not forget this principle in your worldly transaction that the real strength of a man lies in Truth, piety and honesty.

CHAPTER THIRTY-NINE

Purity

The example of a lamp.

Look at the lamp. Why is the light coming out of it? Because the chimney, which is its body, is quite clean and transparent. It is due to this that its inner light is coming out without any obstruction. In the same way, if you also remove the ideas of selfishness, darkness and obscurity from your heart, your inner light will also come out automatically and spread all around.

The King and two painters

A King wanted to test two experienced painters, Ravi and Kavi. To facilitate comparison, they were ordered to display their paintings on the two opposite parallel walls.

According to the order, curtains were put in between the two walls, so that one may not see the paintings of the other. They used to come every day and go away, after doing their daily work on their respective walls After the prescribed period, the king with his courtiers came for inspection of their paintings. When the curtain from Ravi's wall was lifted, they were all stunned by his painting and cried out: Even the Chinese paintings cannot be better.

It was heard from all sides, "Ravi has won full marks. All the scenes of Mahabharata have been painted as real, as if the paintings are just going to speak. Nothing could be thought of better than this. Ravi should be given the reward, There is no necessity now to inspect the painting of Kavi. Wonderful! Wonderful!!"

The king also was so much impressed and satisfied that he too did not like to see the painting of Kavi. But Kavi himself lifted the curtain. As soon as the curtain was removed they were wonder-struck. The king and the courtiers were dumbfounded with admiration, as if they were breathless. They were standing agape. They were so much dazzled with the smooth cleanliness of Kavi's wall that they stood aghast. How could he do the painting two yards inside the wall. It has been well said: The poet (Kavi) can reach where the sun (Ravi) cannot.'

Dear Reader! Could you understand how Kavi defeated Ravi? The distance between the two walls was only about two yards. While Ravi was drawing painting on his wall, Kavi was busy in polishing and cleaning his own wall, so much so, that he made it so smooth as to look like a mirror. The result was as described above: Kavi simply got the entire painting of Ravi reflected on his own wall. According to the law of Reflection of light, the pictures were seen as much inside Kavi's wall, as was the distance between the two walls.

O my friend! You try to see only the exterior. How long will you be decorating your wall like Ravi? How long will you put colours on your exterior surface?

How long would the different colours of your crammed ideas stay in your mind? How could the confused ideas, stuffed into the mind from outside, be useful to you? Education means to give out from within, and not to push in from without.

How long will you act against the very purport of education? Why do you not purify your own heart by proper education and let it be illumined like the wall of Kavi?

Fall of Napoleon

Napoleon was a great warrior and a hero. He was a terror to the neighboring countries. So long as he maintained the purity of heart and character, his success was assured at every step, in all the directions. He was victorious in every encounter of bloody wars. But from his life, it is quite clear that on the eve of the battle of Waterloo, he had allowed himself to be the victim of sensual weakness. He had poured out his vital fluid into the well of voluptuous dissipation. He had thus lost the lustre of his morality into immodesty, because he had imprisoned himself in the immoral love of a moonfaced beauty.

The result is well known to the student of the history. He lost the battle and could never regain his past glory.

The defeat of Prithvi Raj Chauhan

You know the history of Prithvi Raj Chauhan, the Emperor of Delhi. He had once badly defeated the invincible invader, Mohammad Ghori. But the very next year, when he left his palace for the battlefield to fight the same Ghori again, he was girded by a lady of disrepute. He was defeated and taken a prisoner. He could not be victorious in this war.

How could he? The impurity of his character and his inglorious licentiousness stood in the way of his success.

The sad plight of Abhimanyu in Mahabharata

The young and beautiful prince, Abhimanyu, of Mahabharata also met the same fate in the battle-field of Kurukshetra, because on the previous night he had also split his white blood. He was killed in the battle and alas, since then the very generation of the true Kshatriya heroes was annihilated. How sad!

The poet Tennyson says-

My strength is as the strength of ten, Because my heart is pure.'

It is only the purity of heart, which makes a man win. The impure ones are sure to be defeated, insulted and humiliated. They cannot enjoy the glory of peace and dignity of honour. This is the Law.

You can verify it from your own observations and personal experiences.

The greatness of Hanumanji

Why do we worship Hanumanji, the great hero of Ramayana? What lesson do we draw, on seeing the idol of this great Mahabir, the most powerful man of his time? He is respected, honoured and worshipped even today, because, whatever work was entrusted to him, he discharged it successfully with al) sincerity and devotion.

Why was he always successful? Because of his heart being pure and free from sensuality. He never forgot Almighty God, the source of strength. Faith in God or Self can most easily be developed in a pure heart. And he who has faith in God, can surmount the greatest difficulty. He can even cross an ocean, like Hanuman, and can make any impracticable task practicable. Only one should have faith in God, which cannot be achieved without purity of heart. God is clearly visualized only in a pure heart. Also, it is only a pure heart that can enjoy real peace. There can be no peace in an impure heart besmeared with prejudices, hatred, malice, jealousy, desires, passions, emotions etc. Without peace of mind, there can be no concentration, and without whole-hearted concentration, there can be no real success in any job, foe it worldly or otherwise. This is a Law.

The battle of Meghnath with Lakshmana

Take the example of Meghnath, another hero of Ramayana. Nobody could kill him in the battle fijpld, not even Shri Ram Chandra Ji Himself. Only Lakshamana, his younger brother could succeed. Why? Because Lakshmana had disciplined his mind and had been observing celibacy for long. As such, his vital energy was sublimated and he had developed the required strength and the will-force which could not be encountered by Meghnath, who had to go down in fight against Lakshmana.

CHAPTER FORTY

Patriotism

The example of Japanese and others

A tree takes manure from outside, but does not become manure itself. It takes earth, water, air and light from outside, but does not become any one of them. The Japanese assimilated the knowledge of Europe and America but continued to remain Japanese. According to Hindu scriptures, Aryans sent the boy KUGHH to non-Aryans to learn their life-giving knowledge and to acquire it; but he did not become non-Aryan. Similarly, by going to Europe and America to learn their knowledge, you cannot be anything other than Hindus or Indians.

A British doctor's sacrifice for his country

During the Moghal rule, when the British were just traders in India, the king Farookhseer fell ill. All the Indian doctors and quacks treated him without any improvement in his condition. Perchance an English doctor succeeded in curing him completely. The king was overjoyed and wanted to give to the doctor whatever the latter desired. The doctor refused all the precious things offered to him and requested the King to exempt the English goods from the local taxes. The request was readily granted. You will thus see that the English doctor cared more for his country than for his petty gains. Had he accepted the valuable gifts, the King was giving him, he might have become only temporarily rich. But he preferred his country's prosperity to his personal profit. This is what Rama expects of you. The foreigners practice Vedanta in a natural way. Why should they not, then progress?

CHAPTER FORTY-ONE

Devotion to Duty

A gardener's devotion to duty

A man was planting a garden? Somebody asked him, "What are you doing, old man? Will you be able to enjoy the fruits of this garden? Your one leg is already in the grave. Don't you remember the slaying of a saint?"

"Oh Counselor, how can I build a house in this desolate world? When the labourers come to construct my house, I am reminded of the grave-diggers".

The gardener replied, "Others had planted gardens, and we enjoyed the fruits. Now, 1 AM planting the garden, and others will enjoy its fruits after me". That is how the business of this world goes on. Did Christ and. Mohammed enjoy the fruit of their own effort themselves? They willingly made themselves manure for the garden of this world. They could not eat the fruits of the garden planted by them. The fruits which we are enjoying today, even after centuries, are the result of the labour and efforts of the great Rishis of yore, who reduced themselves to dust in the interest of the welfare of their gardens. This is the real motto of religion.

Two servants of a king

Take, for example, the case of two servants of a King. One of them only flatters the King and does not work, while the other discharges his duties faithfully, but has nothing to do by way of flattery. Whom will the king like more? It is clear that he will be pleased with the one who discharges his duties faithfully, because work is of primary importance. Similarly, an atheist may not be using the beads of rosary to repeat the name of God or rubbing his forehead on the ground to flatter God, but, in spite of this, God will be pleased with him, if he has a charitable disposition and does good deeds. Their continued devotion to good deeds is their rosary and their repeated unselfish actions for the good of all are, so to say, the beads. They may not be making a show of worshipping God in temples, churches or mosques, but in practice they do worship God by their good deeds in life.

CHAPTER FORTY-TWO

Progress

Example of running water

Your hand may be fair and strong with pure blood in it. But, if you tie a tight bandage, blood circulation of the hand will stop, and at the same time it will become dirty and impure with the result that the hand will be dried up and thinned. Similarly, those countries which considered themselves to be well off and prosperous and did not like the idea of maintaining contact with the foreigners, taking them to be untouchable or inferior, were themselves segregated with the result that their country starved and they had to face poverty and want. There is a famous saying: *"Running water is pure and stagnant water becomes dirty and impure"*.

It is, therefore, better that the river should continue to flow and the man should continue to progress. If you observe minutely, you will see that those countries which are well off today achieved their affluence by their continued efforts for progress. Take, for example, America. Nearly 45,000 Americans daily stay in Paris.

CHAPTER FORTY-THREE

Self-Help

The example of a short boy

If a school boy does not study well, or say, does not care to help himself, his teacher will not come forward to help him further. It is well known that the teachers are pleased with good students, and that they willingly pay special attention towards brilliant students. Ultimately, those who are favoured by the teacher, get the grace of God automatically. The whole thing boils down to the conclusion that self-help is the foremost duty of a man. Without self-help, neither the preceptor or God will be prepared to help us. There is a well-known saying that "God helps those who help themselves".

1. The example of serving others through self-help

Sir Isaac Newton never thought that he would be serving the world. He was running in pursuit of knowledge, as the moths run towards the burning candle. Because he was doing his duty properly, or say, because he tried to help himself, he ultimately proved himself the benefactor of the world. If a man stands in a field, he can see or make his voice heard up to a limited distance only. But if the same man stands at top of a high tower or a mountain, he can do so up to a far greater area. Rama was once going with a few companions to Gangotri on the Himalayas and lost the way. Their bodies were scratched and bruised by thorns and shrubs. They were all scattered and no one could hear the call of the other. When with difficulty Rama reached the top, he raised his voice, to call them and, as a result of it, they could hear him, and assembled together. Similarly, so long as we are fallen, nobody will hear us, but when we speak from a higher level, all will be able to listen to us.

Now take this small wooden table placed in front of Rama. It cannot be moved, if we try to do so from the farther side or from the centre. But, if we do so from the nearest point, we can pull it to our side very easily. Similar is the relation of the world with a man. A poet says:

"The descendants of Adam are organs of each other, because they are born of the same source".

If you want to move the whole world, you should do so by moving the nearest part of it, i. e. by mov¬ing your own self. If you can uplift yourself, the whole world will be lifted up. I dare say tbat you can move the world to the extent you can move your own self.

Peace

Importance of keeping aloof from the world

Patients, suffering from infectious and contagious diseases, are kept in segregated wards to avoid the diseases spreading to others. So, too, if you are suffering from the infection of worries, woes, anger, spite, jealousy etc., you must also segregate yourself and keep away from the society so as not to spread your agonising malady among others. And so long as you have not calmed down to normalcy, you have no right to infect others. You should keep aloof for your own good and for the peace of others.

CHAPTER FORTY-FIVE

Renunciation

The story of Ayaz - a courtier of Mahmud Ghaznavi

Ayaz, a true friend of King Mahmud of Ghaznavi, was formerly a grass-cutter. But, owing to the friendship with the king, he was promoted to the rank of the prime minister. Some ambitious persons were jealous of his promotion and were on the look-out to disgrace him. They once lodged a complaint against him with the king that Ayaz went to the treasury and took away jewels every day. Mahmud promised to look into the matter. He was accordingly informed, when Ayaz went the treasury at the appointed time. Mahmud followed him stealthily and began to peep through a small opening. He was, however, taken aback to see that Ayaz put aside all his ministerial robes in a corner and, keeping his sickle (grass-cutter) in front, began to offer his prayer to God on an ordinary blanket. He was also heard saying his prayer with all sincerity, "O Lord! This ministry is - Yours and not mine. These ministerial robes are yours and not mine. The strength in the body, light in the eye and what not are all due to you". He was all this time shedding tears of love in complete abnegation to God. In short, he was like white colour and was returning all to the source or origin, God. This is dedication.

So, you see that the first condition of success is to fill your heart with Divine Light. Filling your heart - with Divine Light means dedication or surrender - renouncing everything to God. You are free to act, but are only required to give up the selfish desires attached to your deeds. Not only individuals but the nations also have been successful, following the above process.

Expansion of little self into Universal Self

There is a story. A saint was highly evolved, so much so, that he had attained a stage wherein the worldly objects could automatically serve his daily needs. Once, a man brought him a plate full of *Batashas* (an Indian sweet). The saint on seeing them expressed a desire to have two *Batashas* for himself also. The man then gave him only two Batashas and, considering him to be a greedy person, did not think it worthwhile to give him the whole of it and took the remaining pieces back with him. You will thus see that the saint, by expressing his desire for the Batashas, was deprived of the remaining pieces and was also degraded in the eyes of the man who had brought the entire quantity for him alone. Similarly, even if you deserve a thing, you should not desire it. By so doing, you lose your right to possess it and also you degrade yourself in the eyes of others.

If, however, you want to have the right to be the master of the worldly possessions, you should establish and merge your little (individual) self in the real (universal) Self. It is only, then, that you can become the master of the world, not only of this world, but also of the other worlds. Nay, you will become the Master of the whole Universe, only if you establish yourself in your Atman, the Real Self.

Example of Commissariate Clerk

A commissariate Agent of the army is in charge of rations worth hundreds of rupees. He issues the ration daily and deals with hundreds of soldiers. In spite of it, he is neither ever misled to believe that the entire ration in the godown is his personal property, nor he ever develops any personal attachment with any soldier or soldiers. Even if the supply of ration fails, he has nothing to worry. It is not his headache, even if the godown runs at a loss. And, if it earns good profit, he has nothing to be overjoyed at it. His only responsibility is to discharge his duties faithfully and honestly. Similary, only that man is the true devotee of God who considers his personal property as belonging to God and also who regards his near and dear ones as the responsibility of God. He is there only to look after them on behalf of God, as the commissariate agent looks at the soldiers of the army with no personal love for or attachment with them. Certainly such a man is happy both in this world and in the next one. You have only the right to work with all sincerity and not to bother about the fruits thereof. It is of no avail to worry about your success or failure. It is God's business.

The example of shadow in respect of worldly desires

You might have noticed that if you run to catch your shadow, you can never do so. The shadow will run farther and farther away from you. So, too, if you run after the worldly desires, pleasure or sense satisfaction, they will continue to evade you, howsoever, hard you may try. But, if you walk, turning your face towards the sun, your shadow will run after you. Similarly, if you become indifferent or if you renounce the worldly desires and relations and if you look towards God, the Sun of the suns, all the sense objects and all the worldly pleasures will come to you automatically even without your asking for them.

If you advance towards God, every facility will be at your disposal to help you to attain your Goal. Do not try to make the sun go round the earth. Make the earth revolve round the sun. This is quite natural and also in the fitness of the things. Kama means to emphasize that, instead of making God run after your desires to be fulfilled, it would be fair to make your desires dance around God Himself. Surrender them to Him. This will make you care-free and peaceful.

CHAPTER FORTY-SIX

Anger

The hermit and the shudra (low caste man)

Under the shady trees, there was a neat and clean hut of a hermit by the side of the river, Jamuna. It was decorated with the skins of deer and lions. Ochre coloured clothes were hanging from the pegs in the trees. By chance, a low caste traveller, reached there, and seeing a well-built pucca ghat, he took his bath in the river and washed his clothes. At the moment, the hermit was taking rest inside his hut. When he heard the sound of washing clothes, he came out and saw that his clothes hanging on the pegs were being polluted by the dirty splashes of the washing. Seeing that a man was washing his dirty clothes, he was very much agitated with anger and taking a thick staff, started beating and abusing him. The poor man became unconscious. Even then the hermit continued to kick him, till he himself was tired. After some time, the hermit entered the river to take his bath again.

In the mean time, the shudra (low caste) regained his consciousness, and he also entered the river to take his bath again. By this time the hermit's anger was very much cooled down. . He addressed the poor man and said, 'Why do you take your bath again? Are you not afraid of falling ill or catching cold?'

The man replied, 'You had also taken your bath before. Who do you take your bath again?'

The hermit was annoyed at this retort and said, 'You have the cheek to copy me. I had to take my bath again, because I was polluted by your touch.' The poor man replied, 'I also take my bath again, because I have been touched by a CHANDALA, who is worse than a low caste. I want to purify myself in this river.'

At this reply, the hermit was red with anger. He said, 'What do you mean? You dare abuse me!! Do you mean to call me a CHANDALA?'

The man submitted in a humble tone, 'No Sir. 1 cannot afford to insult you. I have been the victim of your anger. As you already know, this anger is a big CHANDALA. You will please excuse me. I do not mean you, when I say I was touched by a chandala.

On hearing this, the hermit was very much ashamed and he said to himself that the poor man was right in his remarks. I should not have lost my temper.

O dear friend! It is pity that we consider it a pride to indulge in anger, which is, as a matter of fact our worst enemy. It is wonder that we hate a chandala with much greater intensity than what we do in respect of our anger. Anger is the worst emotion. It makes one mad and destroys one's power of discrimination. When God is everywhere and in everything, is it not an insult to God, if we get angry at or insult someone else?

CHAPTER FORTY-SEVEN

Attachment

The Story of Lot and his Wife

It has been mentioned in the ancient books that Lot and his family, including his wife and daughters, were going out of Sodom, leaving the city behind them. But Lot's wife turned back to see the city. The result was that, while others escaped, she immediately turned into a pillar of salt.

O dear! This story proves a law of Nature in respect of man. Lord Byron describes it thus:

"It is his nature to advance or die,

He stands not still, but decays or grows"

Just as a man is continuously growing in his size and intelligence from his very infancy, so, too, it is very necessary that he should also progress spiritually.

Remember that you will be crushed by the wheel of the Law of Nature, if you do not advance i.e., widen your circle of oneness with others. You will fall and face death and destruction. Advance or perish, is the grim watchword of Nature.

Like Lot's wife, when a man refuses to advance, change himself for the better, or to widen his circle to see fresh fields and pastures new, he is condemned. When an individual or a nation indulges in stagnation, or refuses to be progressive, the Divine Providence takes them to task. The individual has to suffer and the nation has to be punished or enslaved.

Egoism

The example of chilled snakes in the Himalayas

While living in Himalayas, Rama has enjoyed the visits to Amarnath, Badri Nath, and Gangotri on foot. A number of times, on his way, he came across snakes which were apparently dead. They were struck with cold and were found coiled up, as if they had no life in them. Rama caught hold of a few of them and, when he gave them a shake, he found them alive. A man once brought to his home a snake which was apparently dead. The children put it in the sun. On being warmed up, it showed life and began to hiss. It also bit a few of the children. Just as the snake apparently looks lifeless for a short time, so, too, your mind also loses its egoism for a short while (by the first process). Your mind, so to say, becomes insensible. At that time you are in a state of self absorption (of Yoga). Control of the mind or turning the mind into such a state, as if it was dead, may enable us to realise God for the time being. But, if the egoism is destroyed for good, that is the union with God. For permanent unity with God, it is not enough to let the snake of mind be temporarily insensible or appear like a dead one. But, if we take out the poisonous fangs of the snake, it does not matter, then, whether the snake is sleeping or waking, living or dead, in senses or out of senses. There is no danger then. When there is no poison in it, it is just the same, whether it is active or inactive. Similarly, the teachings of Vedanta make you harmless, like a snake without poisonous fangs.

One method to make the mind free from egoism for a short while is to sit in the company of saints when the mind will lose its vagaries for the time being, by the cooling atmosphere of their universal love.

But this is only temporary phase and is not enough, for when you return home and face the heat of your domestic affairs in the company of your wife, the seemingly quiet state of your mind is again stirred up to worldly life with the deadly result as it ever was.

Lord Krishna's flute

Someone enquired of the flute the reason for its being so much loved by Lord Krishna who governs the whole Universe. "The great emperors like Arjuna and Yudhishthira are anxious to touch His feet. The dust under His feet in Brindaban is even now being respected and put on the heads by the great Kings and other devotees. The great beauties of the world pine to have a glimpse of His smile. That Krishna, who is All in all, puts you, flute, on His lips and kisses you with love and licking again and again. Why? You are just a small and thin bamboo piece. How could you manage to win so Great Lord? Whence did you get this power to perform such a miracle?"

The flute replied, "I have made myself hollow from head to foot (by destroying my egoism and selfishness). The result is that Lord Krishna Himself comes and kisses me, He kisses me with fondness. Why should 1 not give out pleasant and melodious tunes? I have within me the life and breathe of Rama. My tune is His tune. I have harmonized myself with Him."

Refinement of egocentric desires for attaining eternal life & happiness

You know that, when mercury is eaten in crude form it is not only harmful but may also prove fatal. But when it is refined, after destroying its harmful quality, and eaten as a medical compound in the form of medicine, it becomes life giving. Similarly, when gold is eaten in its crude form, it is also harmful. But when it is suitably refined to be given in the form of medicinal compound, it becomes useful to our health and gives life and strength even to a dying man.

So, too, your crude ego, the Jiva-Bhav or the body and mind consciousness, is definitely very harmful to your spiritual health. It is the root cause of all your troubles. Your egoistic tendencies retard your progress.

Refine your crude, selfish and limited ego and dissolve it and merge it into the Universal Ego of seriousness. You, then, become God yourself, Creator of this universe - Absolute Truth, Absolute Knowledge, Absolute Bliss and Peace Personified.

The End